The Community Called Church

A THEOLOGY FOR ARTISANS OF A NEW HUMANITY

Volumes 2 to 5

Grace and the Human Condition

Our Idea of God

The Sacraments Today

Evolution and Guilt

ORBIS  BOOKS

VOLUME ONE

The Community Called Church

BY JUAN LUIS SEGUNDO, S.J., IN COLLABORATION
WITH THE STAFF OF THE PETER FABER CENTER
IN MONTEVIDEO, URUGUAY

TRANSLATED BY JOHN DRURY

MARYKNOLL, NEW YORK

Abbreviations Used in This Volume

AAS *Acta Apostolicae Sedis.* Vatican, 1909—

Denz. Denzinger-Schönmetzer, *Enchiridion Symbolorum.* Fribourg: Herder, 1963.

DV *Dei Verbum.* Vatican II. Dogmatic Constitution on Divine Revelation, November 18, 1965.

GS *Gaudium et spes.* Vatican II. Pastoral Constitution on the Church in the Modern World, December 7, 1965.

LG *Lumen gentium.* Vatican II. Dogmatic Constitution on the Church, November 21, 1964.

SC *Sacrum Concilium.* Vatican II. Constitution on the Sacred Liturgy, December 4, 1963.

Biblical citations are taken from The New English Bible, with the Apocrypha (New York and London: Oxford University Press and Cambridge University Press, 1970).

Citations of conciliar documents, unless otherwise indicated, are taken from Walter M. Abbot, S.J. (ed.), *The Documents of Vatican II* (New York: Guild-America-Association, 1966).

Wherever possible, other church and papal documents are cited on the basis of translations in *The Pope Speaks* Magazine (Washington, D.C.).

ORIGINALLY PUBLISHED BY EDICIONES CARLOS LOHLÉ, BUENOS AIRES © 1968

COPYRIGHT © 1973, ORBIS BOOKS, MARYKNOLL, NEW YORK 10545

LIBRARY OF CONGRESS CATALOG CARD NUMBER: 72–85794

ISBN SERIES 088344–480–1   VOLUME 088344–481–x

PAPER SERIES 088344–486–0   VOLUME 088344–487–9

DESIGN BY LA LIBERTÉ & RAYNER

MANUFACTURED IN THE UNITED STATES OF AMERICA

THIRD PRINTING

Contents

INTRODUCTION TO THE SERIES   vii

CHAPTER 1. THE CHURCH: A REALITY PARTICULAR AND UNIVERSAL   3
Framing the Question More Satisfactorily   3
CLARIFICATIONS: 13
   I. The Christ-Mystery signified by a Church which is both particular and universal at the same time   13
   II. Does the natural disappear into the supernatural?   16
   III. Linear tradition and dialectical tradition   19

CHAPTER 2. THE ESSENCE OF THE ECCLESIAL COMMUNITY   24
A Different Road or a New Responsibility?   24
CLARIFICATIONS: 34
   I. Is there a Christian anthropology?   34
   II. What is the dividing line between magic and Christian mystery?   37
   III. Is being a Christian a privilege?   40
   IV. The form of the Church embodied in Christendom   44

CHAPTER 3. THE FUNCTION AND NECESSITY OF THE CHURCH   50
The Notion of Mission in Crisis   50
CLARIFICATIONS: 63
   I. Religious practice and the knowledge of God   63
   II. Human experience: precatechesis in the faith   67
   III. Does truth need error?   70
   IV. Is it still true that there is no salvation outside the Church?   73

CHAPTER 4. OBLIGATIONS OF THE ECCLESIAL COMMUNITY   78
Church of the Masses or Sign-Community?   78
CLARIFICATIONS: 87
   I. The relevance of the Grand Inquisitor today   87
   II. Does the Church constitute an aristocracy?   89
   III. The Church and political power   91

CHAPTER 5. CHURCH-WORLD INTERDEPENDENCE   98
              How Do They Dialogue Today?   98
              CLARIFICATIONS: 115

        I.   The long hiatus in dialogue   115
        II. Economic development challenges the Church   118
        III. The Church and the thrust of evolution   120
        IV. The signs of the times and the capacity for
             dialogue   124
        V.   Was the Church's social doctrine a prelude to
             dialogue?   128

CONCLUSION   135

APPENDICES   137
        I.   Pertinent Conciliar Texts   139
        II. A Biblical Tapestry   150
        III. Springboard Questions   169

Introduction to the Series

The type of theology which is being attempted in this series springs from a keenly felt need in today's Church. Indeed that need often finds painful expression. In our age faith is not a tranquil or "natural" reality. It is fraught with anguish, and often subject to deep tensions.   *yes!*

We find groups of Christians who are "losing their faith." Giving expression to the faith is becoming incompatible with their real existence, with their conception of it, the world, and interpersonal relations. But before they reach the ultimate stage of "losing the faith," there is a long road to travel. Today it would seem that among many Christians the process of growing into mature human beings is estranging them from the faith.

Indeed our times could hardly be called tranquil. It is quite possible that we have reached a point in time in which humanity has definitively entered an era where acceleration is a permanent, constitutive element of man's history. As might have been expected, this accelerated pace has profound repercussions on the Christian faith. When the latter is expressed in a language different from that of today, our contemporaries find it alien to them; it is a quaint museum piece. Those who "have the faith" often see it as something that *should be* the most dynamic and meaningful thing for living in today's world. But in fact it is not. All too often it has been transformed into a hideout for people who dare not or cannot live the adventure of *being a human being today*.

The faith of our contemporaries is a *faith-in-crisis,* in the fullest and noblest sense of that phrase. And the unuttered question is: Why do I believe? In what do I believe? These two questions are not situated simply on the intellectual or conceptual level. They are imbedded in the very core of Christian living, creating a faith-in-crisis.

This volume on the Church proposes to tackle the issues on that same level.

Let us try to explore this point a bit more deeply. Our contemporaries have their own vision and real-life experience of the world, other people, and themselves. They are certain, for example, that they possess a long history; that they live amid a humanity launched on a total conquest of the universe; that they live in a world which is pluralistic in both ideological and religious views. They feel a need, not only to proclaim equality and fraternity, but also to achieve these goals in practice. Now this vision of the world, which has many more elements, of course, poses questions to faith. And it does so ultimately because the believer has a conviction, frequently left unarticulated, that his faith can truly give answers to these great questions.

Here we find one of the differences with the apologetics of the nineteenth century. The latter tried to show people in some way that "the Bible was right." And by that they understood a specific conception of man and the universe which was elaborated at a given moment in history. Today we have come to realize that our expression of the faith (and the Bible insofar as it is a vehicle for the faith) is not exhausted by a specific conception of man and the universe; and that a world growing up presents new questions as a new type of human being emerges. The replies that the faith provides as it takes on flesh in these unexpected situations show the believer "what he believes" (the content of his faith) and at the same time *justify* it.

This justification emerges to demonstrate that the content of our faith is a valid response (in faith) to the real problems that form our history. Indeed it is the ability of the faith to inspire initiative and creativity when it confronts the problems of human history that is the contemporary Christian's most persuasive sign of the divine origin of the message proposed to him by the faith.

Thus, only if we are willing to admit that many of our formulations are totally incompatible with the modern mentality, will we appreciate the importance of this type of justification, a justification that emerges from our faith's confrontation with the world.

In this way, and today more than ever before, we can clearly see the difference between a theological discipline divided into many branches and dominated by scholarly experts, on the one hand, and another theology rooted in a faith-in-crisis. Obviously there is no divorce between the two. But it is equally obvious that the former could never serve as the theology for the common run of mortals, whether they be laymen or clergymen. Theology, insofar as it is a scholarly science, will always be the domain of a small minority. Faith, on the other hand, can never be the privileged and exclusive possession of this minority. As the Church sees it, it can be relevant for all men.

Now a theology situated on the level of the Christian's real-life questions possesses its own limits and capabilities. We are not going to describe it in detail in this Introduction. But we would like to point out two characteristics that have the most to do with our effort in this series.

In the first place, this new type of theology is reductive. We do not spell out all the avatars of a doctrine laden with the accumulations of twenty centuries. Thus we reduce the multitude of dogmatic enunciations to certain fundamental mysteries of revelation that give an account of our faith.

Secondly, this type of theology essentially starts with, and takes account of, the world in which our contemporaries live and work. To be sure, it works in close collaboration with its specialized sister theology— note that we do not call her "big sister"—but it retains its own proper and inalienable personality in the task of transmitting the faith.

Our work in this volume and this series is, we repeat, framed within this type of theological effort. It is no more than a first attempt, and we present it as such to our readers. It would therefore be a mistake for the reader to seek a complete theology of the Church or a tract on ecclesiology in the pages that follow. But this does not mean that the issues about the Church not treated here are considered less important or less certain.

Format and Origin of This Series

We have tried to make it easier for the reader to approach this series by using a coherent format. The essential aspects of our reflection on the Church are contained in the initial article under each chapter. They are followed by a section entitled CLARIFICATIONS, in which we try to develop and apply more concretely the central lines of thought, to suggest study topics and related issues, and to go over one or two more points in detail. Notes are given at the end of each of these two main divisions.

The notes are meant to be useful to the reader rather than to be erudite. Many of them are biblical, indicating other passages in Scripture which complement the thoughts presented or which can be used for related meditation. Instead of citing numerous scholarly works, we have limited ourselves to a few more accessible sources: e.g., the *Concilium* series. Our series was originally intended for a Latin American audience, and their needs were uppermost in our minds.

The type of theological reflection presented here can give rise to different discussion formats: full-length courses, study weeks, and the like. But we actually tested it in a seminar approach, involving intensive sessions of study, discussion, and prayer. It may interest the reader to know how our seminars actually operate.

As far as length of time is concerned, our experiences confirmed the feeling that the busy layman benefits more from short-term seminars in which he is actively involved than from long-term courses in which he is generally passive. So now we try to run seminars of three or four days that coincide with a holiday weekend. The aim is to provide five or six sessions of four hours each in a relatively short space of time. We also stress that enrollment in the seminar implies that the individual is willing to involve himself in it totally, to participate in all the sessions, and to remain until it is over. The seminar is meant to be a total experience, not mere attendance at a series of lectures.

Each four-hour session operates pretty much like this. It begins with a lecture (which is reproduced almost verbatim here as the initial section of each chapter). The lecture lasts about one hour, and at its conclusion one or two questions are proposed to the various study groups (see Appendix III). But before they move into their discussion groups, the participants are asked to spend a few moments in personal meditation on the questions. In this way they can make an effort to formulate a personal solution, however provisional it might be, to the questions posed.

The various study groups then spend about forty-five minutes or an hour in discussing the questions. There are no more than ten persons in a given group, so that each individual will participate actively in the discussion. Herein lies the essential aim of the seminar itself, for the participants should move on from formulated truths to a truly interiorized truth. In other words, the discussion represents a confrontation between what they have heard and what they have learned from their real-life experiences; between that which they accepted uncritically as children and adolescents and that which they have put together into a coherent whole as adults.

Thus the questions proposed are not meant to serve as a review of the lecture. They are meant to foster a greater coherence between that which was provided in the lecture and other aspects or facts of Christian experience. To this end, it is highly desirable that the groups be somewhat heterogeneous in makeup, and that their discussion be stimulated by a pointed confrontation with things they may have read in the catechism or heard all their life from the pulpit.

It is also highly useful at this point to have the groups make an effort to reach unanimity on their answers and then write them up as a group project. Such a procedure obliges the participants to engage in real dialogue and to respect differences of opinion. When this period is over, the various groups reassemble at a roundtable forum and each group presents the answers it has formulated. The reply of the group may take one of three forms: a unanimous group response, a set of differing opinions, or a series of questions formulated by the group. It is our feeling that questions worked up by a group are more useful than those which an individual might formulate alone at the end of the lecture.

During the roundtable forum, the lecturer comments on the group replies, tries to respond to the questions of the various groups, and then takes up individual questions if he so desires.

The procedure varies for the final hour. The intellectual effort gives way to a period of prayer and recollection that is related to the theme under consideration. It may involve some form of paraliturgical service or a biblical reading that is not discussed in great detail (see Appendix II).

This pattern is repeated throughout the course of the seminar. As circumstances permit, the final four-hour session may be dedicated to a review of what has been covered and a discussion of possible concrete applications in the local or parochial sector.

As the reader will see from the text itself, our aim is not to move on to a wholly different topic in each four-hour session. Experience has shown that it is more useful to return to the same few basic ideas over and over again, relating them ever more deeply to real-life problems. It is useful, in this connection, to sum up what has gone before at the start of each session. One practical way of doing this is to refer to conciliar texts that relate to the material in question (see Appendix I). While we do not feel that these texts by themselves are enough to encourage this type of reflection, we do find that they are able to shore up and confirm the work already done. For they come from the universal Church gathered together in our day under the special action of the Holy Spirit.

Finally, we would point out that this seminar on the Church is then followed by other seminars covering other fundamental aspects of the faith: grace, God, the sacraments, sin and redemption, etc. Each year a seminar is held on a new topic, and seminars on old topics are held for those who have not yet attended them. In this way we hope to answer the needs of mature persons who are looking for a theology which is equally adult, which is open to exploring new pathways related to their temporal commitments.

The Community Called Church

CHAPTER ONE

The Church: A Reality Particular and Universal

FRAMING THE QUESTION MORE SATISFACTORILY

The first objection raised against the Church was voiced more than twenty centuries ago, and it was clear enough. What could the Church, that insignificant group of people, really offer to a world so vastly superior to it in terms of quantity and antiquity? One had only to listen to Christians to discover that their message had to do with salvation, that is, with the ultimate outcome of human existence. But if it was true that God was truly concerned about the salvation of men, could one possibly agree that he had accorded some exclusive privilege to this tiny community that had only recently appeared on the scene?

Such was the objection raised by men like Celsus and Porphyry in the pagan circles of the Greco-Roman world. The key objection[1] of the latter philosopher has come down to us in this form: "If Christ is the one and only savior, as his followers claim, then why did he come so recently?"

So recently! Porphyry could not have imagined how recent in human history his coming was. The scholarly sciences now tell us that humanity was living on earth for a million years before Christ came. Twenty centuries have passed since Porphyry was alive, and the Church is still something ridiculously "recent" with respect to humanity. If we were to reduce the whole history of mankind to eight hours, then the twenty centuries of the Church would not come to more than a minute![2] Porphyry's objection continues, his opposition gradually giving way to a trace of irony: "How could he come so belatedly, allowing so many people to be lost before that?" And if someone tried to explain that those people were not lost, then he would have to explain why it is proper to call Christ the one and only savior if he did not essentially modify man's possibilities for salvation. And if he did modify these possibilities in some profound way, what was divine providence doing throughout all those prior centuries? If the Christian religion is the one perfect religion (insofar as

3

man's salvation is concerned), then God must be very evil or very weak or very improvident to hold up the remedy for so long. There we have the objection of Porphyry.

Twenty centuries have passed. But have we really answered Porphyry's question, or have we simply forgotten it?

As the Church began to grow and expand in the West, it lost sight of the fact that it had been, and would always be, a minority amid its human contemporaries. It lost sight of the immense multitudes that filled the course of history before Christ. It repeated *ad nauseam* the famous exaggeration of Tertullian: "We are only of yesterday and yet we fill everything!" That was not really the case.

Even if the Church had filled the whole world at a given moment, the problem would still have remained. How could God give an exclusive privilege relating to man's salvation to a community that is so small compared to the whole human race?

Vatican II forced us to confront the world. One of the primary benefits of this fact is that we now must see ourselves as a minority amid the rest of the human race. And we are forced to face the basic problem anew: What is the infinitesimal Christian community supposed to do within the vast community of mankind?

We have two essential facts to work with in trying to frame this question more correctly. The first fact is that the Church has been and *always will be a particular community*.

In the early days of Christianity, Saint Paul was asked to explain who he was in terms of religion. In his answer, he felt obliged to acknowledge the smallness and insignificance of the nascent Church: "This much I will admit: I am a follower of the new way (the 'sect' they speak of), and it is in that manner that I worship the God of our fathers" (Acts 24:14). In other words, Christians were a tiny insignificant group who could identify themselves only as a dissident sect of the Jewish religion, itself a minority group amid the religions of the Roman Empire.

Despite superficial appearances to the contrary in some so-called "Christian" countries, that situation does not seem to have changed very much in the past twenty centuries. Those who are sufficiently Christian to transmit the faith they have received to others are still a small minority in the world. The world has not been converted to Christianity, the human race has not entered the Church. How do we explain this limitation?

The first explanation we hear frequently is that the sins and unworthy behavior of Christians are the cause of the Church's limited spread. But is it possible that Christ, in handing over his work to us, entertained illusions about us?

There is another explanation that goes deeper. The Church follows in the footsteps of Jesus, its founder and God-made-man. The limitation of the Church, then, is not so much the result of its unworthiness as the result of its incarnation. There was no unworthiness in Christ; yet, when he took on flesh and entered our history, he limited himself.

Consider this, for example. Have we given serious thought to the fact that, in a world divided into rival races, the Church must present God incarnated as a white man? When God entered our humanity, did he not know that the white race was exploiting other human races and would go on doing this for many centuries? Did he not know that, by incarnating himself in this particular race, he would put terrible limitations on the future chances of his message being accepted by millions of people? There is no doubt that if he had consulted us, we would have urged him to avoid ties of color and race. And if we pursued this advice to its logical conclusion, we would also have urged him to avoid all similar limitations: e.g., locale, epoch, culture, country, language. In short, we would have dissuaded him from *incarnation*.

He, on the other hand, took incarnation seriously. To become man, he openly accepted our limitations, except those that come from egotism and sin. In a sense Porphyry's question is directed more at him than at Christians, and we could put it this way: "If you have something so enormously important for all humanity, why did you agree to take on a specific race, country, and epoch? Why did you accept a Church that is characterized by these same elements and many others besides?"

Whatever the answer to that question might be, the fact is clear. God, who voluntarily set limits on himself in the Incarnation, also voluntarily set limits on his Church when he put flesh and bones on her: i.e., when he planted her in human history.[3]

The Church was born at a specific moment. And by that very fact, a million years of human existence remained outside her reach. She was born with specific individuals of a certain size and weight. Some exegetes say that Paul, the great preacher of the Church among pagans, was probably a short, stocky man whose outer appearance won little respect (*cf.* 2 Cor. 10:10). And by that very fact, the reach of the Church was limited to those who were capable of overcoming this obstacle. Here we have only one small example from among the many we might cite.

Thus the Church was limited. Or, to put it better, Christ himself limited the Church *forever*. From what we have just said, it should be clear that any talk about a universal Church is utopian if it refers to the number of its members. The Church is essentially limited by the very fact of its incarnation in history. It is a particular reality, destined (not condemned) to be that always by virtue of the elements that go to make it up.[4]

For the Church to be universal in terms of numbers, we would have to presuppose on the one hand that its specific and particular features were erased and that it had neither content, flavor, nor significance of any sort.[5] And on the other hand we would have to presuppose that such an abstraction is relevant for human beings. Such a utopian dream would seem to be found among those who fear any pronouncement whatsoever from the Church, who feel that her chances of reaching all men would be better if she said as little as possible! [6]

What is more, there is another point that is quite decisive here. Let us assume that such an absurd way of proceeding could convince people today or tomorrow to enter the Church. We would still be faced with the same question. What kind of universality would the Church have, when it rules out a million years of human history? Even the absurd dream of all men being converted would still leave us with the inescapable problem: Why so late? Why people of today and tomorrow and not those of yesterday? Why do we find this limitedness and particularity that will never be absent from the Church of Christ here on earth?

Utilizing the approach of theologians in Christology, we can adopt the *communicatio idiomatum* ("transposition of names") and apply to the Church what Saint Augustine said of Christ: "In deigning to be our Way, the Lord did not will to hold us back but to convey us forward." Limited in history, he chose to belong to the past, insofar as we are concerned today, and not to confine us within a perpetual present. The Church, like Christ, is fleshed out in human history. And we can reiterate here the phrase of Pius XII that echoes Augustine, giving it perhaps a deeper inflection: "Men were not made for the Church; the Church was made for men." In short, we must balance out the two ends of the scale. This entity which is a specific and particular reality within mankind must have been created for humanity, that is, in line with a divine plan as vast as humanity itself. This is the case, not the opposite. Humanity was not created to enter a particular reality which it overflows at every turn.

The second fact in this problem seems to contradict the first. The Church will be and always has been universal.

Here we have this infinitesimal group of human beings that first appears in history as a dissident offshoot of Judaism. But what does this group feel it represents in the midst of humanity? All of humanity, no less! They did not call themselves Christians; that is what other people called them. The designation they chose for their little community was "catholic," which means nothing less than "universal." We are astounded by their pretensions: the universal community.

Centuries later Saint Augustine[7] would designate the Church to be "the congregation of the human race." He had no illusions about there being no more pagans in the world. The universality was not based on numbers or geography. Centuries earlier back in Jerusalem the apostles were already "catholic," i.e., *universal*.

We find proof of this belief in the very first decades of the Church. The early Christians believed they were the congregation of the human race, and surely for reasons that go deeper than numerical growth or geographic spread, which were then minimal. In the *Shepherd of Hermas,* one of the first books to appear in Christian circles, the main character has an interesting vision. An old woman appears to him and gives him a small book. Another character asks him who he thinks this old woman is. Guessing to some extent, the main character says she is the Sibyl, the most famous woman known in that age. The other character tells him he is wrong: "She is the Church." Then the main character asks a question that probably would not occur to us today but was perfectly logical then: "Why is she so old?" The other character's reply[8] is central to our present discussion: "Because she was created first, before all else; that is why she is aged. It was for her that the world was made."

Here is the testimony we were looking for. These Christians, who were practically contemporaries of the newly born Church, already considered her to be universal—not because of the number of her adherents but because she embraced the dimensions of humanity itslf;[9] because no reality or human being was outside her frontiers; because she had always been present, even though her limitations as a particular historical reality seemed to indicate otherwise.

That is the answer that Christians would give to Porphyry's objection about their belated entrance on the scene of world history. Without disregarding the particular reality of the Church, incarnated in history even as Christ was, they affirmed its universality as well—not in the light of massive conversions in the future but as its permanent attribute from the beginning.

In short, they simultaneously affirmed the particularity and the universality of the Church. At this point in our reflection we are clearly not in a position to understand how these two apparently opposed attributes could be conceived to be united and simultaneous. But it is equally clear that their framing of the problem was much more realistic and profound than our approach, when we envision the Church's growth to universality in terms of the numerical growth of its members.

Our facile and false solution engenders a set of attitudes that have repercussions on Christian living. Consider some examples. Do we not often feel distressed over our failure to convert the world, feeling that this was Christ's plan and that the only obstacle is our mediocrity, ineptitude, and infidelity? In like manner, do we not have a tendency to adapt our attitudes to those prevalent in our society, not so much compelled by love as by the fear that we shall reduce the popularity and potential of the Church if we differ too much from them? Do we not even go so far as to be sorry that authentic values exist in other religions and even in unbelief, because that means that Christian charity, sacrifice, and solidarity are not enough to attract people to the Church? Do we not fret a good deal about being Johnny-come-latelies in development work, not so much because it suggests sloth and egotism but because the Church thereby loses an argument that could win new adherents and increase her numbers?

What we propose to do, then, is to consider in a more realistic, more theological, and more traditional way, the relationship between these two apparently contradictory characteristics of the Church: its particularity and its universality.

To proceed with this project, we do well to recall that, when we read the Gospel and the rest of the New Testament, we encounter two lines of thought regarding how salvation is obtained. And these two lines of thought bear great similarity to the two aforementioned characteristics of the Church. One line of thought shows salvation to be conditioned by particular, specific means (which only some people seem to possess). The second line shows salvation in its absolutely universal dimension.

Here we need only recall two central texts dealing with these two lines of thought. They are not the only texts we could cite but they are the most well known. They lead the way for a whole series of other passages spread throughout the New Testament.

The first text is in Saint Mark's Gospel (16:15–16). Christ has risen from the dead and he is telling his apostles about the kingdom of God. He tells them: "Go into the whole world and preach the gospel to the whole creation. He who believes and is baptized will be saved; but he who does not believe will be condemned." Here we have a very clear line of thought about salvation, in which salvation appears to be conditioned by the fact of entering the Church through faith and baptism, through faith in Christ's preaching, and through the sacrament which makes one a part of the Church. Salvation is attributed to this.

Clearly this line of thought occasioned the difficulty voiced by men like Celsus and Porphyry. If this is salvation, then what happened before the Church and what will happen to those who do not have a clear notion about her?

Before moving on, let us dwell on the logical consequences of this conception among us. In an established Church, membership in the

Church remains somewhat dubious so long as a person lives. It is not just faith and baptism, through which a person *enters* into the Church, that saves him; it is also his *remaining in the Church* right up to the end. There is thus a tendency to move the stress from faith and baptism to the last sacraments: i.e., from the former to those which ensure that a person ends his life within the Christian community. For a person is not going to be judged for some action performed in childhood but for his last definitive option.

In the same framework of ideas, and for reasons that we saw already, since salvation is conditioned by entering and permanently remaining in this *particular* community (the Church of faith and the sacraments), we inevitably tend to be upset by the limits of the Church and to reduce to a minimum the requisites for belonging to her. Thus we go looking for the basic rudiments necessary so that faith will be valid and the sacraments efficacious. Why? Because the possession of these rudiments will, in theory, allow the greatest possible number of people to meet the particular conditions for salvation.[10]

As we have said, this line of thought is evangelical and crops up in other parts of the New Testament as well. When the frightened jailer saw his prison shaken by an earthquake, he asked Paul and his companion what he had to do to be saved. Paul's reply is practically the same: "Put your trust in the Lord Jesus and you will be saved" (Acts 16:31). And the man is then baptized.

On the other hand, we find that another line of thought appears in an equally central spot in the Gospel where Christ talks about the last days. He is telling his apostles about the last judgment that God will pass on humanity. How is God going to look at the whole of human history in order to decide whether people are to be saved or condemned?

His reply is in Matthew's Gospel (25:31–46), and we are all familiar with the passage. The key factor in the judgment that the incarnate God will pass on all humanity is this: What did you do for me when I was hungry, thirsty, alone, and mistreated? And eternal life will be awarded to those who showed true love, that is, to those who truly aided the God-made-man. We are talking here about actions which merit God himself as a fair recompense (note Christ's "because"!); thus they are divine, supernatural actions, and yet they are required of all men and can be found in them.[11]

Precisely to resolve this difficulty, Christ chose to add an essential aspect to his picture of the judgment: the general surprise. On the scene are people who never saw him, people who passed through history before his coming, people who did not know him during their lifetime either personally or through his Church. So the vast majority of human beings will ask the question that Christ puts on their lips: Lord, when did we see you and succor you, when did we pass you by? His answer is that it matters little that they never met him. The merit of the things they did for other human beings, invested with love, reaches the God who is brother of all and brings them to eternal life.

In other words, the merit that human beings see in mutual love, self-giving, and solidarity is only a shadowy indication of what these attitudes really contain, what they themselves will discover when God passes judgment on them, and what is already known by those who have received from God the revelation of this central mystery concerning humanity.

So here we have a second line of thought regarding salvation, which is intimately related to the universal dimension of the Church. If this line of thought were the only one, our reply to Porphyry would be easy to make. The Church cannot arrive on the scene too late for humanity's salvation because all men are going to be judged by the same criterion: mutual love. The new community called Church does not seem to bring in any decisive element that was lacking before. The judge will pose the same questions to both Christians and non-Christians: What did you do for your brother? What did you do for *my* brother?

But if this response gets us out of one problem, it drops us into another. We must now justify the importance and necessity of this particular community which is fashioned by faith and the sacraments and which has been placed in history by Christ and closely tied up with salvation.

Let us put this another way. The universal reality of the Church and her particular reality seem to be opposed to each other in the same way that the two lines of thought on salvation are. One line of thought attributes salvation to a universal factor such as love; the other attributes it to a particular factor such as entry and permanent membership in the ecclesial community.

Does this mean that we are right back where we started? No. While the two perspectives seem to be opposed to each other, we should be able to find some synthesis. And what we have already said clearly indicates where we should look for a solution. The universal perspective on salvation should clear the way for us to comprehend the significance, value, and necessity of the community called the Church. Paul points the way: "We have set our hope on the living God, who is the Saviour of all men —the Saviour, above all, of believers" (1 Tim. 4:10).[12]

It is clear that Matthew's picture of universal judgment dovetails with this perspective. After all, what distinguishes the Christian in his judgment portrait? The answer is obvious. Only one thing does: the Christian will not be surprised by the criterion used to judge all men.

He will not ask the Lord: When did I see you? For if he is a believer, he is so precisely because he has accepted the revelation of this universal plan which culminates in the last judgment. The Christian is he *who already knows*. This, undoubtedly, is what distinguishes and defines him.

Let us put this in more general terms. Through Christ, God gave every man the possibility of loving others, and he joined all men and every individual in solidarity; he thus put love in everyone's hands as the divine instrument of salvation. This possibility is as vast and as ancient as humanity itself. It does not date from A.D. 1 or 30. Nor is it limited by the historical limits of the ecclesial community. Through Christ, it reaches all men. The more traditional strains of theology have always echoed these perspectives: The redemptive work of Christ, carried out within history, goes beyond the limits of time and dominates the whole unfolding development of the universe—both its past and its future.[13]

But there is something that begins with Christ and that moves out solely toward the future: namely, the revelation of this plan that suffuses all time.[14] The Christian is not the only one to enter into this plan. But he is the one who knows it. He knows the plan because he has received not only redemption but also revelation.[15]

The Christian is *he who knows*. Does this definition give us the key we need to unite and synthesize the universal perspective of salvation with the foundation of a particular community called the Church in the framework of history? That is what we shall try to see in the following chapters.

NOTES TO CHAPTER ONE

1. Henri de Lubac, *Catholicism* (London: Burns, Oates, 1950), pp. 126 and 137. Various pieces of historical information from this important work are utilized in this chapter. See especially Chapter II and Chapter VIII of this work.

2. *Cf.* Yves Congar, O.P., Lecture on Schema XIII, Rome, October 12, 1965. See *Dialogo* I, No. 1 (Montevideo, Uruguay).

3. "Just as Christ carried out the work of redemption in poverty and under oppression, so the Church is called to follow that same path in communicating to men the fruits of salvation" (LG 8).

4. "However, until there is a new heaven and a new earth where justice dwells (*cf.* 2 Peter 3:13), the pilgrim Church, in her sacraments and institutions, which pertain to this present time, takes on the appearance of this passing world" (LG 48).

5. We might recall here the question posed by Christ: "When the Son of man comes, will he find faith on earth?" (Luke 18:8). We know that in the mind of the evangelists the universal proclamation of the gospel was not identified with numerical universality because they associated this proclamation with

persecution (*cf.* Mark 13:9–13). The division inherent in Christ's very message will last to the end: "Do you suppose I came to establish peace on earth? No indeed, I have come to bring division" (Luke 12:51).

6. We must not confuse two principles here. One is that concrete incarnation in specific forms—cultural, racial, and so forth, is essential to the Church and entails a perduring particularity for her. But we cannot use this principle to deny the principle of spiritual poverty that should guide the Church. In carrying out her mission, the Church must see every concrete form of incarnation in time and space as relative and precarious.

7. De Lubac, *op. cit.,* p. 20.

8. *Ibid.,* p. 27.

9. "All men are called to belong to this new People of God. Wherefore this People . . . is to be spread throughout the world and must exist in all ages" (LG 13).

10. *Cf.* "Pastoral Latinoamericana, hora de decision," *Mensaje* (Santiago, Chile), No. 127 (March–April 1964).

11. See CLARIFICATION II below: the natural and the supernatural.

12. "All men are called to this catholic unity of the People of God . . . There belong to it or are related to it in various ways . . . all who believe in Christ and indeed the whole of mankind. For all men are called to salvation by the grace of God" (LG 13).

13. See CLARIFICATION III below.

14. "It is he who brought us salvation and called us to a dedicated life, not for any merits of ours but of his own purpose and his own grace, which was granted to us in Christ Jesus from all eternity, but has now at length been brought fully into view by the appearance on earth of our Saviour Jesus Christ. For he has broken the power of death and brought life and immortality to light through the Gospel" (2 Tim. 1:9–10; see also Titus 1:2–3).

15. "The Christian man receives the 'Spirit . . . as firstfruits of the harvest to come' (Rom. 8:23) by which he becomes capable of discharging the new law of love. Through this Spirit the whole man is renewed from within, even to the point of setting our bodies free (cf. Rom. 8:1–25). All this holds true not only for Christians, but for all men of good will. . . . Such is the mystery of man . . . as seen by believers in the light of Christian revelation" (GS 22).

CLARIFICATIONS

I. THE CHRIST-MYSTERY SIGNIFIED BY A CHURCH WHICH IS BOTH PARTICULAR AND UNIVERSAL AT THE SAME TIME

The Church is simultaneously an historical movement, a sign, and sacrament (i.e., a particular reality) on the one hand, and the salvation of humanity (i.e., a universal reality) on the other hand. In short, it is an expression of the mystery of Christ himself. The historical pageant of the "incarnate" Christ, prepared by the Old Testament and prolonged by the visible Church, embraces and manifests the mystery of God's unfolding plan for all humanity.

To begin with, what does this plan consist of? Biblical revelation spells out simply this: the plan of God who is the savior of the world. Essentially the plan involves allowing human beings to share God's own life in and through Christ.

Saint Paul puts it this way to the Ephesians:

> Praise be to the God and Father of our Lord Jesus Christ, who has bestowed on us in Christ every spiritual blessing in the heavenly realms. In Christ he chose us before the world was founded . . . and he destined us—such was his will and pleasure—to be accepted as his sons through Christ Jesus . . . For in Christ our release is secured and our sins are forgiven through the shedding of his blood. Therein lies the richness of God's free grace lavished upon us, imparting full wisdom and insight. He has made known to us his hidden purpose . . . to be put into effect when the time was ripe: namely, that the universe, all in heaven and on earth, might be brought into a unity in Christ (Eph. 1:3–10).

Thus God's plan is eternal ("before the world was founded"). It has its moment in history for fulfillment ("when the time was ripe"). And its content is adoption into divine sonship through Christ. All the mysteries in the life of Christ, who is the savior and reconciler (Col. 1:20), are the carrying out of God's plan when the time was ripe. But two mysteries in particular point to the reality of Christ as the heart of the world, through whom everything acquires its consistency and salvation. Those two mysteries are the Incarnation and the Paschal Mystery.

1. The Incarnation establishes the era of the fulfillment of God's plan. It establishes Christ in solidarity with human life and human realities.[1] But obviously it involves more than just the biological or moral solidarity which every human being shares when he comes into this world. The

unanimous feeling of the Church Fathers is that Christ's entry into human history represents a betrothal between divinity and humanity. Basing their view on a series of biblical texts that present Christ as the new Adam, as the reconciler of all history, they see Christ establishing a real, original relationship with every single human being.

It is an original relationship because there is no similar model for it in human relationships. It is also original because it gives rise to something new: through this relationship, Christ engraves the feature of sonship on the fate of every human person. It is unthinkable that God would call someone into human existence, within this historical plan, without the person having this Christian destiny and vocation.[2]

The relationship of each human being to Christ is also real. In other words, it is not extrinsic or juridical; it intrinsically and ontologically affects the very significance of the human person.

By virtue of this relationship, man is a mystery which can be discovered only through faith.[3] Pascal puts it pointedly: "Not only do we know God through Christ; through Christ we come to know ourselves as well." This Christian mystery concerning our personal relationship with Christ is something that we will discover fully at the moment of our death; and all humanity will be surprised to learn it at the second coming of Christ, when we will all see "God's sons revealed" (Rom. 8:19). So through the mystery of the Incarnation, in which Christ enters a personal relationship with every human being, he becomes the heart of the world from the start of history to its finish.

This alone explains certain statements of Christ: "Anything you do for one of these, you do for me." All human history has touched his heart, as the final judgment scene in Matthew's Gospel clearly indicates (Matt. 25:31–46). The actual carrying out of the mystery of Christ's Incarnation in a specific time and place is the visible, historical moment of the universal mystery of his personal relationship with the whole of human history. By virtue of this universal mystery, everything "subsists in him," in accordance with the plan which God freely devised before creation.

When we look at the whole of human history, we clearly see in it a process of socialization and concentration with respect to interpersonal relationships. This ascending thrust of human history cannot be the fruit of egotism and sin, which lead to separation and division. As with all the deeper dimensions of the human person, this process echoes the original bond which every person has with Christ. Through this bond, the world is being suffused with the process of filiation that will reshape the human family into the family of God.[4]

2. The Paschal Mystery of Christ, that is, his death and resurrection, also reveals to us the Savior's relationship with sinful humanity.

The redemption has often been viewed as a ransom operation, but the reality of it is much more than that. It is the "passing of the Lord": i.e., passing from the death that derives from sinful Adam to the life that comes only from God.

If the vocation of every man is one and divine (cf. GS 22), then sin is its annihilation. This is not the nothingness from which all things were created; it is the nothingness that places in doubt the very ground of human existence. When man slips off the track and proceeds to destroy his true destiny, he follows an irreversible route that can be corrected only by someone who has the power to re-create.

Jesus emptied himself to reach man in the distant depths of his fall. He did not come to man by sinning himself, but by subjecting his human life to all the consequences of sinful alienation, even to the point of death. Having arrived at that point, only Christ has the power to provide "passage." Hence the great salvific happening is his "passover." Christ is the only one who has made this passageway; we participate in this new creation when we are incorporated into him.

Redemption is not something extrinsic to man. It is not some juridical fiction whereby God is moved by the merits of Christ or hides our sins under the mantle of his blood. Redemption is our intrinsic transformation into one "body" with him, whereby we live the divine life. This filial adoption, which decides the essence and the destiny of the human person, had remained open to question because of sin. But in Christ and through Christ, the paschal man, the plan of God is fully realized in us human beings.

So once again when we consider the mystery of redemption afresh, we find that it is through Christ and through communion with his life that human existence is enabled to flourish in accordance with the Father's will. Everything subsists in Christ, and in him everything finds its supreme source of fulfillment, significance, and value. The visible steps of "passing over" in Christ's historical life have repercussions on all of human history. While Christ is a particular reality in terms of his human life, his mystery takes in the universality of human beings.

Thus God's plan has an empirical aspect, which is *salvation history*. This history finds its origin in Abraham and reaches its culmination in the earthly life of Christ. After Pentecost, the paschal Christ continues his visibility and presence in the Church, which is "a visible assembly and a spiritual community" (GS 40). The Mystical Christ (i.e., the Church as a particular reality) and the Cosmic Christ (the Church as a universal reality) are inseparable aspects of the one and only Christian reality.[5] They differ only in terms of faith and the sacraments (visible signs and awareness of the Christian mystery); they do not differ at all in salvation content. Both are inseparable, as are the sacramental sign and the grace signified, as are the historical Christ (who is particular and visible) and his universal salvation mystery. The paschal Christ is the Mystical Christ and the Cosmic Christ at the same time. The Church, as a particular reality, is the conscious and visible sign of the presence of Christ the Savior in the heart of each human being (the Church as a universal reality). Thus by starting with the incarnate Christ and his mystery, we make clear the distinction between, and the inseparability of, the particular reality and the universal reality of Christ's Church.

These brief considerations stress the social implications of Christological dogma. They point up the incompleteness of any consideration of the Christian mystery and of any devotion to Christ that does not include his relationship to the Church and humanity. With their help, Christians can usefully explore the Christological presuppositions they bring with them to any examination of the Church. Is our interest in the life of

Christ centered around stories and anecdotes? Do we read the Gospel to find good examples—that is, in the same way we read lives of the saints? Do we read and ponder the rest of the New Testament, which clearly points up the ecclesial and cosmic aspect of the Christ reality? In our interior life what concrete content do we give to "personal union with Christ"? Is the major feature of our interior life an effort to get closer to the historical Jesus through our imagination and emotions? Do we see Christ's resurrection and ascension as alienation and separation?

Such questions as these are very important if we are to get a proper picture of the reality that continues and signifies the mystery of Christ: that is, the Church.

II. DOES THE NATURAL DISAPPEAR INTO THE SUPERNATURAL?

Quite logically, any effort such as this to present the Church within the universal mystery of salvation presupposes a certain conception of the relations between the natural and the supernatural. It is not surprising, then, that this distinction should be posed as an objection to this first chapter, and hence, to all the chapters which follow from it.

How is the objection presented? It starts right off by identifying, in general terms, the supernatural plane with participation in the faith and sacraments of the visible Church. The identification is not seen as total, of course, since the Church has condemned the view that invincible ignorance represents a privation of grace (cf. Denz. 1647, 1677, and 3866–73). But the existence, activity, and positive outcome of supernatural factors outside the Church is indeed seen as a very abnormal case (cf. pages 30–31 on the sacraments of desire). Outside the boundaries of the Church, this view sees the existence of natural factors as the normal state of affairs. Thus philanthropy is distinguished from charity, and the "natural" virtues of pagans from the "supernatural" virtues of Christians. Even within the Christian way of life, some find room for the same distinction. A much-read Christian author tells us that "the vocation of many militant Christians is based more on natural generosity than on a supernatural spirit."

Speaking from a theological point of view, it does not seem easy right now to justify this distinction or opposition set up within the whole complex of human attitudes. Right at the start we have the clear statement of Christ in his description of the last judgment: he will give eternal life as a reward for actions that were not consciously related to him. We also have the whole Johannine theology about the God who is Love, who gives his life for men, with the result that "every man who does right is his child" (1 John 2:29). John's words are clear: "We for our part have crossed over from death to life; this we know, because we love our brothers" (1 John 3:14); "Everyone who loves is a child of God and knows God" (1 John 4:7); "God himself dwells in us if we love one another" (1 John 4:12); "He who dwells in love is dwelling in God, and God in him" (1 John 4:16).

Only within such a perspective can we explain a universal divine plan whereby God is truly and effectively "the Saviour of all men—the Saviour, above all, of believers" (1 Tim. 4:10), a plan that involves a final judgment in which everyone will be judged on the same criterion, a criterion which has decisive and supernatural value: "Come, enter and possess the kingdom that has been ready for you since the world was made. For . . . you gave me food" (Matt. 25:34–35).

The same message is expressed in different imagery in 1 Peter. After his death, Christ goes to preach to the dead and to pass new judgment on their lives:

> In the body he was put to death; in the spirit he was brought to life. And in the spirit he went and made his proclamation to the imprisoned spirits. They had refused obedience long ago, while God waited patiently in the days of Noah and the building of the ark, and in the ark a few persons, eight in all, were brought to safety through the water. . . . Why was the Gospel preached to those who are dead? In order that, although in the body they received the sentence common to men, they might in the spirit be alive with the life of God (1 Pet.: 18–20; 4:6).

Using imagery, this passage indicates that there is another judgment in Christ which is deeper and more just than that of human beings; before Christ's judgment seat, even unbelief can show up as a salvation judgment in the deeper light of the gospel.

The controversy with the heresy of Semi-Pelagianism also helped the Church to broaden her horizons, to see the normal and effective presence of grace where more simplistic tendencies tended to see nothing more than "the natural." What we do, in effect, is project our own limitations on God. Where we are concerned, anything gratuitous is rare, infrequent, uncertain, and often absent altogether. So we tend to feel that the supernatural cannot be that which we see every day in the lives of human beings. We feel that love and self-giving must be "natural" because we see these features every day. Well, in its debate with Semi-Pelagianism, the Church defined that the initial attraction which laid hold of a person and brought him to the submission of belief was supernatural, precisely because it was already under the influence of God's gift. So the controversy did not deal with the initial steps to faith insofar as they were understood to be the acts immediately preceding the act of faith. It dealt with them as the slow journey of a person, motivated by a desire to do what is good and right, toward the good news of revelation.

Finally, we would say that *today* it is not easy to maintain that man's normal, everyday existence outside the Church is carried out on the natural plane. For Vatican II clearly and expressly teaches the following:

> The Christian man, conformed to the likeness of that Son who is the first-born of many brothers, receives "the first-fruits of the Spirit" (Rom. 8:23) by which he becomes capable of discharging the new law of love. . . . Linked with the paschal mystery and patterned on the dying Christ, he will hasten forward to resurrection in the strength which comes from hope. All this holds true not only for Christians, but for all men of good will in whose hearts grace works in an unseen way. For, since Christ died for all men, and since the ultimate vocation of man is in fact one, and divine, we ought to believe that the Holy Spirit, in a manner known only to God, offers to every man the possibility of being associated with this paschal mystery (GS 22).

Against these arguments is raised an objection that is no less serious on the intellectual level. The phrase above which talks about one divine vocation would seem to exclude *in reality* any possible distinction between a natural order and a supernatural (or divine) order, since everything is caught up in the latter. Do we not thereby erase the distinction between nature and grace? In the end, are we not eliminating grace by converting it simply into a part of reality rather than a gift that is radically above and beyond the scope of nature?

To reply to this question, we must take account of some of the ideas advanced in present-day theology to deal with some of the imprecise formulas used during the era of the "nouvelle théologie" (around the end of World War II). One feature of that new theological tendency seemed to deny the distinction between the natural and the supernatural, without seeking to deny the essential gratuitousness of grace and the supernatural. In the debate which ensued many theologians, such as Karl Rahner and Leopoldo Malevez, arrived at conclusions that were both clearcut and traditional. We can sum up these conclusions in general terms here.[6]

It is theologically necessary to make a distinction between the concepts of nature and the supernatural. But this does not mean that the distinction has to be historical or chronological. In trying to envision the natural we do not have to envision what *existed before* grace arrives on the scene. All we need do is envision what *might have existed* if grace had not been intermingled with man's life from the very first moment. To truly appreciate and affirm the gratuitousness of the supernatural, we are obliged to relate it to a person who would not have received this gift. This person could have existed and lived a normal existence, but it is useless to imagine such an existence on the basis of *our* human existence, which is intrinsically modified by grace. We must also grant the possibility of a person in whom grace would not be a gift but something demanded by human nature itself. But it is not licit to pass on, without further ado, from the possibility to the actual existence of either sort of person or the existence of a time when man might have lived without the gift of grace. The controversy with Semi-Pelagianism already tells us that we will not find this person in the pagan.

To avoid useless discussions in this area, Rahner proposed a term which the Council translates in its phrase about man's vocation being "one and divine." Rahner's term is "supernatural existential." It signifies that the human beings we know are born within an existence whose structure is supernatural; in it everything is related to man's one and only destiny, and man can do nothing that does not have positive or negative value vis-à-vis eternal life. This does not mean that grace and nature are confused with each other. The two concepts are different. And this forces us to remember at all times that man could have existed without the gift which God, *in reality,* made to him from the very beginning in calling him to a supernatural existence.

Now we cannot close our discussion of this topic without alluding to another conception that poses great obstacles to a proper understanding of the mystery of the Church. It is an ingenuous but widespread view which views the relationship between nature and grace in what we could call *chronological* terms. Creation and its overall design, for example, is

conceived as being entirely unrelated to the Incarnation and the Redemption. The latter were decided upon at a later date, as it were, as a replacement solution. Or, at the very least, they were selected with another aim
in view which has its own proper order of values and instruments. In
this view, grace comes to a nature that is already perfect and operational,
thus having an adventitious and accidental character. Baptism would
succeed a state of nature which, if perpetuated, would lead to limbo, an
intermediate place cut off from the positively or negatively supernatural
destiny of the rest of mankind.

These more or less primitive and infantile ways of turning a distinction between concepts into a time gap (which could be usefully explored)
would not be serious if they did not radically impede our effort to frame
the Church within the destiny of the human community throughout the
ages. Everything that follows depends on our ability to get beyond this
obstacle.

III. LINEAR TRADITION AND DIALECTICAL TRADITION

The notion of Church universality presented here is rooted in the
existence of a divine salvation plan that is common to all humanity. It
is not rooted in the numerical expansion of a Church which is regarded
as the exclusive bearer of salvation, and which theoretically should reach
all humanity if it were not for the resistance of non-Christians or flaws
in the witness of Christians themselves. Thus the notion presented here
cannot help but seem to be something new and suspect in our day.

In the Church, however, *Tradition* does not signify mere repetition
of objective formulations of the faith. It signifies an ever deeper exploration of the revealed Word, through which the awareness of the Church
sheds greater light on the content of this divine revelation.

Thus revelation is not a formula entrusted to the Church for safe-
keeping. It is rather a living Word which calls out to human existence
in every age. And man's understanding of it advances as humanity itself
grows and deepens through its own questioning.

So we can talk about an historical conditioning, not only of the faith
in general but also of the awareness which the Church has of herself and
her relations with the rest of mankind. Through the contingent aspect
of historical reality, the faith continues to open up new pathways for
itself. It continues to explicate and reformulate itself in order to maintain its character as a response to God's summons to man.

The continuity of Tradition will be verified, not so much by a logical
concatenation of formulas as by the ever deeper effort of the Church to
remain faithful to the Spirit and to find a response to the questions that
are posed by new situations in history.

Right within the New Testament itself we find an example of a
profound change in outlook, framed within the deeper continuity of the
Spirit. It concerns Christian awareness with respect to the matter of
universality. It is worth our while to analyze the period of expansion
that immediately followed our Lord's ascension and the Pentecost gift
of the Holy Spirit. What did the newborn Church think about itself?

In trying to answer this question, it would be anachronistic to cite
the sermons of Jesus that are set down in the Gospels (*cf.* Mark 16:15).

The Gospels are not the first-written books of the New Testament, chronologically speaking. Moreover, they presuppose a faith-inspired growth in understanding of the words and deeds that the apostles experienced during their three years with Jesus. If we want to lay hold of the early outlook of the newborn Church, we must rather have recourse to the Acts of the Apostles, where the first questions of the nascent Christian community are conveyed to us in all their vitality. Like the new life that was beginning for these people, their process of reflection and formulation would gradually take shape and prepare to confront the experiences and opinions of the community members.

Let us consider briefly the principal stages in this process. In the first stage Christians, newly sprung from Judaism, did not take note of the *absolute novelty* of Christianity vis-à-vis the religion of Israel. Immediately after its account of Pentecost, Acts tells us this about the Christians: "They kept up their daily attendance at the temple, and, breaking bread in private houses, shared their meals with unaffected joy." (2:46).

The reference to the temple and the Eucharist suggests an unquestioned coexistence of Judaism and Christianity. In the speeches of Peter, Christ shows up as the definitive fulfillment of all that had been proclaimed by the prophets, without this fulfillment presupposing any rupture with the religion of Israel: "And so said all the prophets, from Samuel onwards; with one voice they all predicted this present time" (Acts 3:24).

Confronted with the problem of universality, the Christian outlook of the newborn Church will evince all the limitations of the view that held sway in contemporary Israel. Despite the universalist message of some prophets, despite the spirituality of the sapiential books which transcends all ethnic barriers, the religion of Israel continued to be a particularist, national religion from the sociological point of view. To be sure, with the passage of time Yahweh ceased to be one god among many, the localized God of the nation, and became the Lord of the universe. But humanity continued to be divided up into Jews and gentiles; and the Jews, failing to view themselves with explicit reference to the latter (i.e., with a function to perform for them), tended to view *election* as a privilege that *conferred exclusive rights on them.* Saint Paul undoubtedly refers to this situation when he addresses the following words to the pagans in the Church of Ephesus: "You, Gentiles, as you are outwardly, you, 'the uncircumcised' so called by those who are called 'the circumcised' (but only with reference to an outward rite)—you were at that time separate from Christ, strangers to the community of Israel, outside God's covenants and the promise that goes with them. Your world was a world without hope and without God" (Eph. 2:11–12).

Within this framework and without any other possibility being posed, the first Christians preached the Good News *solely* to the Jews (*cf.* Acts 11:19). This in fact was their first response to the problem of universality regarding those destined to receive the message: that message was destined for the Jewish people.

But Acts also alludes to something that would be decisive in opening up a new vision within Christianity. In the Christian community there was present a group of Hellenistic Jews who had lived outside Palestine, and who had their own synagogues in Jerusalem where they read the Bible in Greek. This fact was gradually freeing them from Jewish religious prejudices and making it easier for them to glimpse the novelty of Christianity. One of their number, the Deacon Stephen, was the first martyr of the Church. He would be condemned to death precisely for preaching that Christians were liberated from the practices of the Israelite religion. Here is the accusation made against him: "This man is for ever saying things against this holy place and against the Law. For we have heard him say that Jesus of Nazareth will destroy this place and alter the customs handed down to us by Moses" (Acts 6:13–14). The statements were not slanderous at all. It was just that Stephen had begun to see what Paul would later spell out in his letters: the liberation of Christianity from the religion of Israel and its total novelty vis-à-vis the latter. Paradoxically enough, Paul was present at Stephen's execution and "was among those who approved of his murder" (Acts 8:1).

But Christian awareness would have to travel a long road before this idea was definitively spelled out.

The second stage in this process involved the conversion of a pagan named Cornelius, which is reported in Acts 10. In a vision Peter sees a huge canvas filled with all kinds of animals, whose meats were prohibited to the Jew because of his religious notion of legal purity. A voice tells him: "Up, Peter, kill, and eat" (Acts 10:13). Peter, speaking from the depths of his Jewish religion, replies: "No, Lord, no: I have never eaten anything profane or unclean" (Acts 10:14).

The reply to Peter's protest has implications that would gradually take explicit form in Christian awareness: "It is not for you to call profane what God counts clean" (Acts 10:15). In other words, in Christ is eliminated the religious distinction which opposes the profane and impure to the sacred and pure—not only with respect to food and objects but also with respect to persons. As Paul would spell out later (cf. Eph. 2:14–17), there is no longer any distinction between a chosen people (the Jews) and the gentiles.

Peter came to understand this, at least to some degree, under the pressure of real-life events. Before entering the house of Cornelius, he says: "I need not tell you that a Jew[7] is forbidden by his religion to visit or associate with a man of another race; yet God has shown me clearly that I must not call any man profane or unclean" (Acts 10:27).

For Peter, however, this is but the first hazy glimpse of a reality that is breaking into the picture which he held unquestioningly before. What follows will reinforce the impression on his Jewish outlook. Peter transmits the Good News to Cornelius. Then "the Holy Spirit came upon all who were listening to the message. The believers who had come with Peter, men of Jewish birth, were astonished that the gift of the Holy Spirit should have been poured out even on Gentiles" (Acts 10:44–45).

Faced with this intervention by God, they could not hold on to any religious prejudice: "Is anyone prepared to withhold the water for baptism from these persons, who have received the Holy Spirit just as we did ourselves?" (Acts 10:47).

So the conversion of Cornelius is a decisive leap forward for Christian awareness in the process of acquiring a deeper understanding of Chris-

tianity as something that supercedes the Israelite religion. But it is only
one leap forward. When Peter returns to the community of Jerusalem,
he is criticized by Jewish Christians for having entered the home of gentiles and eaten with them (cf. Acts 11:3). He is forced to give a detailed
explanation of everything that happened. When he comes to talk about
the coming of the Holy Spirit upon the gentiles, he adds this: "Then
I recalled what the Lord had said: 'John baptized with water, but you
will be baptized with the Holy Spirit.' God gave them no less a gift than
he gave us when we put our trust in the Lord Jesus Christ; then how
could I possibly stand in God's way?" (Acts 11:16–17).

This remark of Peter produces the same impact on the brothers in
Jerusalem that the actual events had produced on him and his compan-
ions: "When they heard this their doubts were silenced. They gave praise
to God and said, 'This means that God has granted life-giving repentance
to the Gentiles also' " (Acts 11:18).

Let us stop for a moment to examine the process that has taken place
in Christian awareness. They started with the unquestioned position that
Christianity was to be preached solely to the Jews, but new situations
and events posed new questions. When these questions came up, they
remembered the words of Jesus which they had not understood before.
On the basis of these words, they elaborated the formula that "God has
granted life-giving repentence to the gentiles also." This formula was
not only different from but actually opposed to their earlier view.

The doctrinal problem was not resolved, but this did not forestall
a reaction from Judaizing factions which could not accept the extension
of their privilege to pagans. When Paul and Barnabas were sent to
Antioch in Pisidia, they began by preaching in the synagogues to the
Jews. But eventually, at the request of pagans, they preached to the whole
city. "When the Jews saw the crowds, they were filled with jealous resent-
ment and contradicted what Paul said, with violent abuse" (Acts 13:45).

This reaction marks the start of Paul's apostolate to the pagans, whose
theological basis finds expression especially in Romans and Galatians.
Here is his reaction to the incident at Antioch: "It was necessary . . .
that the word of God should be declared to you first. But since you reject
it and thus condemn yourselves as unworthy of eternal life, we now turn
to the Gentiles. For these are our instructions from the Lord: 'I have
appointed you to be a light for the Gentiles, and a means of salvation to
earth's farthest bounds' " (Acts 13:46–47).

The Acts of the Apostles thus opens the door to Paul's letters, which
we cannot analyze here. Let us simply point out one thing that relates
to the problem we are considering here. The notion of universality which
was beginning to dawn in Christian consciousness came about through
their overcoming of a particularistic notion about a chosen people and
their liberation from the practices of the Israelite religion. It is a universality which relates explicitly and primarily to those at whom the
message is directed. No one is excluded a priori from the community of
believers, and there are no ethnic barriers that separate people from
each other. In his own flesh, Christ "annulled the law with its rules and
regulations, so as to create out of the two a single new humanity in himself" (Eph. 2:15).

But if we were to ask Paul or contemporary Christians whether they thought this unity would be achieved through the entry of all men into the Church, they would probably reply that this question had not been formulated. It is certain that in Paul's ponderings we find elements upon which we today, through our own questioning, can ground the notion of universality proposed here. But it is no less certain that the central pre-occupation of the Church in its expansion phase, confronted with a pagan world which it must progressively penetrate, is the urgency of communicating to all "the unfathomable riches of Christ" (Eph. 3:8). It is this rather than posing the problem of the situation of those who do not and will not belong to the Church. The latter problem faded before the urgent task of immediate evangelization.

In analyzing this discovery of a certain universality within the New Testament itself, we were not interested in depicting the ultimate development that this notion could undergo. We simply wanted to show an example of the first step in a maturation process which, under the influence of the Spirit, often takes forms that appear to be a denial of what went before but which actually represent a deep continuity. The same process is involved in moving from many preconciliar conceptions to ones which alone permit authentic dialogue between the Spirit-guided Church and the "signs of the times."

NOTES

1. "For by His incarnation the Son of God has united Himself in some fashion with every man. He worked with human hands, He thought with a human mind, acted by human choice, and loved with a human heart" (GS 22).

2. "The ultimate vocation of man is in fact one and divine" (GS 22).

3. "The truth is that only in the mystery of the incarnate Word does the mystery of man take on light . . . Christ, the final Adam, by the revelation of the mystery of the Father and His love, fully reveals man to man himself" (GS 22).

4. Christ "taught us that the new command of love was the basic law . . . of the world's transformation. To those, therefore, who believe in divine love, He gives assurance that the way of love lies open to all men and that the effort to establish a universal brotherhood is not a hopeless one" (GS 38).

5. We use the word "mystical" here, prescinding from the distinctions made after Pius XII's encyclical, *Mystici Corporis Christi*. Leaving aside any discussion of terms, we feel that the content is clearly established by identifying the visible Church with the Mystical Body and salvation outside its visible limits with the Cosmic Christ. Something similar applies to the expression "People of God." Although this term was thought up to refer to the universal dimension of the Church, a particular usage today, and indeed its origins in the Bible, tend to make it synonymous with the Church as a particular reality. We feel that in these pages the meaning will be clear from the context; long terminological discussions are not needed.

6. Karl Rahner discusses this point in *Theological Investigations*, Vol. I: *God, Christ, Mary and Grace* (London: Darton, Longman & Todd; Baltimore: Helicon, 1961), pp. 304–311, and 356, Note 1.

7. It is worth noting that Peter defines himself as a Jew. He had not yet perceived the radical consequences of the Christ event on his condition as a Jew.

CHAPTER TWO

The Essence of the Ecclesial Community

A DIFFERENT ROAD
OR A NEW RESPONSIBILITY?

Porphyry posed a decisive question for us, and present-day history is forcefully reminding us of it. Our first response to it was that the limitations of the Church do not obstruct the universality of salvation.

We are not too late on the scene or too few, because all men are included within a salvation reality. At this point Porphyry could raise another objection: Why have you come at all? What critical function can belong to the community called the Church within this unfolding universal reality?

Answering this question presupposes two steps. Firstly, we must determine more clearly what exactly this Church of which we speak is. Only then can we move on to the second step, asking ourselves what is its function, contribution, and necessity.

These two steps are more or less interwoven into the passage in Saint Mark's Gospel which we considered a central text for one line of thought on salvation (Mark 16:15–16): "Those who believe it and receive baptism will find salvation." The necessity and essence of the Church are expressed here in summary form, the former by "will find salvation" and the latter by "believe it and receive baptism."

In effect the Church is the community of faith and the sacraments (baptism being the initiation into them). Frequently people add the element of authority or jurisdiction to these two basic elements mentioned by Christ himself. But they are not really adding one more factor because authority was established, not for its own sake, but precisely to regulate faith and the sacraments.

Now if we take this as the essential makeup of the Church, we can ask this question: Does it fit in with the definition we formulated in the preceding chapter as a key to understanding the function and necessity of the Church: the Christian is he who knows? In that chapter we saw that what distinguishes the ecclesial community within the universal salvation plan, which is as broad as all humanity in all ages, is the fact that it knows this plan through revelation. Thanks to the latter, we can say that the community called Church possesses the secret of what is happening in human history, knows its warp and woof, and understands the stakes that are being played out.

Now when we confront this definition with the essential components of the Church, i.e., faith and the sacraments, do we confirm our definition or not? Is it enough to say that the Church is the community of those who know the secret of human history? Or must we add something else? Does the word "know" take account of the total reality of the community called Church?

To answer this question, we shall examine in turn the two essential elements alluded to by Christ himself.

First let us consider faith. The Church is the community of believers, that is, of those who have faith in what God has revealed.

But what is it that God has revealed? Is it perhaps a series of truths that are useful and even necessary for salvation and that relate to a divine world which only tangentially touches human realities in this world? To answer this question we must grasp the message of the New Testament in some summary and essential form.

"It was there from the beginning; we have heard it; we have seen it with our own eyes; we looked upon it, and felt it with our own hands; and it is of this we tell. Our theme is the word of life." Here we have almost an echo of the prologue to the Fourth Gospel: "No one has ever seen God; but God's only Son, he who is nearest to the Father's heart, he has made him known" (John 1:18). John thereby sets up an opposition. On the one hand there is what was known about God through the Old Testament and rational understanding, all this being a knowledge of God *from outside.* On the other hand there is this knowledge of God *from within,* which only the incarnate God himself could communicate to us. The three Synoptics delivered a message through the sayings and deeds of Jesus. In the Fourth Gospel, John delivers this message through deeds and events charged with meaning and symbolism. Now, in his First Epistle, he delivers the same message in a few basic ideas. His approach seconds our task here.

Looking at John's epistle, we see that he tells us that the revelation of the Word can be summed up in the clear expression: *God is love.* John tells us this explicitly on two occasions (*cf.* 1 John 4:8 and 16), and says it indirectly in many other spots. The only thing is that we have emptied this expression of much of its content by placing God's love solely in the fact that he gives us the existence we possess. When we speak of love we mean the giving of oneself, not merely of a gift that can be recalled. Thus when the God who is love gives something he gives himself too. Now this is what Saint John wanted to indicate. He writes that a person who did not have any experience of what loving was could not appreciate who God was (1 John 4:8). Further on he expressly spells this out, saying that we know charity not because God has given us something but because he gave up his very life for us (1 John 4:9–10; 3:16). God became love for us to the point where he chose to suffer our death; he took our death upon himself. He truly suffered and died, as more traditional theology compels us to say.

Thus the expression "God is love" signifies something very concrete. It signifies not just that God gives something that he has but that he gives himself. And John adds something that is very important: that God gave us his very own life. He did so not just because he died for us but also because he passed his life on to us. It is a victorious gift, unlike our gifts which often end in the mere act of giving and are not actually received by the person we are giving them to. The gift of his life to us is a victorious gift from God; it is passed on to us so that we have the same life as he does.[1] And what sort of life is this? Self-giving. Because of this we too are able to give ourselves, and this is a divine and eminently supernatural possibility for Saint John (1 John 4:7). Man does not give himself naturally. By nature he is simply a being who needs everything and who seeks out what he lacks on every level of his existence. Because he has divine life in him, however, he is capable of taking what he has, forgetting about himself and what he lacks, and giving it to others. This possibility is so divine that John sees it as an experiential sign of the fact that we are in a new creation, that is, in the supernatural order: "We for our part have crossed over from death to life; this we know, because we love our brothers" (1 John 3:14). This for him is the sign that divine life has been passed on to us, because without this life we would not have the capacity to love.

Thus, for Saint John, the main thing is to exercise this divine life, to practice self-giving. In the life of the average person, it begins with love for another visible person: one's neighbor. Real self-giving, genuine and showing itself in action rather than in mere words (1 John 3:18), begins with the giving of oneself to another visible person who needs our being. John has no confidence in the person who claims to love God alone: "If a man says, 'I love God,' while hating his brother, he is a liar. If he does not love the brother whom he has seen, it cannot be that he loves God whom he has not seen" (1 John 4:20). What matters most to John is not the object of love but the fact that it is *really practiced*. In origin love is divine. For the man who practices love, who practices self-giving in any degree, exercises the divine life that is in him (*cf.* 1 John 4:7). Now we can understand the logical jump that Saint John makes at various points in his epistle: "If God thus loved us . . . we in turn are bound to love one another" (1 John 4:11; 3:16). We expect him to conclude by saying that we ought to love God, but instead he tells us to love one another.

Now we can understand Christ's commandment as it is given in John's Gospel. When Jesus was asked what the chief commandment was, he spoke about loving God; but he also implied that there was another commandment in the same category, namely loving other human beings (*cf.* Matt. 22:34–40). But when he comes to leave his testament to us, when he tells us what is essential just before returning to his Father, he bequeathes his own commandment to us on the eve of his passion. Saint John is very explicit about it. It is the very commandment of the Word which comes from within God, which reveals the essential thing to us and provides an orientation for our whole life. And what does his commandment bid? "Love one another; as I have loved you, so you are to love one another" (John 13:34; see John 15:12–13; 13:13–14). This does not seem important to us, because we are wont to count on this possibility of divine life dwelling in us. This habit indicates that man presently has this possibility because God gave it to him; but it does not suggest that it is *natural.* So we should realize that any love man shows for his fellow men, however simple it may be, is divine in origin thanks to the timeless gift God has given to all men. It is therefore supernatural in itself and conducive to eternal life.[2]

We can also realize that not only is the source of this love between human beings divine but that its object is always God as well. God loves each one of us immeasurably, even to the point of enduring our sufferings and sharing our death. So what we do for any person is accepted by him without anything being lost at all, for he loves us without measure. Thus the *source* of all real love between human beings is God, the divine life within man. And what is more, the *object* of all real love between human beings is God as well as the person loved.

Now we can return to the vision of the final judgment presented by Christ in Saint Matthew's Gospel. God is going to judge all men in terms of the way they have practiced self-giving and real love throughout the history of mankind. Why? Because this gift is God's life in man, the power that God has given to human existence. And all men will be judged in terms of this power given to them.

From what we have said so far, we can conclude that revelation is both a revelation of God and of what is happening with the human race.[3] Saint Paul indeed describes Christian revelation as knowledge of the *mystery.* And for him, mystery signifies a divine plan, hidden but universal in its operation, that runs throughout history.[4] This plan of love, centered around the historical Incarnation and redemptive work of Christ, has two planes as it were. On one plane, the Incarnation and Redemption operate from the beginning of humanity to its end. On the other plane, *knowledge* of this loving plan operating as a mystery in the Incarnation and Redemption is at work solely from the time Christ came into human history.

Let us consider here two central texts of Saint Paul. The first deals with the plane wherein the grace of Incarnation and Redemption surpasses all time:

> Mark what follows. It was through one man that sin entered the world, and through sin death, and thus death pervaded the whole human race, inasmuch as all men have sinned. . . . death held sway from Adam to Moses. . . . But God's act of grace is out of all proportion to Adam's wrongdoing. For if the wrongdoing of that one man brought death upon so many, its effect is vastly exceeded by the grace of God and the gift that came to so many by the grace of the one man, Jesus Christ. And again, the gift of God is not to be compared in its effect with that one man's sin; for the judicial action, following upon the one offence, issued in a verdict of condemnation, but the act of grace, following upon so many misdeeds, issued in a verdict of acquittal. For if by the wrongdoing of that one man death established its reign, through a single sinner, much more shall those who receive in far greater measure God's grace, and his gift of righteousness, live and reign through the one man, Jesus Christ.
>
> It follows, then, that as the issue of one misdeed was condemnation for all men, so the issue of one just act is acquittal and life for all men. . . . where sin was thus multiplied, grace immeasurably exceeded it (Rom. 5:15–20).

The second text deals with the plane which begins in history with the redemptive Incarnation and goes on from there through history. It is man's sharing in the mystery, thanks to revelation:

> Paul, apostle of Jesus Christ, commissioned by the will of God, to God's people at Ephesus, believers incorporate in Christ Jesus. Grace and peace from God our Father and the Lord Jesus Christ. Praise be to the God and Father of our Lord Jesus Christ, who has bestowed on us in Christ every spiritual blessing in the heavenly realms. . . . In Christ our release is secured and our sins are forgiven through the shedding of his blood. Therein lies the richness of God's free grace lavished upon us, imparting full wisdom and insight. He has made known to us his hidden purpose . . . to be put into effect when the time was ripe: namely, that the universe, all in heaven and on earth, might be brought into a unity in Christ. . . .
>
> I, Paul, who in the cause of you Gentiles am now a prisoner of Christ Jesus—for surely you have heard how God has assigned the gift of his grace

to me for your benefit. It was by a revelation that his secret was made known to me. I have already written a brief account of this, and by reading it you may perceive that I understand the secret of Christ. In former generations this was not disclosed to the human race; but now it has been revealed by inspiration to his dedicated apostles and prophets, that through the Gospel the Gentiles are joint heirs with the Jews, part of the same body, sharers together in the promise made in Christ Jesus. Such is the gospel of which I was made a minister, by God's gift, bestowed unmerited on me in the working of his power. To me, who am less than the least of all God's people, he has granted of his grace the privilege of proclaiming to the Gentiles the good news of the unfathomable riches of Christ, and of bringing to light how this hidden purpose was to be put into effect. It was hidden for long ages in God the creator of the universe . . . This is in accord with his age-long purpose, which he achieved in Christ Jesus our Lord. . . . With this in mind, then, I kneel in prayer to the Father, from whom every family in heaven and on earth takes its name, that out of the treasures of his glory he may grant you strength and power through his Spirit in your inner being, that through faith Christ may dwell in your hearts in love. With deep roots and firm foundations, may you be strong to grasp, with all God's people, what is the breadth and length and height and depth of the love of Christ, and to know it, though it is beyond knowledge. So may you attain to fullness of being, the fullness of God himself.

Now to him who is able to do immeasurably more than all we can ask or conceive, by the power which is at work among us, to him be glory in the church and in Christ Jesus from generation to generation evermore! (Eph. 1:1–10 and 3:1–21).

Thus the message is not an a-historical one. It is essentially historical in the sense that it lets us know about God loving and operating in humanity and humanity acting with God even though men may not know it.[5] We also know the mechanism at work in God's activity with humanity: love.[6] We not only know in some vague way that God has a salvation plan. We also know how this plan works itself out. This, in summary form, is the faith of the Church, which is the mystery of Christ. To believe in Christ is to do all the things that Jaime Diaz relates to the "Amen" we utter at Mass: "It is, before everything else, our personal surrender to the Son of God, in whom God was pleased to reveal the hidden mystery to us. *Therefore* it is our total acceptance of God's salvific plan, of his will for us, of charity as the supreme law." That in effect is the message we receive. It is in summary form the *whole* mystery—not just a part of it.

Thanks to the wisdom of which Saint Paul speaks, the Church is the consciousness of humanity as it were. She is humanity arriving at full awareness of what is taking place in it.[7] Thus, as we have already seen, the Church is all humanity in a certain sense. She is the congregation of the human race, just as that which is conscious in us represents our whole being.[8]

The totality of church dogmas are not magical formulas that pass on salvation. They are the explication of this central revelation, which is both a revelation about God and a revelation about man at the same time. It provides access to the divine mystery and to the mystery of mankind and human history.[9]

Well, some one might say, at least the *sacraments* add to this knowledge an exclusive feature: efficacious means of grace and salvation. Thanks to them, the Christian would seem to be one who confronts humanity not only as one who knows but also as one who receives grace— as one who receives it in abundance at any rate.

But here we must recall some items from the Church's traditional theology. We know that the sacraments are not the only means by which God grants his grace. The same theology of the sacraments tells us that there are sacraments of desire which correspond to the visible sacraments. Baptism can be sacramental baptism, that is, received through the visible sign instituted by Christ; but it can also be a baptism of desire for those who for some reason cannot receive the sacramental sign. These latter receive the grace of God without the visible sign, directly from the heart of God to their heart as it were, as God's response to the good intention which God himself placed in them. The principle underlying the whole theology of grace is that "God does not deny his grace to anyone who does his part." This same principle is also valid in the whole theology of the sacraments.

Having reached this point in the theology relating to the sacraments of desire, we must of course be careful not to minimize their scope and effectiveness. When we view them in terms of the Church and the sacraments which are fully such, the very term "sacraments *of desire*" may invest them with the connotation that they are extraordinary means for exceptional situations and therefore presumably inferior in effectiveness to those which Christians normally use.

But this is not the case. To begin with, we must not think that baptism of desire is only the desire of a man who already believed in the Church and died before having the time or means to get himself baptized. Theology has always understood that baptism of desire is a much broader reality: namely, an acceptance of God even without knowing the Church. We should not becloud the word "desire" as if it meant simply "desire for the waters of baptism." For in fact it signifies a much more general response to God.

What is more, we know this as well from the other sacraments. When a person cannot receive absolution, contrition is enough to receive the grace of pardon. And this contrition is not found solely within the visible Church, into which a person can go physically to make his confession. Contrition is a much more general expression, indicating that "God does not deny his grace to the person who does his part." Nor does he deny his pardon to that person. The same holds true for spiritual communion and other such things.

In other words, while it may be exceptional for God's grace to come through the sacraments of desire where Christians are concerned, this is the normal situation for humanity. This is how God's grace operates in the daily lives of human beings. The sacraments of desire are nothing more than the countless expressions of man's good will which find echo in God, of the same God who is the origin and object of this same good will.[10]

Karl Rahner justifiably remarks that there is no theological reason for thinking that the grace received in this way is any less than that which Christians receive in the sacraments of the Church.[11] And if we want to avoid talk in quantitative terms where grace is concerned, we might say that there is no theological reason for thinking that the person who lives in the normal atmosphere of the sacraments of desire is disfavored in his quest for salvation.[12]

What is more, all our theological reasons, starting right with the serious intent of God's universal salvific plan, lead us to avoid any such minimization. Vatican II is explicit on this point: "We ought to believe that the Holy Spirit, in a manner known only to God, offers to every man the possibility of being associated with this paschal mystery" (GS 22).

It is precisely the phrase of the Council that permits us to respond to the question that springs up spontaneously here, even as it did in the preceding chapter: What then is the difference between receiving grace and its power for love and salvation directly from God on the one hand, and receiving it through the full sacraments of the Church on the other hand?

Our answer is the same as that which we indicated in Chapter I, as the one suggested by the Council. Only God knows the grace that operates through the sacraments of desire; it comes to man in a *mysterious* way. By contrast, the sacrament not only confers grace on the Christian but also *signifies* it: it lets us know it. In essence and mission, the Christian is he who knows, he who is acquainted with the hidden reality of God's gift which passes our way without men knowing it.

It was for this reason that God wanted us to have faith in general and the sacraments in particular. With them the Christian does not acquire a monopoly on grace (which reaches others too, and in abundance); but he does come to know it and to live it consciously. Thus we should not be surprised to find that the term *sacrament* is simply the Latin translation for a key Greek word in Saint Paul's writings: *mysterion*. Through faith and through the sacraments the Christian comes into possession of this secret which remains mysterious but nonetheless efficacious for the rest of humanity.

Combining the elements we have discussed so far, we can try to form a synthesis between the two lines of thought on salvation that we encountered in the New Testament. We were surprised to find that in the text of Matthew cited earlier, salvation is attributed to love, while in the text of Mark it seems to be attributed to something else: i.e., faith and the sacraments. But after what we have just seen, we must conclude that faith and the sacraments do not designate another reality but the very same one: i.e., love lived in the Christian way, which involves possession of its *mystery*.

Thus the obligation of the Church is none other than the obligation of love. And if, in loving, each and every person gives the being that he is, then the Christian, in *truly* doing this, must include what he is in the Church; in short, he must give his awareness of the mystery through faith and the sacraments.

In the next chapter we shall see that this knowledge is a powerful factor for love. Right now, however, we shall simply point out that our remarks force us to make an important change in the picture we frequently have about relations between the Church and mankind. That picture sees humanity travelling on an erroneous path which of itself does not lead to salvation. It is only believers who, by some privilege from God, have found the right road. Marked out by faith and the sacraments, this road will take them away from other men and lead them to salvation.

Considering what we have just discussed, we are forced to rectify this picture. Unless they fall back through evil intentions, all men travel the same road, and it leads them to salvation: it is the road of self-giving through love. The journey is common to all men, who are turned in the right direction by a law that God has placed in their hearts. The only thing is that some people on this road, through God's revelation, know something that relates to all; they know the mystery of the journey.[13] And what they know, they know in order to make a contribution to the common quest. What does this contribution involve in concrete terms? That is the theme of Chapter III.

NOTES TO CHAPTER TWO

1. "This likeness [between all men and God] reveals that man . . . cannot fully find himself except through a sincere gift of himself" (GS 24).

2. "The Christian man . . . receives the first-fruits of the Spirit by which he becomes capable of discharging the new law of love. . . . All this holds true . . . for all men of good will in whose hearts grace works in an unseen way" (GS 22). See CLARIFICATION I in Chapter I.

3. "Faith throws a new light on everything, manifests God's design for man's total vocation, and thus directs the mind to solutions which are fully human" (GS 11).

4. "It is, finally, through the gift of the Holy Spirit that man comes by faith to the contemplation and appreciation of the divine plan" (GS 15).

5. "And thus directs the mind to solutions which are fully human" (GS 11).

6. Christ "taught us that the new command of love is the basic law of human perfection and hence of the world's transformation" (GS 38).

7. "And yet I do speak words of wisdom to those who are ripe for it, not a wisdom belonging to this passing age [i.e., one that has its source in created realities]. I speak God's hidden wisdom, his secret purpose framed from the very beginning, to bring us to our full glory. . . . God has revealed [this wisdom] to us through the Spirit. . . . so that we may know all that God of his own grace has given us" (1 Cor. 2:6–12).

8. The Christian lives between two "manifestations" or epiphanies: that of the grace of our savior God and that of the glory of the savior God (cf. Titus 2:11–13). Thanks to the mystery which we possess, our function for God comes to involve praising him for the glorious favor he has bestowed and recognizing his glory even now, before its final epiphany (cf. Eph. 1: and 11–12). Christians have the conviction that created realities reach their fulfillment in them; their place and function within this arc of time is recognized.

9. "Christ . . . by the revelation of the mystery of the Father and His love, fully reveals man to man himself" (GS 22).

10. "It is not always necessary [for salvation] that the person be de facto incorporated into the Church as a member. But it is required that he at least be united by desire or intention, even though it is not even necessary for this desire to be explicit" (Letter of the Holy Office to Archbishop Cushing of Boston; American Ecclesiastical Review 127 (1952), pp. 307–311; cf. Denz. 3866, 3873).

11. See Karl Rahner, Theological Investigations, Volume II, Man in the Church (London: Darton, Longman & Todd; Baltimore: Helicon, 1963), pp. 113 ff.

12. But this is how we should interpret Paul's phrase in which he explains that being a Jew is not a privilege over against the non-Jew with respect to justification. His phrase is "God has no favourites" (Rom. 2:11). On this point see CLARIFICATION III below.

13. "The Church, at once a visible assembly and a spiritual community, goes forward together with humanity and experiences the same earthly lot which the world does. She serves as a leaven and a kind of soul for human society" (GS 40).

CLARIFICATIONS

I. IS THERE A CHRISTIAN ANTHROPOLOGY?

Under the whole relationship between revelation and anthropology there is framed a series of problems which were discussed in some way by Vatican II, especially in its decree *Gaudium et spes*. Here we should like to offer the reader a summary overview of this complex of questions.

The point of departure here is the gap between faith and life in the world. Vatican II expressly indicated that this divorce is not Christian: "This split between the faith which many profess and their daily lives deserves to be counted among the more serious errors of our age" (GS 43). This whole problem area has taken shape in the face of a "desacralized" world. The world has been desacralized in a profound sense. In effect man has taken cognizance of his power to fashion himself as man (anthropogenesis). The new form taken by criticisms of religion is framed within the level of anthropogenesis. Marx criticized religion as a mask of fear supporting a situation wherein man exploited man. Nietzsche criticized religion as a mask of weakness against the will to power. Freud criticized religion as a neuroticism tied up with the father figure.

The great seer into this new situation was the Protestant theologian, Dietrich Bonhöffer. He maintained that criticism of religion as a human failing and a source of alienation is an indispensable condition for the faith of our contemporaries. His theme has been taken up by a whole series of Protestant and Catholic theologians, and it has culminated in the recent "death of God" movement. Undoubtedly this is a major question in current theological literature because of its transcendent pastoral implications.

Gaudium et spes tells us this: "Christ, the final Adam, by the revelation of the mystery of the Father and His love, fully reveals man to man himself and makes his supreme calling clear" (GS 22). This is one of the key ideas in this conciliar document; in revealing himself as Love, God also reveals to man his inmost condition. Every theological statement, that is, every statement about God, is at the same time a statement about man.

Here then we have the first response of the Council to the problem posed by the breach between faith and human living. In accord with this affirmation, the same conciliar document offers us a perspective on man, a vision of him. The whole first chapter discusses the dignity of the human person, the makeup of man, the dignity of his ability to understand truth and wisdom, the grandeur of his liberty, the dignity of his moral conscience, and other such things.

This brings us to the second link in our chain. On the basis of the Council's affirmation cited above, can we infer the existence of a Christian anthropology, of a Christian theory about man? Or, to put it another way, does revelation offer to the believer a finished picture of man, a science of man? Does revelation make its adherents "superior" in this respect? Alongside those who painfully seek to know the mystery of their existence, would Christians be supplied with a *revealed science?*

It is undeniable that a somewhat "triumphalist" and magisterial tone in the Constitution (*Gaudium et spes*) provides a foothold for such an interpretation. But such an interpretation is incorrect in our opinion.

Revelation does not offer us an anthropology, no more than it offers us a cosmology. To be sure, the Bible does have a conception of man. Or, to put it better, it has several conceptions of man, depending on the era in which its books were edited and the contemporary currents of thought. But this anthropology, this conception of the world, is not a revealed datum. In the last analysis, what revelation tells us is that man, *as he appears in the course of history,* is borne along by the love of God, who never reneges on his gift of love.

"The sin-laden history of humanity shows us that God's love for sinful man is a love that liberates and pardons. And the human life of Jesus reveals that the only adequate response to God's love is radical love for one's fellow man—a love so radical and absolute that in itself it bears witness to God's love for man." [1]

This revelation is expressed through an anthropology. To paraphrase a patristic thought: Revelation "waited" for human experience to grow and mature sufficiently so that it could be "God's alphabet." But this "alphabet" is man himself as he has developed over the course of history.

So revelation does not teach us an anthropology that dropped out of the heavens. It enlightens us on the meaning of our existence. Looking at it from this angle, we must acknowledge that the Christian possesses a light which the nonbeliever lacks.[2] For this reason we can truly talk about a Christian understanding of life but, strictly speaking, we cannot talk about a Christian anthropology.

> Thus the Christian does not possess a separate human anthropology. As a Christian, he knows that man, as he is, is drawn up into the mystery of God's gratuitous love. So at bottom the mystery of man is the very mystery of God as seen in its human reflections. As history unfolds and develops, man discovers the dimensions of his existence. At each new stage of this self-discovery, he looks for the light of this unique revealed datum; and in each new dimension thus discovered, he integrates a love for his fellow men that is sustained in its depths by God's absolute and gratuitous love. As for anthropology, its formal structure will be fashioned by the terrestrial experiences of human Christians and non-Christians. Revelation, in turn, invites us at every turn to carry out our mission of love within the realm of this anthropology.[3]

This reflection leads us to the third link in our effort to form a synthesis.

Doesn't what we just said involve an exaggerated reduction of revelation? Does it not involve both doctrinal and moral relativism?

The effort to clarify this question, or at least to pose it more exactly, has major importance with regard to the transmission of the faith. So we shall attempt it here.

It is obvious that the image of man has evolved dizzily in this century. The Industrial Revolution, technology, Marx, Freud, Einstein, and many other factors have transformed it profoundly. None of the basic views which man had of himself have been left standing. It is also evident that the faith had been expressed within a conception of man that is now abandoned—both in the Bible and the magisterium. The famous conflict between science and faith maintains its force precisely because of the power science has to transform the image of man and the universe.

The Christian, and especially the Catholic, has been in the rearguard of this progress. He has been more a passive onlooker than an active participant. And those Christians who kept steady pace with the march of progress often encountered difficulties with religious authorities.

The conflict between science and faith was (is?) a painful process of purification through which contemporary Christianity passed. And it has brought with it this "retreat" by revelation. Many things which were believed to be immutable, and many teachings which appeared to belong to the deposit of faith, were reduced to the relative status of "vehicles" of faith. And all this happened in a very brief space of time.

This process has provoked waves of fear in the Catholic Church. Progress has not proceeded calmly but in sudden bursts, with strong tensions on both the left and the right. We may still not be mature enough in the faith to see it subjected to the "anxiety of our day" without feeling afraid. We have come out of a hothouse, and it is an effort for us to accept the fact that our faith is to be lived in the midst of this world, in the city of man. The feeling that revelation has been relativized or reduced in scope may result from this initial contact with the strong currents of our world, with "the joys and the hopes, the griefs and the anxieties of the men of this age, especially those who are poor or in any way afflicted . . ." (GS 1).

It may result from our first steps toward purification, which is to be followed by the next stage: construction.

This brings us to the final link in our effort to fashion a synthesis. The *retreat of the faith* is one moment, one condition, for a faith that is rooted in life. The mold, like the Word of God, remains ever relevant and powerful. It is the very work of the Spirit.

If the Christian is out on the same quest as every human being, if revelation gives him only enlightenment on the meaning of existence, then he must express his faith in this common quest. Precisely because faith can no longer be professed through an outdated image of man and his relations with the cosmos, the Christian inevitably faces the urgent task of fleshing it out in his world through *his* questions and *his* hopes. But this is possible only on the condition that the Christian has made a prior act of poverty and has died to an expression that is not the embodiment of "his life in the world."

So the Christian must confront this question: How am I to express this gift of self (which is radical and absolute and which finds its support only in the gift of God's definitive, pardoning love) in my world and my circumstances?

And the reader should note that once again the faith will find expression through a conception of man that is precarious and transitory. Our task is not definitive but provisional. Perhaps our world, with its greater changes, has made us a bit more truthful. Perhaps it is easier for us to accept the transitory aspect of our effort, because we live a human life that is on a high-speed train.

But this provisional task is *essential*. Without it there is no faith. A faith that does not become incarnate fades away. It disappears, and simply ceases to exist. Incarnation is the first law of revelation. God manifested himself through a concrete people and a concrete anthropology; then he delivered himself up fully in a man who was completely inscribed in history and geography. The world will believe in a faith that is fleshed out in today, not in a faith that takes refuge in some abstract, inoperative spiritualism, not in a faith tied up with other conceptions of man.

That is how faith is transmitted from generation to generation. That is how the grandeur of the Word is revealed to us through man's own progress. To the extent that humanity grows and matures, it becomes capable of serving as a better vehicle for the gift of God. In this way the work of every human being to form a human race and a universe that is more human and fraternal helps to reveal "the divine secret kept in silence for long ages but now disclosed" (Rom. 16:25–26).

II. WHAT IS THE DIVIDING LINE BETWEEN MAGIC AND CHRISTIAN MYSTERY?

The view of the Church presented in this chapter sees faith and the sacraments as expressions of the mystery of God revealed to men.

But there is no doubt that this conception clashes, if not with theory, then at least with many practices (most of them popular practices but some cultic ones as well) in which faith and sacrament appear in a very different context.

As we shall see in CLARIFICATION IV of this chapter, it could not be otherwise when the Christian way of life was lived in an overall regime called Christendom. In passing from a Christian practice rooted in conversion, in which God's revelation appealed to liberty, to a mass Christianity, the formulas of faith and the ritual formulas tend to be simplified and made more immediate. Simplification, a typical byproduct of mass living, makes them appear as possessing a value which can be ascertained with material exactness.

The notion of immediacy refers to the tendency to attribute to these formulas an automatic effect, one which achieves its purpose without involving the creative power of liberty.

Now in this conception, not only the sacraments but also and primarily the faith come to form part of attitudes that are *magical* in nature. Why?

Magic, reduced to its essential elements, consists of the quest for an

efficacity that goes beyond man's power. It achieves this by having recourse to superior powers, whom it tries to get to operate in a specific way
through symbolic gestures. These gestures, taking on superhuman power
but nevertheless controlled by man through symbolism, will produce the
proper effect directly. It will be all the more automatic insofar as the
efficacity is not the human, common effectiveness of an ordinary concrete
action.

If one is trying to cause the death of his enemy, he will resort to a
spell so that his trivial act will be tied up with a superior power. With
this combination of deeds and words one expects an automatic result that
is out of all proportion to the action performed but that is controlled by
the symbolism of it.

Now this approach, which appears in coarse form among primitive
peoples, is transformed but does not disappear on more developed levels
of existence; for it is a deeply rooted dynamism. Thus it tends to reappear
even within Christianity, although in more subtle forms.

1. In the case of faith, the desire to determine once and for all the
minimum that can and should be demanded of the masses has led to
attitudes that are equivalent to magical ones, even though they are garbed
in fine theoretical robes. It is worthwhile, and even necessary, to seek
them out.

Consider, for example, the apparent solicitude of some people for
"orthodoxy," by which they mean that what we say must dovetail outwardly with dogmatic formulas. Is there not a magical approach underlying this solicitude in some way? Does it not attribute to a formula a
salvific effectiveness that it does not possess? Salvation in reality comes
from God and transforms man through his acceptance *in faith,* i.e., insofar as man accepts revealed data and converts it into real-life existence.
Thus it involves a creative, personal process rather than the mere repetition of something that has been taught. We do not sign a blank check
which God and the Church can fill in as they wish.

The blank-check approach seems to offer automatic security. On the
other hand, any quest for coherency in the faith and any criticism of the
solutions fashioned in our dialogue with the world, which are thus inadequate by their very nature, seem to jeopardize salvation. This is another
indication that their efficacity is being looked upon in a magical way.

Here we must also include the anxiety produced by the postconciliar
tremors in the Church. People demand to know, once and for all, *what
they must believe.* They want these necessary beliefs to be distinguished
from those that can still be debated. In effect they are attributing to
formulas a salvific value that is magical in nature, because it is automatic,
impersonal, and disproportionate to the effect desired (salvation).

This latter tendency is characteristic. When Cardinal Lercaro was
commenting on a celebrated address of Pius XII to Italian jurists, he said
that religious liberty involved *respect,* not so much for error as *for truth.*
This remark goes to the core of one of the most difficult transformations
required in Christian living. In effect he was saying that man does not
possess truth simply by repeating it. To possess truth means to run the
risk of making a mistake. Mathematics is not learned by rote but by trial

and error. And in this area Christian renewal requires that faith be a truth whose effect (salvation) is proportionate to the cause employed: truth actually possessed and converted into a way of life. This frees dogmatic truth from its magical character. It allows us, and even obliges us, to run the risk of thinking for ourselves where the message of faith is concerned.

2. Now consider the sacraments. We all can readily see that they, by the very fact that they involve acts and gestures, are a noticeable realm for magical deviation. Since the sacramental life is to be the theme of a later volume, we shall not delve deeply into sacramental theology here. But let us indicate briefly the mechanism whereby one arrives at magical attitudes in this area.

There is nothing intrinsically magical in the fact that the *sacraments* are *efficacious* channels of grace. A gift, accompanied by a gesture, is efficacious. So is the very gesture of affection alone. No one would say that we are caught up in magic when we say that a handshake establishes friendship and signifies it.

In the controversy with Protestantism, the Council of Trent defined the *ex opere operato* efficacity of the sacraments. In so doing, it wished to express two realities that are closely tied together: (1) that the sacramental act is not simply a reminder or commemoration of a gift obtained from God, that in it the gift is really given; (2) that God gives this gift *unfailingly.*

In stressing these two points, the Council of Trent did not introduce magical factors, but it did open the way for them. It might seem, on the one hand, that God needed the sacraments to communicate his grace. But if the sacraments are necessary, it is not because their absence would mean the absence of grace in the world. It is because without them the grace conferred would not be *signified.* To insist on their signification character is not to deny the aspect of efficaciousness; it is simply to indicate the why and wherefore of the Christian sacraments (*cf.* SC 7). If a person receives the sacraments without comprehending their signification, then he will receive grace by virtue of his presumed good will; but it will not be Christian grace accompanied by knowledge of the mystery.

Secondly, the infallible conferral of grace leaves room for some people, who seek to find a special privilege in the Church, to imagine that in the sacraments they have an instrument of grace which they can manipulate. Human beings are accustomed to regard anything personal as a variable reality, so they cannot get used to the sacramental relationship. It is indeed infallible, given without strings attached and for good; but it does not thereby cease to be a personal gesture calling for an equally personal response. Its infallible quality is linked up with the mechanical and the automatic. And so by degrees this nonphysical mechanism is degraded to the automatism and impersonal nature of the magical.

By contrast, we can adopt a different outlook. We can see the sacraments as personal gestures of humanity's Savior, as gestures through which he reveals to us his activity in every man's life and summons us to collaborate with him in the new creation. If we do this, we shall have drawn an uncrossable dividing line between magic and the sacraments.

III. IS BEING A CHRISTIAN A PRIVILEGE?

The occidental distinction between knowing and living, between understanding and doing, between truth known and holiness actually lived, introduces a difficulty here that is usually expressed in terms of ascetical theology. If faith and the sacraments are understood to be correlates of the revelation of the mystery, can they still be translated into terms of *holiness* and *perfection?* Even if they only involve *knowing* what God had kept hidden from men in earlier centuries (*cf.* Eph. 3:5), is there not in our vocation to the Church a privilege, a greater perfection, a special reason for giving thanks to him who has summoned us to "share the heritage of God's people in the realm of light" (Col. 1:12).

We feel that the succeeding chapters of this volume will dispel any effort to interpret Christian knowledge, a response to the revelation received, as a privilege that fashions an intellectual elite. We shall see that it makes sense only when it is viewed as the source of a work of service on behalf of all men, making us "Christ's subordinates and stewards of the secrets of God" (1 Cor. 4:1). This will be discussed further in later chapters (see the main article in Chapter III on Christian knowledge and the main article in Chapter IV on the necessity of the Church as a sign).

However, this is only the first step. It removes one obstacle but the essence of the difficulty remains. Paul says to the Romans: "Through him [i.e., Christ] I received the privilege [i.e., was graced] of a commission" (Rom. 1:5). In other words, we have received grace (or favor) and apostleship, a gift and a commission, a privilege and a responsibility. Even if we readily admit the aspect of responsibility in the Christian vocation, we still must try to establish the proper relationship between these two terms or synonyms. Let us see what we can do here.

That the Christian vocation involved an *election* on God's part is a datum that formed part of the daily life of the primitive Church. The early Christians knew they were "chosen" or "elected" (*cf.* 1 Cor. 1:27–28; Rom. 8:33; 1 Pet. 1:2; James 2:5). Using the term in a way that is somewhat different from our usage today, they called themselves "saints." For them, as for the Old Testament in general, it meant "consecrated" or "united in a special way to God." In this union with God they saw a proof of God's love and a reason for giving thanks. The most significant passage in this respect might well be this one from Paul's Epistle to the Colossians: "Then put on the garments that suit God's chosen people, his own, his beloved: compassion, kindness. . . . To crown all, there must be love, to bind all together and complete the whole. Let Christ's peace be arbiter in your hearts; to this peace you were called as members of a single body. And be filled with gratitude" (Col. 3:12–15).

Here we must make a theological observation that is important for understanding what follows. The contemporary expression of Christian thought, as reflected in the writings of the New Testament, did not see any special importance in distinguishing between the thanks they owed God for reasons relating particularly to their status as Christians and the thanks owed by all men to him if they knew what Christians knew. This is what we see in the text above. Only on rare occasions do the early Christians give thanks to God *specifically* for what relates to them as Christians.

Thus when the Christian gives thanks to Christ for having redeemed him, he is not implying that non-Christians are not redeemed. It is just that the problem was not posed, all the more because other men could not give thanks for something they did not know. For this very reason, it is up to Christians to give thanks for (i.e., in place of) all the rest of mankind who are unwitting beneficiaries of the same grace (*cf.* 1 Tim. 2:2).

Thus we are still left with the problem of trying to find out whether the early Church saw the peculiar and constitutive Christian element as a supplementary perfection, a benefit, and a special reason for giving thanks, or simply as a responsibility shouldered. In other words, when Paul refers to grace and the apostolate, is he making a real distinction between that which all men receive from Christ (i.e., a benefit, a perfection, a grace for which they should give thanks), and the responsibility that is introduced into the life of the Christian through his new-found knowledge of the mystery (i.e., his being sent to serve others, his apostolate, which would not entail thanks since it is hardly a benefit in itself).

In several places Paul expressly deals with the specific and distinctive aspect of the Christian vocation. He begins his Epistle to Titus this way: "From Paul, servant of God and apostle of Jesus Christ, marked as such by faith and knowledge and hope—the faith of God's chosen people, knowledge [*supergnosis*] of the truth as our religion has it, and the hope of eternal life. Yes, it is eternal life that God, who cannot lie, promised long ago, and now in his own good time he has openly declared himself in the proclamation which was entrusted to me by ordinance of God our Saviour" (Titus 1:1–3).

Here, as in the Epistle to the Ephesians, the fundamental difference between Christian reality and that which it is not shows up clearly in every passage that alludes to the phase of God's plan embodied in revelation and the commissioning of some men to propagate it.

But this difference, which makes the receiver a collaborator and administrator of what he has received (*cf.* 1 Cor. 4:1–2), is also conceived by Paul as a *grace,* a favor. And it is so immeasurable that it overflows into full knowledge of the mystery. This is described beautifully in one passage of the Epistle to the Ephesians. It begins with an act of thanksgiving which, as we saw earlier, does not seek to distinguish the specifically Christian reasons for giving thanks: "Praise be to the God and Father of our Lord Jesus Christ, who has bestowed on us in Christ every spiritual blessing . . . in Christ he *chose* us before the world was founded, to be dedicated and without blemish in his sight, to be full of love; and he destined us . . . to be accepted as his sons through Jesus Christ" (Eph. 1:2–5).

Here we have the plan which dominates the whole history of the world and of which creation itself is an instrument (see CLARIFICATION I, Chapter I). But this plan is not a scheme affecting only Christians. Paul goes on to contrast the aspects of this plan that touch all and the aspects of it that cover the specific position of Christians within this plan: "For in Christ our release is secured and our sins are forgiven through the shedding of his blood. Therein lies the richness of God's free grace lavished upon us, imparting full wisdom and insight [i.e., not speculative knowledge but knowledge of the real world]. He has made known to us his hidden purpose—such was his will and pleasure determined beforehand in Christ . . ." (Eph. 1:7–9).

Here Paul clearly states that it is the immeasurable generosity of God's favor which makes us responsible for communicating the message, which turns grace within us into a message for other men.

This is the culmination of God's plan of grace and salvation. Henceforth, now that this mission exists, it will contribute the element that truly directs and guides the universe. This total synthesis of knowledge and wisdom will turn God's plan into an awareness that will mold human history.

Here we find the two points of view that will allow us to resolve the apparent contradiction between that which is a grace but not a privilege on the one hand, and that which is a responsibility but also a perfection on the other. The two elements in question are (1) the man who receives grace and (2) God's plan which acquires greater depth through its insertion into human history.

It is not easy to frame these two realities in one and the same language. Paul himself encountered this difficulty when he tried to discuss the import of the revelation of the Law to the Jewish nation. Somehow through this incomplete but real revelation of the mystery, the Jewish nation would gain something that distinguished them from other peoples. It would put them in a position in relation to other peoples that was analogous to the position of Christians in relation to others.

In his Epistle to the Romans, Paul poses the problem and enunciates the fundamental principle underlying the personal or subjective aspect of perfection: "There will be trouble and distress for every human being who is an evil-doer, for the Jew first, and for the Greek also; and for every well-doer there will be glory, honour, and peace, for the Jew first and also for the Greek. *For God has no favourites*" (Rom. 2:9–11).

But if there is no personal advantage involved, wherein lies the difference? In an objective quality, of course: "In the law you [i.e., the Jew] see the very shape of knowledge [*gnosis*] and truth" (Rom. 2:20). Here objectively there is a value, a perfection: the Jew can "teach" (Rom. 2:21), even though he may interpret this quality wrongly. Thus it is an objective advantage: "Then what advantage has the Jew? What is the value of circumcision? Great in every way. In the first place, the Jews were entrusted with the oracles of God" (Rom. 3:1–2). Only in this way do we reach the point where a certain reality, hidden but real, is elevated to the level of conscious knowledge. And this is important even though in the case of the Jews, as Paul sees it, the reality discovered was a negative (but necessary) one in God's plan: i.e., sin. "Law brings only the consciousness of sin" (Rom. 3:20).

Here we have a higher stage in God's plan, a perfection acquired by the divine design in its historical working out. But we must not confuse this objective quality with a guarantee or a personal advantage accruing to the person who lives in this stage. That was the error of the Jews: "What, then? Are we Jews any better off? No, not at all! For we have already drawn up the accusation that Jews and Greeks alike are all under the power of sin" (Rom. 3:9).

Now let us try to sum up what we have just seen in conceptual form, using a few outside examples.

There exists an equality of *subjective* possibilities for all men with regard to salvation, holiness, and perfection. For each person they will ultimately come down to imitating the example of God, who gave his life for us (*cf.* 1 John 3:16–18). Being holy means giving everything that one is and has, be it much or little. To give halfway, even when it involves a magnificent gift, is to be only halfway holy.

In Bernanos's novel, *The Diary of a Country Priest,* the main character is sick and goes to see a doctor. After examining him and asking him questions, the doctor asks him if he still believes he was created with free will since he has a terrible heritage of alcoholism. The priest's response is substantially this: I don't know what dosage of liberty I have, but I will always have enough to give back to God in the form of love.

It is certainly true that the infirm person who offers his meager dosage of liberty without reserve is as holy as someone like Francis of Assisi, assuming that he offers to God all that he had to give. This is the holiness of which Jesus speaks when he compares the size of the gifts offered in the temple from a subjective viewpoint: "I tell you this, this *poor* widow has given more than any of the others; For those others . . . had more than enough, but she, with less than enough, has given all that she had to live on" (Mark 12:43–44).

The French psychologist Beirnaert has written an important article on the potentialities for holiness in those whose capacity for liberty is diminished by some disease or psychic imbalance. He uses the ideas we have just seen to resolve a problem which did not crop up in earlier times, because people assumed that all men had an equal store of personal liberty and responsibility. We can truly say that progress in psychology, which has pointed out diminutions in personal responsibility, has shown us the full theological merit of Christ's parable about the talents entrusted to different individuals (*cf.* Matt. 25:14–30).

But there is another side to the coin here. Receiving more or less, being well or sick, and knowing or not knowing what God has revealed, is not and should not be considered an indifferent matter. It has decisive *objective* importance. Why? Because there does exist a divine plan for the history of humanity (as we shall see more clearly in the succeeding chapters of this volume). And where this plan is concerned, it is most important that all have at their disposal as many possibilities as they can, so that they can contribute them to the formation of the new heaven and new earth.

Receiving something will always entail a danger for the receiver, as we know from the Gospel (*cf.* Matt. 25:30). But this danger should be considered a *grace*. Indeed there is no grace that is not a danger and a personal responsibility as well. For it is through grace that God's plan acquires the possibility of being objectively carried out. What is more, the aim of God's gift is not to quiet us or smother us but to make us fully free and creative, thus associating us with God's own work. In giving thanks for grace we are not giving thanks for the closer proximity of holiness or salvation. We are thanking God for giving us what he himself holds most dear: the destiny of the beings he loves, the destiny of all mankind.

All this is summed up concisely in a passage written by Péguy, which describes the whole course of God's grace in human life: "Mystery, danger, bliss, misfortune, divine favor, unique election, terrible responsibility, the whole grandeur of our lives . . . It depends on us whether the eternal Word will sound out or not . . . It is not enough that we have been created, reborn, and made faithful . . . It depends on us whether hope will suffuse the world or not . . . He has placed his eternal hope in our hands—frail, transitory, and sinful." [4]

IV. THE FORM OF THE CHURCH EMBODIED IN CHRISTENDOM

It is a fact that for centuries in the West the majority of people in the Church crossed the dividing line between Christian mysteries and magical attitudes. It is also a fact, dovetailing with the preceding one, that in these circumstances Christianity was lived as a privilege which people tried to ensure to as many as possible.

These two facts are commonly subsumed under the name of Christendom. So far we have hinted at what we might call the *theological* roots of this phenomenon. If we want to understand this phenomenon better, it is no less important that we take into account the conditionings of a *sociological* nature that accompanied the spread of the Church. For in a specific period they helped to give her a *form* which, though far from being immutable and eternal, still weighs heavily on our efforts at renewal in the present day.

How did we end up with this overall situation known as Christendom? What characteristics were displayed by the Church in that period? What implications does this historical situation have for us today? Let us begin by providing a brief analysis of the sociocultural context in which Christendom arose and developed.

First there was a pre-individualist period. The individual did not define himself as an individual but as a member of a group: i.e., a clan, a people, a family, a corporate group. In short, he defined himself in terms of some general category.[5] Is it not significant that the unit was defined in terms of its affiliation to a group by the term "individual," which means inseparable and indivisible? [6] In those circumstances the group to which one belonged constituted a closed circle. It set limits at the same time that it offered protection. It exercised strict control at the same time that it offered the security of firm roots. In short, the group transmitted traditional values and norms which, in a relatively stable period of history, enabled the individual to confront the foreseeable situations of life.

Another feature relating to social structure must be added to this picture. There existed a system of highly differentiated classes, each one closed in upon itself and eventually considered to have the same immutability as the laws of nature. A person was born, grew up, and died in the same status within an unchangeable social structure.

Finally, the continuity of this situation was ensured by the isolation in which the various human groups lived. The individual generally was confined to the narrow geographical horizon of his day-to-day life. He found himself in a position of dependence both with regard to nature and to society, strictly controlled by his natural environment (lacking dominion over nature) and by the strict laws which his group imposed on him. The result of this situation was that there was a very restricted realm for individual liberty, but also a feeling of security because the element of unpredictability was reduced to the maximum.

It was in this context that the Church lived out its process of institutionalization, and we must examine this process in the light of the *milieu* in which it took place.

Normally any religious group must confront the problem of survival and unity when its founder disappears and its membership starts to grow. This is particularly true when its geographic expansion is rapid and widespread, as was the case with Christianity.

The response to this problem is to bolster the institutional aspects which permit it to organize and control its members. In itself this procedure does not offer any great difficulties. Any human group must be organized if it wants to perdure, particularly when it has many members. However, the convergence of a number of factors that were concomitant with the institutionalization process tended to vitiate the deepest aspects of the Christian message.

The first factor was that new members no longer entered Christianity through personal conversion but rather through the simple process of birth. Thus the process of selection effected through a conversion to the faith, with all that this involved in terms of a profound change in human attitudes, was gradually replaced by mere vegetative growth. Conversion gradually came to be the rare exception.

The second factor was what we might call a shift of stress with regard to aims and goals. The aim of Church institutionalization is to ensure the earthly survival of the *new life* which was communicated by Christ and which summons men to freedom. But by virtue of its own dynamism, the institution tends also to set itself up as an end in itself, i.e., to make its own stability the one and only aim. In laying stress on the element of group *stability,* the institution introduced a new motive that was paradoxically opposed to the authenticity of the new life lived in the freedom of Christ. It tried to reduce the unpredictable elements in its members' behavior patterns to established routine forms. In short, the institution tended to become polarized around its normative function: i.e., regulating the conduct of its members, fixing goals and limits, and prescribing or proscribing for the purpose of ensuring stability.

This new element, combined with the element of growth through birth rather than personal conversion, gave rise to a fundamental change in the thrust of the Church. From a missionary outlook which sought to transmit a revelation that questioned human existence and called for a total response, it shifted to an outlook preoccupied with the idea of "preserving" the faith of people who had been born into Christianity and who were therefore presumed to be active and operative as Christians. The presentation of the message as a summons to conversion was replaced by an effort to *teach* a faith that was already hereditary. This faith was to be explicated through formulas that were handed down and that were presumed adequate in themselves to evoke the subjective experience from which they arose. In other words, the formulary aspect of assent to faith was given precedence over the richer aspects of New Testament thought, which saw this assent as the total consecration of man to God by way of response to his summons.

To carry out this function of ensuring and safeguarding the uniformity of its members' faith, the Church relied on a third decisive factor: its ability to institutionalize not just its interior life but also its visible presence in the temporal order. When Constantine declared Christianity to be the official religion of the state, the Church came out of the catacombs with a new element that would give rise to ambiguities throughout her history. That element was power. Henceforth the visible aspect of the Church in human society would be manifested through civil educational institutions, guilds, and other organisms whose function would be to protect and keep control over the faith-life of her members. This formed the bedrock of the phenomenon known as "Christendom." It crystallized a sociological milieu that was capable of conserving and transmitting the faith; and this faith was not the product of a painful conversion process but rather of simple birth and life in this sociological milieu.

The visibility of the Church in civil institutions completed the aspect of ambiguity in the phenomenon known as Christendom. Not only had the faith lost its dynamic character by being identified with the culture in which it was expressed (first factor). Not only had it been made routine and uniform for the sake of institutional stability (second factor). Now, by being transformed from a state of anticipation for God's eschatological kingdom into a *Christian society*, it was also transformed into a well-knit ideology that defended the established order. It could count on all the force embodied in a power that was spiritual in nature and hence superior; but it exercised this power ambiguously in the temporal order. This was the wellspring of all the historic conflicts between the Church and the civil authority.

Finally a fourth factor will complete our analysis of Christendom. It was the geographic spread of Christianity throughout the West, so that the political boundaries of the Empire coincided with those of the Christian world. Oneness of faith was no longer an isolated phenomenon; it embraced Western culture as a whole.

This new element was undoubtedly decisive for the church theology that was elaborated within the framework of Christendom. The universality of the Church was envisioned in quantitative terms. The Church was universal because all men belonged to her. The chief byproduct of this view was that missionary activity ceased to be the task of *each and every* Christian. The pagan was no longer someone whom you lived with or near; in a Christian world there were no pagans, just good or bad Christians. The pagan was someone living beyond the borders of the West, specifically in the Islamic world challenged by holy crusades.

When the discovery of new worlds and ancient cultures brought perplexity to the ingenuous Western mind, the subsequent questions never reached the point of challenging the status of the church establishment. In reality the missionary work initiated in this period did not try to incarnate Christianity in the new cultures. Instead it took its inspiration from the situation known as Christendom that prevailed in the West: Westernizing and Christianizing were inseparable. Where circumstances permitted missionaries to reproduce the phenomenon of Christendom (e.g., in Latin America), the Christianization process "triumphed." Where age-old cultures resisted this Westernizing effort, the Christianization process came to nought.

Underlying these four factors already analyzed was another fact. Christianity had become a religion of the masses, a mass process whereby a growing number of "Christians" were incorporated into the Church *without ever being evangelized.* The Church was thus confronted with the task of taking in a mass of people and organizing them and then controlling them; and Christianity, by its very content, was incapable of doing this without losing the most authentic elements of its message. This is precisely what happened. The four factors already discussed are simply aspects of this process whereby Christianity was transformed into a Christian society, whereby the Church undertook an impossible *tour de force* and tried to take in a mass of nonevangelized Christians without vitiating its message.

In this section we have presented this whole process as a sociological phenomenon. This might suggest to some that it involved an insensible transformation under the impulse of some uncontrollable determinism. But that is not true. History, and that includes the history of Christianity, is fashioned by options and choices that are more or less clearly seen together with their implications. However it is not our intention here to go into a "subjective" analysis of the conscience of the Church in this whole process which culminated as Christendom. Our aim here is solely to see this phenomenon as a fact of past history, because it continues to affect the outlook of today's Christian.

Our analysis has been very summary, to be sure.[7] But two facts should be clear: (1) Christendom is primarily a sociological phenomenon, the product of a unique and precise moment in human history; (2) however, on the basis of this historical situation there was elaborated a theology which, to some extent, was meant to be its justification. The great prosperity enjoyed by the Church in the regime of Christendom validated the regime itself and the theology which arose in it, as Father Liégé indicates. It was considered an ideal that should be preserved. When the sociological (i.e, politico-cultural) substrate on which Christendom rested underwent change, as it has radically in the last five centuries, Christians resisted the idea of accepting this change. They could not see what was called for: a new form of ecclesial incarnation and a different process of reflection on the life of the Church—the latter now being situated in the world in a new and unexpected way.

The period of transition in which we are now living is woven specifically of the tensions and conflicts between two different factors: (1) the elements of Christendom that still persist in the structures of the

Church, her pastoral activity and, above all, in the minds of Christians;
(2) the new forms of ecclesial incarnation called for by a revitalized
theology, which are trying to make their way slowly and painfully into
the lives of Christians and into the visage that the Church presents to
today's world.

Our pastoral effort faces an important problem. It must find out how
to help Christians to make the transformation from a Christendom mentality to a more profound (and conciliar) conception of the Church's
function.[8] Those in charge of the pastoral effort must therefore try to
figure out at what point their own community is in this process. We do
not intend to propose a detailed sociological methodology for examining
this problem, but we should like to offer some general guidelines.

The "Christendom" mentality involves a whole series of attitudes
toward different things. Here we shall offer some questions that might be
asked about people's conception of the faith and concern for security.

1) **Their conception of the faith:**
   a) To what extent is the faith basically viewed as an intellectual pro-
      nouncement that is the object of formal assent?
   b) To what extent does the individual *passively* wait for the Church
      to propose this pronouncement, without any personal search on
      his part?
   c) To what extent does the Christian yearn for clear formulations
      and fear to take on any personal responsibility with regard to the
      faith? This attitude finds expression in the attitude of those who
      feel that conciliar renewal merely involves a change of formulas:
      "Tell me what I must believe."
   d) To what extent is unanimity and uniformity of expression valued
      above everything else, while those who do not express things in
      "traditional" terms are criticized severely?
   e) To what extent do people feel real perplexity over the confused
      situation that has followed upon the Council?
   f) To what extent do people see Christian education of their chil-
      dren as a process of teaching them the truths of faith and precise
      patterns of conduct, without leaving any room for the free choice
      of the child at the proper time?
   g) To what extent would parents feel shattered if one of their chil-
      dren were not Catholic?

2) **The problem of security.** The Christendom outlook places great
value on *security,* both in the realm of faith and the realm of action.
This security seems to be threatened by various factors that challenge
deeply rooted attitudes. Pertinent questions here would be:
   a) To what extent does the Christian feel threatened by the super-
      ficial or profound changes taking place in the Church?
   b) To what extent does he prefer the preconciliar situation, where
      things were more clearcut, stable, and well defined?
   c) To what extent does the Christian want Christians to be pro-
      tected from any and all non-Christian ideologies that might jeop-
      ardize their own certitudes?

d) To what extent is he intolerant of those who think differently from him, his intolerance being a defense mechanism against his own insecurity?

e) To what extent does he fear to assume personal responsibility and prefer to rely solely on the authority of the priest?

This questioning process could also focus around other attitudes that are basic elements in the Christendom mentality, such as people's refusal or inability to assume the consequences of personal freedom. It is up to the individual to decide what form these questions should take.

NOTES

1. Edward Schillebeeckx, "Foi Chrétienne et attente terrestre," *Schema XIII: Commentaires* (Tours: Mame), p. 147.

2. Does this light turn the Christian into a privileged aristocrat? For a treatment of this question see CLARIFICATION III below.

3. Schillebeeckx, *op. cit.*

4. Charles Péguy, "Le porche du mystère de la deuxième vertu," *Cahiers de la Quinzaine*, Oct. 22, 1911.

5. See Jacob Burckhardt, *The Civilization of the Renaissance in Italy* (New York: Macmillan, 1921), p. 129.

6. Raymond Williams, *The Long Revolution*. Cited by Eric and Mary Josephson, ed., *Man Alone: Alienation in Modern Society* (New York: Dell, 1962), Introduction, p. 19.

7. To preclude irrelevant objections here, we should like to point out that our analysis deals solely with some of the general characteristics that typify the phenomenon of Christendom. It is thus an oversimplification. We do not deny or denigrate the spiritual riches, authentic holiness, or aesthetic values that flourished during that period. We are staying on the level of the "ideal type," which admits of variations in its historical manifestations.

8. It is worth noting here that we are not claiming to pass judgment on the past. In every age the Church lives out her history in accordance with the clarity and profundity she has attained with regard to revelation. As Vatican II tells us about Tradition: "This tradition which comes from the apostles develops in the Church with the help of the Holy Spirit. For there is a growth in the understanding of the realities and words which have been handed down. This happens through the contemplation and study made by believers . . . through the intimate understanding of the spiritual things they experience" (DV 8). But there is no doubt that the growth in understanding at a given moment does indict those Christians who hang on to outdated forms of the past. This is not to deny that psychological limitations do prevent many from having the flexibility necessary for the change. But this is a pedagogical problem, not a theological one.

CHAPTER THREE

The Function and Necessity of the Church

THE NOTION OF MISSION IN CRISIS

We often hear it said that the points already raised in this volume or, if you will, the change of face alluded to in the preceding chapter, raise questions about the notion and value of a *missionary* Church.

It frequently happens that long-time Christians, and even more importantly young people, evince a curious reaction when they reflect deeply on the function of the Church in the world. When they see all its cosmic dimensions, when they realize that the Church is meant to be the universal sign of salvation, instead of leaping enthusiastically into the task that these perspectives open up, they respond with a sigh of relief: "So the Church is necessary after all!"

It is paradoxical that, for some people, the moment they begin to understand the full meaning of the elements that constitute the life of the Church they begin to lose interest in them, a situation that at times produces sacramental and dogmatic crises.

Does this mean that they have misunderstood? Not necessarily. Is it, then, that they do not fully accept what they have heard, or that confrontation with other equally free opinions in the Church produces a certain skepticism? No, that is not true either. After Vatican II it should be clear that it is not dangerous to hear things which the majority of bishops have discussed freely and accepted.

Experience would indicate that two factors lie behind this crisis. And it is, moreover, a crisis of maturing which may not affect everyone tangibly but which is more widespread than some might think.

One factor is more emotional in origin. It involves the difficulty tied up with passing from individualistic motivation to a communitarian, social, and universal one.

This involves a crisis because we were wont to hold on to the Church, her dogmas and sacraments, as the indispensable instruments of our own personal salvation. And when we hear that Christianity is something to give away, and that the Church was not instituted to save those within her but to perform a work of service for all humanity, then we are gripped by the feeling that the Church is not as important as we thought it was. Even before we reflect on how necessary our Church may be for others, the very fact that she is not related to our personal salvation as if she were an indispensable recipe produces this feeling of welcome relief. Initially at least, a social motivation is never as strong and all-absorbing as a personal, individualistic one.

This does not prove that one should be more prudent in his exposition or that many Christians are not prepared to take this new step. It proves how necessary and urgent it is to free our Christianity from the absorption of our own egotism, which is radically opposed to the message and mandate of Christ. Essential crises must be faced and lived through. There is no other way. Otherwise everything will disintegrate from within.

A second factor, related to the first, is on a more intellectual plane. It deserves closer scrutiny, greater stress, and fuller clarity. From what we have said already, we may not immediately see the magnitude of the service that the Church can and should offer to humanity. We describe it in various ways: passing from the implicit or anonymous to the explicit, from ignorance to knowledge, from spontaneous living to reflected living. Now these descriptions may be philosophically and theologically exact. But they do not imprint on our imagination the magnitude of the transition. They do not make clear to us how essential and decisive for humanity may be this work carried out by a part of the human race.

And to the extent that we do not give more concrete content to the Church's contribution to the world, the first factor mentioned above is reinforced, as it were. Since the Church is less directly tied up with my own personal salvation, and since she is ultimately a part—even though a highly perfect part—of a plan that goes far beyond her visible limits, she may not appear to me to be endowed with the all-absorbing and almost magical importance that I once attached to her.

According to Vatican II, our religion must pass through this "crisis," so that it may acquire in us that depth without which it will never become authentic service to the world.[1] The moral development of any human being faces a critical moment when that person has to move on from an infantile and magical morality ("Tamper with that and see what happens!") to a moral life based on the validity and usefulness of one's actions for the aims intended. And it is a critical moment precisely because the relationship of a system of means to an end initially does not have the psychological power that fear of immediate consequences does. Only slowly, as we grow to maturity and reflect on what experience tells us about the consequences of our immediate behavior patterns, do we lose the inborn tendency to judge things on the basis of terrible consequences: "So it is not as terrible as they said, and I can do what I want."

It is impossible for Christianity to avoid passing through this crisis! But in so doing it must ask two questions: (1) What is at stake personally for the Christian in reaching and maintaining full awareness of God's salvation plan for all men? (2) Why is it so important for this overall plan and history that the Christian operate on this level of full awareness which is proper to the ecclesial community? These two questions will be examined in this chapter.

We have already had occasion to point out that Christ used two different formulas to describe the road which leads to salvation. When he was referring in general to God's judgment on humanity, the thing required of man was simply real love. When he referred to the function of the Church and spoke about it to the apostles, he tied in salvation with faith and the sacraments. As we have already said, Christ was talking about the same thing in both texts: real love. But real "Christian" and ecclesial love is lived out with faith and the sacraments: i.e., with full awareness of what is what, thanks to God's revelation. This comes down to saying that if man is saved by human love, then the Christian is saved by Christian love, love lived out in the realm of faith and sacraments.

But then someone might raise an objection: Does it not seem that Christ attributed excessive importance to the qualifying adjective (Christian) in the latter case? Is it not exaggerated to attribute salvation explicitly, not only to love itself but also to faith and the sacraments which are the Christian *way* of living it? Can we not say that a difference in *method or manner* cannot be so decisive, that the obligatory nature of the Church has therefore been greatly exaggerated?

Obviously this difference of manner cannot be so decisive in terms of an overall view of history. Hence Christ himself mentioned only love in talking about the general judgment. But is it true that the manner matters little from *my* point of view?

We can make a side observation here which may clarify the matter for some readers. It relates to Teilhard de Chardin's overview of evolution. Teilhard points out that from one point of view life itself may seem to be the essential thing, while the form it takes (i.e., animal or human) would seem to be something secondary and accidental. But he stresses the fact that from another point of view the attainment of the human level effects such a profound cosmic transformation of life on this planet that today the world can be viewed as the world of man, with animal and vegetable life being elements of this world. In short, if one takes due account of this reflexive turning in on itself that occurs in evolution when consciousness appears, so that the thrust of the whole universe is now assumed within it, the seeming adjective suddenly becomes a substantive factor even though it remains only a small portion of the universe in terms of quantity.

This same point can and should be applied to the Church and the Christian, ecclesial way of living the love which is common to all men of good will. The "little flock" may remain such, but it can recapitulate the universe and thus be the most decisive and substantial factor in human history.

But let us get back to our main questions. Can this Christian, ecclesial way of loving, involving faith and the sacraments, constitute something truly critical for salvation insofar as the person who has arrived at this level is concerned? Writing specifically about the sacraments, Rahner offers an image that can help us to answer this question. He asks this question: If grace is also conferred by God without the sacraments, can the latter be something truly essential and obligatory for the Christian? His answer is this:

> The whole process can be compared to the life shared in common by two lovers. Everything they do is sustained and transformed by this love and is its—very discreet, almost imperceptible—expression, even the insignificant, ordinary things which seem to have quite a different meaning and purpose from love and which would have to be done even if there were no love between these two persons. And yet, sometimes, and even often, they must tell each other their love openly, in words and by gestures which are nothing but the expression of love—of a love which was already finding expression in everything they do. It is as if the hidden law of the whole of their two lives united together must continually bring forth new formal, outward expressions (Gestaltwerdungen) of their love, in which this love, which after all is always there, realizes itself ever more fully and in ever new forms. These are only gestures, not love itself—gestures "which do not really seem to matter" compared with the proving of one's love in deed and in truth; and yet love lives by them. Love would die if it were not for these expressions which are not love at all and which those not in love consider superfluous "formalities" . . . But the everyday course of love will always go on concentrating itself in such gestures and love itself will always draw new life from them.[2]

With this example Rahner introduces us into the paradoxical world of the human, its peculiar set of values and its distinctive obligations. Human friendship is translated into acts of help and companionship, among other things. Would it not seem logical that a person could refuse to give a handshake, just out of laziness, and claim that it mattered little since the substantive reality remained the same? Why is this not the case? Why is the visible sign important?

Now consider our proclamation of the faith which is, in the last analysis, nothing more than a complex of sounds symbolizing a reality that is infinitely more substantial. Would it not be equally logical to deny any critical importance to this proclamation, since the underlying reality would presumably perdure even without the sign complex? What madness drives people to kill or be killed over a group of sounds that say yes or no, or over series of pencil marks that signify a personal signature? [3]

The point is easy enough to see. The Church, the visible community with its formulas of faith and its sacraments, is to the cosmic community of God's People what the aforementioned signs are to the reality they signify and convey.

From one point of view they can seem to be nontranscendent as compared with the underlying reality, the latter being implicit but real and as vast as the universe. But if a person were to presume to conclude from this that one could dispense with them, he would be surprised to find that their roots are imbedded in the essential reality and that they cannot be separated from it by anyone who arrives at that level.

The Council said this expressly at one point: "The Church, now sojourning on earth . . . is necessary for salvation. . . . therefore, whosoever, knowing that the Catholic Church was made necessary by God through Jesus Christ, would refuse to enter her or to remain in her, could not be saved" (LG 14). If we are to appreciate this, we must *first of all* ponder the aspect of the human condition to which we have just alluded: i.e., man cannot whimsically return to the instinctive level because the dawning of conscious awareness, explicitation, and reflection in him is not simply a higher perfection but a whole new world. It is the world of the human where man plays out what he once played out on the level of instinct; it is a system of relationships which, through their signification, affects and determines the very roots of life.

To give just one more example, we can cite the importance of a banknote. It is simply a piece of paper with a precise signification. Depending on what this signification is, it is recognized by another person and interpreted accordingly. The life and death of billions of people on this planet depend on this network of signs.

This teaches us, in the second place, that we cannot fully handle the problem of the Church's necessity or obligation without solving the question of its contribution to humanity. In other words, we have already seen that the transition from the implicit to the explicit, from the anonymous to the conscious, from the spontaneous to the reflected, is not something that can be taken or left (as opposed to the essential) without radically altering the result. Now the question is: What concretely makes it so important for humanity that Christianity, or better, the grace of God shifts from its anonymous reality to conscious, explicit, reflexive reality through the Christian community?

Since the necessity of the Church cannot be fully appreciated except in terms of its essential contribution to the world, we must explore more deeply the relationship that exists between "the community of those who know" the mystery of love and those who practice this love without yet knowing the mystery behind it. Is it simply that both are engaged in a common task, one group having the faith and the other group not having it? One group knowing what is involved, the other group not knowing? If that were the case, then the essential thing would be cooperation, not dialogue; and dialogue itself would have to be regarded as an effort at conquest and proselytism. Is that really the case?

In line with an age-old theology in the Church, Vatican II sees the building up of the world through human good will as something more than an anonymous Christianity or simply authentic, saving love. It sees this effort as a "preparation for the gospel." In other words, it sees it as a journey toward an encounter, as the opening up of a dialogue between a question that is moving forward and the "good news" ("gospel") that is waiting hopefully (LG 16).

As we have just said, this has to do with an old theme in Christian theology. In the time of Saint Augustine, when Christianity was still a relatively new thing, a strange theological opinion arose among Christian monks. It held that God's grace was not necessary for keeping the moral law and gaining salvation.

It was an attitude characteristic of monastic circles. As the professional athletes of moral perfection and sanctity, monks were inclined to denigrate the grace of God. This supernatural help appeared to militate against the struggle for holiness and emulation. A British monk, Pelagius, championed this opinion in a famous letter to Demetriades. The latter was about to enter the novitiate of a monastery, and he had asked Pelagius for spiritual counsel. The most important thing, said Pelagius, is to recognize the wondrous powers of human nature; they by themselves suffice for the practice of virtue.

Pelagius was condemned, and his opinions came to form a heresy known as Pelagianism. Against him the Church maintained that the grace of God, the gratuitous supernatural gift that Christ gave us, was absolutely necessary for man if he was going to achieve his divine, supernatural goal and to practice the divine law that brings us to God.

Other monks broached the Pelagian viewpoint in a more subtle form, for which reason they were called *Semi-Pelagians*. They said one could not deny the presence and necessity of grace in any spiritual effort when it involved someone who was already a Christian. But they pictured another route where victory was granted only to greater effort, for only that counted. It was the route of a man moving toward the Church *before he entered it*. It was, in short, all the virtues practiced by the non-Christian as he approached faith and baptism. There nothing seemed to be added to human effort. After all, there did not seem to be any doubt that many pagans in every age drew near to the faith in a wondrous way. There were philosophers like Socrates and Diogenes, and the saints of the Old Testament, who did not belong to the People of God.

Well, Semi-Pelagianism was condemned too.[4] It was declared that the Church saw man's whole journey under the guidance of conscience as the *start of faith,* presupposing an already present attraction toward full knowledge of the divine message; hence it had to be regarded as supernatural, even as faith itself is.

To put it another way, the relationship between the man of good will and the Christian who was working for the betterment of the world—the one divine vocation of all men—did not simply mean that they were collaborating from their different levels of knowledge: one having anonymous, implicit, spontaneous knowledge and the other having precise, explicit, and reflected knowledge. It also meant that this work was the start of faith for the man of good will. It was a journey toward an encounter, the preparation for a dialogue, the gradual formulation of a question that sought, with the ever-growing intensity of love itself, the good news that the Christian had to give.[5]

Now if love is faith that is beginning, this faith is made to dialogue with the full faith.

Useful as they are, these statements are still relatively general. They do not adequately enlighten us on the features of this encounter, of this dialogue which our unique divine vocation prepares with the help of man's conscience and good will.

Here we shall try to delve more concretely into what happens when a man opens up to self-giving. This brief phenomenological analysis will show: (1) why all authentic love is a faith-beginning; (2) that if love is to overcome its intrinsic obstacles, this beginning faith must pose questions and encounter the corresponding answers that can only come from full-fledged faith.

When love moves beyond the initial stage of enthusiasm and instinctive attraction, it gradually becomes aware of what self-giving really is.

It begins to realize that self-giving is the most serious, demanding, unpredictable, and irreversible adventure that can happen to a human being. This gives rise to the first basic and essential question: Is love worth the effort?

This question stays with us whether we are pondering basic love for people or the decision to commit our love forever to a person whom we will never wholly know. To love means to lose our autonomy and to become dependent on another. And this dependence may end up one day as disillusionment and heartbreak, leaving us empty inside. All love is a gamble, wherein we risk the best and deepest part of ourself.

There are no guarantees in this world to cover the gamble. We either accept or reject love. For this very reason every act of love is more than an act of good will; it is an act of trust, an act of faith. It is an act of faith launched into the air, without any precise name or clear content.[6] It is a belief that love is worthwhile, which defies fate and blind indifference to the importance of self-giving.

The point is that *we* know that this trust is well placed. We know that it is placed in good hands: i.e., that there is Someone who has responded with a yes and that this gesture is not lost in a void. We are those who "have believed in love," as Saint John says, because we know the name of him who is the origin and object of all love.[7]

That is why the Church tells us that through love the grace of God prepares faith; because all love is a faith beginning. The greater the love, the deeper is the initial faith and the more it demands a response.

This brings us to something else, which is the second point mentioned above. We must expect crises in the normal development of love. We will encounter challenges and questions that are more and more explicit and critical. Let us look at some of these questions, by way of example, for then we shall see more concretely how love prepares faith, how it prepares the encounter and dialogue with what the Christian knows.

Perhaps the most general, and at the same time the most demanding, question of love has to do with its trust and *hope*. Is love worth the effort, when it is so probable that it will be shipwrecked? Would it not be more prudent not to turn irrevocably to another with our innermost depths, since this person can move away from us, die or, worst of all, gradually shut himself up in incomprehension, superficiality, fear of life, or infidelity?

It gives us food for thought to see couples entering marriage whose own parents, godparents, and relatives are the clearest proof of love's failure. Someone might suggest that it is the rest of us, not they, who question whether love is worth the effort? But that is not the case, as is evident from the fact that an ever-growing number of couples are consciously or unconsciously approaching marriage as an experiment. The result of this crisis of hope is that they do not invest in the experiment the decisive and total resources which love would require to be truly victorious. If only Christians would realize that their notion of indissoluble marriage is not a motive for separation, and certainly not a condemnation of any other form of love or marriage! If only they would realize that it is an expression of hope that must be echoed by anyone who knows the mystery of love, in the face of human beings who do not have the same assurance and who have doubts about the demands and possibilities of self-giving!

We can find the problem of hope in love on other planes. Do we not see it in the whole question of choosing the means with which to improve local, national, and world society? It is most important that the Christian recognize these elements for dialogue in the events that take place around him. The Sino-Soviet dispute within communism, for example, stems from differing appraisals of the proper methods to be used in bettering humanity's lot. One Russian statement[8] puts it this way: "As they see it, the main thing is to put an end to idealism as soon as possible. How and *at what price* this is to be achieved is a secondary question. But for whom is it a secondary question? For the millions of people who would be destroyed in the event of a nuclear war?" The important thing for us to realize here is that their disagreement is ultimately rooted in a different attitude toward hope. It is as if God's grace were preparing a dialogue with the faith that springs from his revelation. If this dialogue does not take place, it is our fault. We shall have missed an appointment.

And it is a meeting where we would have had something decisive to say. Do we not know that no love is ever lost? We know from our faith that what love constructs is not destroyed by any obstacle, even though it may seem to be. Authentic love builds the new earth in some unseen way. And in that new world we will be astonished to see standing the things that we thought had been destroyed over and over again.[9] This does not give us concrete solutions.[10] But it does mean that the solutions which we must seek out with the rest of humanity[11] bear the stamp of certainty which springs from our faith.

Another question which love formulates sooner or later as it progresses has to do with the *scope* of love. Is love worth the effort when you go beyond the narrow circle of the family or those who think the same way as you do? Is it worth it outside the boundaries of the same class or race, or religion or nation?

It is logical for a person to wonder about the possibility and value of giving himself to those who belong to other circles and will not appreciate his gift. They will oblige him to see this love through to the end, to become a member of this new sphere. To extend one's self-giving beyond familiar circles is to lose all the security of one's own way of life and confront unknown demands. Not long ago, when a natural catastrophe left countless children homeless, Catholics were advised not to give them shelter in their own families. Why? Because the homeless children came from other life-styles and moral circles, so that they could logically jeopardize the moral life and Christianity of one's own children.

Here we see the temptation enticing every man to put controls on love and not let it have free play. We must not let it jeopardize the life we are leading, the system of values we hold, the well-being of persons we already love. This temptation, as we noted, is rooted in what we know. But for the man of good will, it is one of the problems of existence. And a response to it becomes all the more urgent as good will occupies an ever larger place in our life.

It is our feeling that today the affluent and developed countries, to cite just one example, have firmly decided not to let their yearnings for solidarity get out of control. They will not share their fortune and prosperity on an equal basis with others who are impoverished. Does the Christian have anything to say about this? Is he saying it?

It is not that the Christian has a precise response to give here. He too must ask questions of himself and others when confronted with a concrete problem. But he does know something: That the least of men has absolute value and hence an absolute right to be loved, whatever the price may be: "Anything you did for one of my brothers, however humble, you did for me" (Matt. 25:40).[12] And that which he knows is an essential element of the dialogue in which human beings ask themselves what to do with a love whose demands never end.

We could go on indefinitely analyzing and counting off the questions raised by love, a love which is already a shadowy but demanding faith. They are the questions of the day that speak to us through actual events and long to dialogue with that which our faith tells us.

The dialectical course and rhythm of love, the preparation of human beings for love, the possibilties for love when people do not even have the means to make it effective: all these topics and many others are occasions for dialogue between that which is a "preparation for the gospel" and the gospel itself, between faith beginning and full-fledged faith, between the world and the Church.[13]

If this dialogue is to exist, the Christian must be prepared to recognize the "signs of the times," [14] that is, he must be capable of analyzing contemporary happenings in relation to the divine plan that paves the way for this saving dialogue.

What we want to do right now is point out the tieup between what we have just said and our initial issue: the necessity of the Church. We have just seen that the attainment of full awareness of that which was once instinctive and spontaneous cannot be considered as simply a higher perfection from which we may choose to prescind. It is rather something new and definitive, creating a new balance upon which everything else will depend from now on.

As we noted, this holds true not only on the level of the individual but also on the level of the human community as a whole. Thus the Christian faith is not a knowledge granted for the personal profit of the receiver; it is granted so that he may give something to others. Whether he does or not depends on whether or not his good will (which may seem to be something more solid and basic than Christian faith) gives way to exhaustion in broaching the radical questions of love. Inevitably the moment for formulating such questions does come, and dialogue must be initiated if love is not to retreat or be lost entirely.[15]

Rahner makes a very pertinent remark in his book, *Mission and Grace*. It will help us to appreciate both the scope and the necessity of this dialogue between love (i.e., faith beginning) and faith itself. Sometimes, Rahner remarks, the Christian response to love's questions is a complete and perfect one. Such is the case when a man receives and accepts the full Christian response, accepting the faith and becoming an active agent of this dialogue henceforth. But Rahner points out that the Christian response also reaches human beings in *partial doses*.[16] Even though a person may not allow for the whole scope and hopefulness of Christian love, the very fact that he lives among men who do love with full-fledged hope and unreservedly will often cause him to resolve his doubts in favor of love. Thus love will have been fully fleshed out, and it is for this purpose alone that God revealed his mystery to men. On the day of final judgment, man will hear some such statement as this from his judge: "Come, blessed of my Father, because I was hungry and your love had sufficient scope and hope to feed me . . ."

Herein lies the necessity of the Church. Here we see why it is so indispensable in the salvation plan for humanity. In the midst of the human race there must be people who know the mystery of love, who will meet and dialogue with those who are moving toward the gospel and confronting the questions raised by love.[17] As humanity progresses on its journey, we have been slow to formulate the questions which, at the right time, would arouse people to the need for dialogue. And this dialogue is essential for what Teilhard called the "piloting of history." Vatican II poses this dialogue to us. It demands that we undergo a profound transformation so that we may engage in it.

NOTES TO CHAPTER THREE

1. *Cf.* GS 7 and 10.

2. Karl Rahner, *Theological Investigations,* II, *Man in the Church* (London: Darton, Longman & Todd; Baltimore: Helicon, 1963), pp. 129–130.

3. "If a man will let himself be lost for my sake and for the Gospel, that man is safe" (Mark 8:35).

4. The Council of Orange (A.D. 529), which did this, was not an ecumenical council. But its condemnation represented Christian doctrine and was not re-iterated by later ecumenical councils such as Trent. Vatican II declares: "Nor is God Himself far distant from those who in shadows and images seek the unknown God, for it is He who gives to all men life and breath and every other gift (*cf.* Acts 17:25–28), and who as Savior wills that all men be saved (*cf.* 1 Tim. 2:4). Those also can attain to everlasting salvation who through no fault of their own do not know the gospel of Christ or His Church, yet sincerely seek God and, moved by grace, strive by their deeds to do His will as it is known to them through the dictates of conscience. Nor does divine Providence deny the help necessary for salvation to those who, without blame on their part, have not yet arrived at an explicit knowledge of God, but who strive to live a good life, thanks to His grace. Whatever goodness or truth is found among them is looked upon by the Church as a preparation for the gospel" (LG 16).

5. The differing situations of human beings on this road leading to the Church and salvation are pictured both in the Gospel and the other books of the New Testament: "As he was stepping into the boat, the man who had been possessed begged to go with him. Jesus would not allow it, but said to him, 'Go home to your own folk and tell them what the Lord in his mercy has done for you'" (Mark 5:18–19). "Just as formerly you were disobedient to God, but now have received mercy in the time of their disobedience, so now, when you receive mercy, they have proved disobedient, but only in order that they too may receive mercy. For in making all mankind prisoners to disobedience, God's purpose was to show mercy to all mankind" (Rom. 11:30–32).

The latter text shows us that there are two divine mercies, as it were: one in the faith of Christians, the other in the nonfaith of the Jews. They are two distinct situations on the same road.

6. "For man . . . cannot live fully according to truth unless he freely acknowledges that love and devotes himself to his Creator" (GS 19).

7. "Such a hope is no mockery, because God's love has flooded our inmost heart through the Holy Spirit he has given us" (Rom. 5:5).

8. Reply of the Russian Communist Party to the Twenty-Five Points of Mao Tse-tung.

9. "What was sown in weakness and corruption will be clothed with incorruptibility. While charity and its works endure, all that creation which God made on man's account will be unchained from the bondage of vanity. . . . indeed all the good fruits of our nature and enterprise, we will find them again, but freed of stain, burnished and transfigured" (GS 39).

The phrase "will be clothed with incorruptibility" (1 Cor. 15:42, 53) echoes the central text of Saint Paul on Christian hope: "Our troubles are slight and short-lived; and their outcome an eternal glory which outweighs them far. Meanwhile our eyes are fixed, not on the things that are seen, but on things that are unseen. . . . For we know that if the earthly frame that houses us today should be demolished, we possess a building which God has provided—a house not made by human hands, eternal, and in heaven [i.e., because it is not man's but God's life in us which he is building up]. In this present body we do indeed groan; we yearn to have our heavenly habitation put on over this one—in the hope that, being thus clothed, we shall not find ourselves naked. We groan indeed, we who are enclosed within this earthly frame; we are oppressed because we do not want to have the old body stripped off. Rather our desire is to have the new body put on over it, so that our mortal part may be absorbed into life immortal. God himself has shaped us for this very end; and as a pledge of it he has given us the Spirit" (2 Cor. 4:17—5:5).

10. *Cf.* GS 43.

11. *Cf.* GS 16.

12. "This Council lays stress on reverence for man; everyone must consider his every neighbor without exception as another self . . . In our times a special obligation binds us to make ourselves the neighbor of absolutely every person . . . recalling the voice of the Lord: 'As long as you did it for one of these, the least of my brethren, you did it for me' (Matt. 25:40)" (GS 27).

"For by His incarnation the Son of God has united Himself in some fashion with every man" (GS 22).

13. "Hence, giving witness and voice to the faith of the whole People of God gathered together by Christ, this Council can provide no more eloquent proof of its solidarity with the entire human family . . . as well as its respect and love for that family, than by engaging with it in conversation about these various problems" (GS 3).

14. GS 4; *cf.* GS 11.

15. "By contrast, when a divine substructure and the hope of life eternal are wanting, man's dignity is most grievously lacerated . . . The riddles of life and death, of guilt and of grief go unsolved, with the frequent result that men succumb to despair" (GS 21).

16. Karl Rahner, *Mission et Grâce,* Vol. I (Paris: Mame, 1962), p. 223.

17. Some might object that this comes down to posing Prophyry's complaint once again. The Church has come belatedly if, for a million years, human beings have had to pose these questions for which only she had the response. So here we must make an important observation. The Church was established in the world during the first period in which peace took the place of violence in a considerable portion of the planet. It is certainly true that Roman law did not touch a large underlying substrate of injustice and violence. But the very fact that for a time the most extreme weapons of violence were set aside was a necessary prerequisite for the appearance and formulation of the questions based on love for which the Church brought an answer. Hence there is an intimate relationship between the foundation of the Church and the historical moment in which it took place. This suggests to us that the saving dialogue is conditioned both by the Church and the world. We find this same fact formulated in a slightly different but related way in the social teaching of the Church (see Leo XIII, *Rerum novarum,* n. 27; Pius XII, Pentecost Radio Message, June 1, 1941).

CLARIFICATIONS

I. RELIGIOUS PRACTICE AND THE KNOWLEDGE OF GOD

In this chapter we have attempted to clarify and explain the necessity of the Church. Hopefully we have added more understanding to the phrase that is often repeated in this book: "The Christian is he who knows." But it is quite likely that the reader may still have some difficulties with regard to non-Christians, not about their situation and status as regards the salvation plan but about their knowledge of this plan. For if we say that the Christian is he who knows, we can also say that the non-Christian is he who does not know. So the question is: Is this *not-knowing* compatible with a knowledge of this plan? It is a legitimate question, since it is obvious that man cannot go along groping in the dark about something as critical as salvation. God does not save man in spite of himself, nor lay hold of him in a distracted state. Both for the Christian and the non-Christian, salvation is eminently a reality of a personal and free nature. What then does the non-Christian know? And how does he come to know it?

In reality our text has already given us an answer to this problematic issue. But we do well to spell it out more clearly. One might well ask himself this question about non-Christian religions: Should they be considered as a form of revelation by God? Or, at the very least, should they be considered as a preparation for Christian salvation, so that the religious non-Christian makes progress on his journey toward the faith by being faithful to his own religion?

The significance of these questions will be readily understood if one realizes what has been said in certain sectors of Christian apologetics. Some currents of apologetics have regarded non-Christian religions—the more highly evolved ones if not the more primitive ones—as a means of reaching some sort of contact with the divinity. It is admittedly inadequate, but it presumably predisposes man to accept the true God when he is presented to him in Christian proclamation. For this reason some are wont to praise profoundly religious people (e.g., those in India) without going on to ask what relationship their religious practice has with acceptance of the Christian message.[1]

In so doing, they tend to cite as support the words of Saint Paul in the Areopagus of Athens. After all, doesn't Paul begin by praising the religious conscience of the Athenians? Here are his words: "Men of

Athens, I see that in everything that concerns religion you are uncommonly scrupulous. For as I was going around looking at the objects of your worship I noticed among other things an altar bearing the inscription 'To an Unknown God.' What you worship but do not know—this is what I now proclaim" (Acts 17:22–24).

It would seem, then, that in taking their religious awareness as the point of departure for his preaching Paul considered Christianity as the culmination of this pre-existing religious practice. But actually the very opposite is true. For Paul follows this introduction with further remarks which present Christianity as a veritable rupture from any sort of religion: "The God who created the world and everything in it, and who is Lord of heaven and earth, does not live in shrines made by men. . . . As God's offspring then, we ought not to suppose that the deity is like an image in gold or silver or stone, shaped by human craftsmanship and design" (Acts 17:24 and 29). In his whole speech, which is interwoven with the artifices of Greek oratory, there is no appeal at all to religious awareness. Instead he summons the Athenians to repentance and to faith-based acceptance of the Lord Jesus who died and rose (cf. Acts 17:30–32).

What then are we to think about the whole religious movement of humanity, wherein non-Christians can have some knowledge of God and his plan without knowing about his revelation?

Paul himself gives us his reply in the Epistle to the Romans. We can sum it up briefly. In the light of the full revelation in Christ all religions, including the religion of Israel (cf. Rom. 2:1), involved idolatry. Does this mean that every attempt by man to enter into a relationship with God, outside of positive revelation, is condemned to failure? Not at all. But it does signify that the possibility of such a relationship is not realized precisely through religion itself but through other pathways that we must now analyze. It also signifies that we cannot attribute to religion the certain knowledge of God and his salvation plan that we are seeking outside positive revelation.

What might these other pathways be? In his Epistle to the Romans Paul tells us that man is not totally in the dark in this world insofar as knowledge of God is concerned. There is a revelation which we could call natural, coming through creation, history, and man himself: "For all that can be known about God lies plain before their eyes; indeed God himself has disclosed it to them. His invisible attributes, that is to say his everlasting power and deity, have been visible ever since the world began, to the eye of reason, in the things he has made" (Rom. 1:19–20). But this spontaneous knowledge of God ("knowing God"; Rom. 1:21) is ambiguous. It can take one of two dimensions. Man can acknowledge God and offer him praise and thanks. Or he can engage in idolatry (i.e., turn God into an object), estranging himself from God and reducing himself to a subhuman state (cf. Rom. 1:21–32).

Now the point is that it is not religion specifically which brings the spontaneous knowledge to its full flowering in praise and thanksgiving: i.e., to a personal relationship with God. Quite the contrary is true. Religion is the root of a thrust whereby man, who once knew God, turns him into an object in man's own service. God is turned into images made by human hands, temples made by human hands, and even more subtle things such as the law and legal prescriptions of the Israelite religion. This is called idolatry by Paul, and he attributes idolatry to both pagans and the Jews.

What is it, then, that allows man's spontaneous knowledge of God to open up into a personal relationship with him where non-Christians are concerned? What accomplishes this in people who do not have explicit faith in the revelation of Jesus?

In looking for an answer to this question, we will find two lines of thought in the Bible—as far back as the Old Testament itself. They converge to establish a close reciprocity between man's relationship to God and his relationship to his fellow men.

The first line of thought points up the relationship between idolatry, i.e., the fundamental sin of man, and his sins against others. Idolatry is the fundamental disorder from which follow, as an inevitable consequence, our sins against human beings. The book which opens the Old Testament shows us the deep tieup between "the sin" and "sins"; and it does not do so in a theoretical way but by presenting us with an unfolding story. Whatever may be the interpretation of the original sin, one thing is indubitable: beneath the symbolism of the story of man's fall, we are shown a radical change in the relations between man and God. And, in Genesis 4, this is immediately followed by the story of Cain and Abel. The sin against another human being is presented as a consequence of the original sin. By the same token, the listings of sins in both the Old and the New Testament (especially in Paul's descriptions of the works of the flesh) always present this duality: there is a fundamental sin, idolatry, and there are sins against others (cf. Gal. 5:19–21; 1 Cor. 5:11; etc.).

Now this first line of thought in Scripture could suggest to us that the tieup between the fundamental sin and other sins is an extrinsic one: i.e., that the former simply preceded the latter historically. But the danger of adopting this interpretation is ruled out by the second line of thought in Scripture. It stresses the mutual tieup between *knowledge* of God and *love* of neighbor in both negative and positive form. Negatively speaking, he who *does not love* his neighbor *does not know* God; positively speaking, he who *loves* his neighbor already *knows* God.

We need not go into an analysis of John's first Epistle, which truly does represent the culmination of this progressive revelation, in order to see this. For we can find astonishingly clear texts in the Old Testament itself. Let us examine a few.

Isaiah summons Israel to a spirituality that goes beyond mere cultic formalism, describing her sin this way: "O sinful nation, people loaded with iniquity, race of evildoers, wanton destructive children who have deserted the Lord, spurned the Holy One of Israel and turned your backs on him. . . . Your countless sacrifices, what are they to me? says the Lord. I am sated with whole offerings of rams and the fat of buffaloes. . . . The offer of your gifts is useless, the reek of sacrifice is abhorrent to me . . . Though you offer countless prayers, I will not listen" (Isa. 1:4, 11–15).

In other words, all the enumerated acts whereby man seeks to establish a relationship with God—sacrifices, prayers, offerings, assemblies, and trips to the temple—do not reach him. What stops them? Isaiah tells them. Picturing it in the Old Testament terms of justice toward the poor and other distressed people, Isaiah says it is their lack of love for their neighbor: "Wash yourselves and be clean! Put away the evil of your deeds, away out of my sight. Cease to do evil and learn to do right, pursue justice and champion the oppressed, give the orphan his rights, plead the widow's cause" (Isa. 1:16–17).

Lack of this love does not simply diminish the value of the ritual acts mentioned earlier. It actually cancels their relationship with God. Where there is no love of neighbor, there is no knowledge of, or relationship with, God.

Hosea is even more explicit in this passage: "Hear the word of the Lord, O Israel, for the Lord has a charge to bring against the people of the land: There is no good faith or mutual trust, no knowledge of God in the land" (Hos. 4:1). And where we would expect a long list of sins against God, Hosea mentions only sins against our neighbor: "Oaths are imposed and broken, they kill and rob, there is nothing but adultery and licence, one deed of blood after another" (Hosea 4:2).

As we were just saying, he who does not love his neighbor does not know God. The point is also put in positive form in the Old Testament. Jeremiah puts it this way in speaking to King Joachim about his father: "He dealt justly and fairly; all went well with him. *He dispensed justice to the lowly and poor;* did not this show he knew me? says the Lord" (Jer. 22:15–16).

Those who *do not know* "the breadth and length and height and depth" (Eph. 3:18) of the love with which God loves us and we love other men do not walk in total darkness along the pathway of salvation. They too do know God, but not precisely through the religious structures that man has created as a surrogate for God, nor even in the conscious plenitude of faith. They know him by giving assent to the deepest dynamism that God has placed in man: love of one's fellow men.

And so we have just travelled another route to arrive at the theme of this chapter: love prepares the way for faith. Perhaps now it may be clearer to us that we should not seek out the traces of God's activity and presence in the world in the religious monuments of the past or present; that we do better to look for them in all the gestures—be they religious or not—whereby man responds to the urgent obligations and demands of love. And, in a more general context, it may be clearer that they are to be found in the whole process of maturation and interiorization whereby men come to realize the full implications of this obligation that begins from their *neighbor* to eventually acquire a planetary dimension.

This does not rule out the possibility that non-Christian religious elements, and even more those of the Israelite religion, introduce people to a genuine knowledge of God to the extent that they foster love. But it should be noted that this preparation does not come through the religious element as such. It comes through something that transcends the religious aspect and passes judgment on it: i.e., the capacity for inspiring and fostering love and justice. This is *vita recta,* according to Vatican II:

the authentic preparation for the gospel with its twofold dimension of goodness and authenticity (*cf.* LG 16).[2]

Within the context of this CLARIFICATION we can formulate certain questions, the response to which will help us to define our position with respect to the problem we are examining.

Suppose, for example, that we are trying to evaluate the situation of Christianity or its potentialities in atheistic, laicist, or materialistic societies. Do we focus our attention primarily or exclusively on the religious elements (e.g., the affluence of places of worship) that are surviving in them? Do we see them as the activity of God resisting all attempts at eradication by the political authorities? In determining the potentialities of Christianity, do we give equal or primary value to certain nonreligious dimensions: e.g., solidarity and disinterested dedication to the effort to improve society and diminish inequalities between human beings? Where do we tend to pinpoint "preparation for the gospel" in most cases?

Consider the continent of Latin America and the possibility of evangelizing its masses. What value do we place on efforts at human betterment that seek to salvage man from his marginal existence? Do we see them as projects in which charity is practiced, as ways of attracting the masses to Christianity and protecting them from other ideologies, or as intrinsically worthwhile efforts for developing man's personal and communitarian values? In using the mass communications media, do we rely on the religious character of the programs or do we prefer to evoke values related to human betterment? What principles underlie our preference?

We might also consider the pastoral organization of a society in which the Church is already implanted, such as is the case in Latin America. Where do we invest our main concern, the largest portion of our personnel, and our greatest efforts at trying to understand a given situation? Do we restrict ourselves for the most part to saving the faith of "simple souls," equating their religious practice with Christian effort *à outrance?* Or do we leave room for other activities that may be a preparation for the gospel, such as that of people who do not profess religion but do commit themselves sincerely to the transformation of society? Which of these two situations do we regard as being closer to a mature Christian faith?

II. HUMAN EXPERIENCE: PRECATECHESIS IN THE FAITH

We Christians believe that any pathway toward authenticity in our being and life is a preparation for the gospel. Man is not fashioned into full being independently of grace. The latter is not a reality that comes to us at the end of a journey; it is our intimate and inseparable companion throughout our human journey.

Here our aim is to look at things from a pastoral point of view. The community called Church has, as its fundamental mission, the transmission of the faith. It is commissioned to proclaim that the Kingdom is already here in our midst. In our day this perennial task of the Church entails fundamental obligations.

During the centuries of Christendom, evangelization was carried out chiefly by *impregnation.* Public customs and ways of thinking were "bathed in Christianity," so that becoming a part of society almost automatically meant becoming a member of the Church. Today that situation has changed radically, due to the fact that people live in a pluralistic situation where the presuppositions of a former day no longer hold sway. For example, it is quite likely that all the summaries of our faith right from the New Testament formulas on presuppose a listener for whom the conceptual and existential signification of God is correct, or at least adequate for less demanding generations. Our era is different, so that the preacher must ask himself where are the reference points that will enable his contemporaries to grasp the content of faith conceptually and existentially.

We feel that these tieup points must be looked for in life itself, in man's real existence. And it is in this sense that we speak of the major human experiences as being a precatechesis in the faith.

1. Every profound human experience, and by that we do not mean to imply that they are rare, opens out into a question on the meaning of existence. The most natural form is a question charged with wonder and anguish: Who are we? What are we? Such questions surface during forceful moments that fill us with sensations and sharpen our awareness.

It should be noted that this question focused on the meaning of our existence acquires real depth and solidity only at the end of all the pathways that lead us into the truth of our being. It is a difficult and costly task to reach that point without cheating life, skipping steps, lying, or allowing ourselves to be taken over by facile solutions, ideologies, and escapist mechanisms. Thousands of subterfuges are offered to us. We can act to avoid the risk of thinking, and we can latch onto religion as insurance for the beyond. To live life deeply, to take our existence in our own hands, to fashion ourselves consciously and fully: this is the difficult road to take, the "narrow gate" that leads us to a simple but unendingly profound question: Who are we?

This process of maturing experience in the bosom of a truly human relationship causes the believer and the nonbeliever to traverse the same road, forcing upon them the same obligations of authenticity and communication. In this process speech and language go through a deep ascesis until the person truly arrives at the major question indicated above. It is at this latter point that one can insert the proclamation of the Good News. Without this process of dialogue, without this growth in authenticity, and without this experience of communication, the proclamation of the faith is in danger of being turned into an ideology or a myth that is unacceptable to our contemporaries.

Thus the proclamation of the faith is meant to give reasons for our hope within the context of the major question we have arrived at through our common journey. Its proclamation will be the explication of a testimony that we have given throughout our process of encountering other men.[3]

2. Now this process of precatechesis also fulfills a very important function within the Church itself, a function of purification.

Our faith runs the risk of being transformed into mere words or into an ideology. The Creed must be verified on the level of our real-life existence. Otherwise we will serve the letter and kill the spirit. Our morality must be rooted in this perduring confrontation if it is not to be enslaved to the law once again.

The process of precatechesis, a privileged focus point in a missionary Church, puts our faith into action and calls forth the authentic theological problems. The re-examination of life practiced in many movements was and is an important step in the search for the "truth" of our faith. But perhaps today we see more clearly that the primary source of this progress in the truth is in a dialogue with the nonbeliever, which will inevitably bring down our superstructures. Above we said that the proclamation of the faith is a summons to the nonbeliever. Here we would add that the process of precatechesis is a purification, a call to conversion on a wide scale, for the Christian himself.

Consider, for example, our moral code with regard to the sexual relationship. There is certainly no doubt that in this area revelation enlightens us on the mystery of our sexual life. But neither is there any doubt that we have frequently fallen into the sin of pharisaism, propounding a set of taboos and psychic deformations under the Christian label. Now we discover that our contemporaries possess quite a different vision of the sexual relationship. Today people's experience of sexuality has acquired very definite characteristics, due to the investigations of depth psychology, studies of the sexual function, and the mass media which convey them to the general public.

The precatechesis dialogue, not as an isolated process but as a more intense form of dialogue with the world, is enlightening the Church on the existential content of its message. It is obliging the Church to move away from her traditional formulas and to get at the reality of her faith which always possesses an inexpressible core. This dialogue is forcing the Christian to realize that many of his positions on this subject are not products of the Good News but atavistic remnants of social prejudice, inertia, psychic distortion, and crypto-heresy which have been masquerading under the cloak of faith.

The Christian now sees himself obliged to undertake the difficult work of disengagement and updating. To put it bluntly, he must undertake the difficult task of maturing as a human being. This broader perspective, gained in his contact with the nonbeliever, is then brought in contact with the sources of revelation and the magisterium where its urgency becomes more pressing and its connotations become richer. Only then can the Christian grasp and communicate the inexpressible message that revelation offers us about sex, and the Good News it proclaims about this all-encompassing and anxiety-ridden aspect of our experience.

These two facets of the basic human experiences as precatechesis in the faith are interrelated. If the believer is honest in his dialogue, he will note that the nonbeliever possesses a curious kinship with him inside himself. He will notice that the nonbeliever frequently formulates disturbing questions which he himself never was able or never took the trouble to formulate. Thus the dialogue with the nonbeliever becomes an interior one inside the believer himself. It is precisely this kinship capacity that makes the dialogue possible. The proclamation of the faith to our nonbelieving brother is, at the same time, a proclamation of the faith to the nonevangelized areas of our Christian existence. Thus the power of the Word shines out through our frailty.[4]

III. DOES TRUTH NEED ERROR?

In the previous chapters, and perhaps even more in this one, the reader may have noticed a false dichotomy in the terms we employ. We have been talking about things such as "what the *world* gives to the *Church*" and "what the *world* demands of the *Church*." We are moving within the church-world dialogue that has become fashionable since Vatican II.

But even when we are using this dichotomy in terms of interdependence and mutual aid (*cf.* GS 40 and 44), it is obviously not precisely exact. In reality the Church does not dialogue with *the world* for the simple reason that she is not outside the world. She dialogues with *the rest of the world,* with the rest of humanity, since she herself is part of the world and part of humanity. The Council itself says this at one point (GS 11).

From this point of view, the real interlocutors in this dialogue are "believers and nonbelievers" (GS 12). Here is the real dichotomy; and it is between these two sides that we should talk about mutual aid and interdependence.

It may be worthwhile to ask why we have not always utilized this more correct form of expression. Many reasons might well be offered, but we might well wonder whether some underlying theology was not at work here. As we all know, the conciliar documents do not present the unified style that results from perfect unanimity of thought. We are all aware that different opinions existed at the Council. Their traces are evident not only in what was not said but also in many small details of what was actually said. One of these details is the terminology to which we have just alluded.

We feel that it is easier to speak of mutual aid or interdependence between the Church and the world (or between the Church and humanity) rather than between believers and nonbelievers. Why? Simply because the terms *world* and *humanity* are ideologically neutral, while the term *nonbeliever* alludes to error. It is invincible error in the case of men of good will, culpable error in other cases, according to the current terminology.[5] Thus if we were to speak about interdependence between believers and nonbelievers, we would in practice be posing the problem of truth. What kind of truth do we possess? If the Catholic possesses the truth, then to what areas of existence is this mutual aid with a person in error restricted? And is there not a danger that the needs and obligations of collaborative effort will eventually lead us to pose the problematic issue of some sort of interdependence between truth and error?

The most interesting thing to note is that such an interdependence does in fact exist, according to the Council. Let us consider some passages of *Gaudium et spes.*

In section 4 we read that the Church has certain duties in carrying out her mission: "To carry out such a task, the Church has always had the duty of scrutinizing the signs of the times and of interpreting them

in the light of the gospel. Thus, in language intelligible to each generation, she can respond to the perennial questions which men ask about
this present life and the life to come, and about the relationship of the
one to the other" (GS 4). Now if a person were to read this passage in
isolation, apart from the context of the whole document, he might think
that all the questions come from the rest of humanity while all the
answers are readymade, needing only to be fitted to the different mentalities of different ages and generations.

But in section 11, the Council goes a step further. It poses a series of
questions and indicates that they still await an answer: "What does the
Church think of man? What recommendations seem needful for the up-
building of contemporary society? What is the ultimate significance of
human activity throughout the world? People are waiting for an answer
to these questions. From the answers it will be increasingly clear that the
People of God and the human race in whose midst they live render
service to each other" (GS 11).

Thus, in offering an answer the Church will come to realize what she
owes to the nonbelievers who formulated or helped to formulate the
questions. And to say this is to recognize that without these questions
the truth possessed before was at least inferior to that which results from
dialogue. In other words, the answer is not prepared and readymade
beforehand. We arrive at it only through an analysis of the real-life questions formulated by humanity in its effort to fashion itself further. Thus
these questions have come to form part of a truth which is no less
revealed for all that. And so between believers and nonbelievers we begin to see emerging an interdependence and mutual aid with respect to
the truth itself.

Now the question is: What kind of truth does the Christian possess
if he does not engage in dialogue? At this point we must go another step
forward. The Council does this in connection with a specific but highly
significant issue: dialogue between believers and atheists about God.

In section 19, after pointing out that atheism as a whole is not a
spontaneous development, the Council goes on to describe it this way:
"For, taken as a whole, atheism is not a spontaneous development but
stems from a variety of causes, including a critical reaction against religious beliefs, and in some places against the Christian religion in particular. Hence believers can have more than a little to do with the birth
of atheism. To the extent that they neglect their own training in the
faith, or teach erroneous doctrine, or are deficient in their religious,
moral, or social life, they must be said to conceal rather than reveal the
authentic face of God and religion" (GS 19).

The important thing to point out here is that, strictly speaking, the
last-mentioned cause (i.e., being deficient in their religious, moral, or
social life) could be compatible to some extent with a proper idea of God;
but that does not hold true for the first two causes mentioned. If the
Christian conceals the face of God out of poor formation or poor expression of the message, it is because it is veiled inside himself. Thinking
that he knows God, he actually knows and propagates an idol that the
nonbeliever cannot recognize. In other words, he does not possess the

Christian truth even though he may repeat word for word the dogmas of faith or the articles of the Creed.

To formulate a truth in words and to really possess it are two distinct things. Let us consider an example suggested by the Council itself in connection with our dialogue with atheism. The Church affirms that "the recognition of God is in no way hostile to man's dignity, since this dignity is rooted and perfected in God. For man was made an intelligent and free member of society by the God who created him. Even more importantly, man is called as a son to commune with God and to share in His happiness" (GS 21). Now this is an undeniable truth. But is the truth really possessed by someone who repeats formulas and lives a slave morality, making it look as if worship of God means obeying a catalogue of preformulated do's and don't's? Saint Paul says no.[6]

So then we might well ask this question: Would the Church possess the truth in any case, even if she did not dialogue with the world? We are not afraid to answer "no," even though each and every word of Christ and each and every conciliar and papal definition would continue to be true in themselves. We would say that the Church would not possess the truth because her whole being would perish in such isolation; for her very *raison d'être* is to be a leaven amid the rest of humanity (*cf.* GS 40).

In reality, however, we believe that the truth defined by the Church was never such without being related to the world and its problems. In her own way, and with the limitations imposed by her outlook and her contacts with the rest of mankind, the Church has never turned totally into herself.[7]

But in every epoch of history, the truth possessed by the Church cries out for the complement she needs to be fully real: ever new dialogue with nonbelievers, i.e., with her fellow citizens on earth. The Council tells us: "While rejecting atheism, root and branch, the Church sincerely professes that all men, believers and unbelievers alike, ought to work for the rightful betterment of this world in which all alike live. However, such an ideal cannot be realized without sincere and prudent dialogue" (GS 21).

Thus not everything is positive about this dialogue, since the Council calls for prudence. The person dialoguing can lose his truth without assimilating the other side. So why run this risk?

Because the opposite danger is even worse. The truth which the Church possesses is constantly in danger of becoming mere words if it is not fleshed out in dialogue. In other words, the Church is constantly in danger of losing her truth if she does not seek for it with other men. Thus possessing the truth and seeking the truth are not opposed courses. They are essentially related, and their relationship goes by the name of the Spirit, who guides the Church. That brings us to the conciliar passage which may well be the most scandalous one for those who harbor a false conception of tradition and regard it simply as the repetition of truths: "In a wonderful manner conscience reveals that law which is fulfilled by love of God and neighbor. In fidelity to conscience, Christians are united with the rest of men in the search for truth . . ." (GS 16).

What truth must be sought jointly by Christians, nonbelievers, and atheists? At first glance it does not seem to be the great truths of revelation. The common quest operates on a more immediate and concrete terrain: "in the search for truth, and for a genuine solution to the numerous moral problems which arise in individual life and from social relationships" (GS 16).

What is involved here is the truth that is fleshed out in everyday human activity. But this fleshing out is not presented merely as the application of the truth to a welter of individual cases. The Council does not say: in search of the *truths* derived from the truth. It says: "in the search for *truth*" (singular). This signifies that revealed truth itself is seeking its incarnation in the final truth, the truth of everyday human activity which prompts and demands dialogue.

God revealed the mystery of his being, the mystery of history, and the mystery of man so that this final truth might exist. "For faith throws a new light on everything, manifests God's design for man's total vocation, and thus directs the mind to solutions which are fully human" (GS 11).

Now in this context we might well ask if we should not add a new element to the whole concept of the Spirit helping the Church in order to ensure the infallibility of this journey toward an ever fuller possession of the truth that God confided to us. As we have seen, this journey is not accomplished without all of humanity contributing the questions which arise from a sincere search. That being the case, then it seems that this very quest and the whole journey of humanity ought to be subsumed under this divine assistance.

The movement directed by the Spirit of Christ does not stop with a formula. It leads the Church to an ever greater comprehension, whose essential ingredient is dialogue. So the Spirit must also be in the heart of all those who dialogue—not to prevent them from making mistakes but to ensure that their quest ends up in a dialogue with revealed truth. Only thus will they gain "a genuine solution to the numerous moral problems which arise in individual life and from social relationships."

IV. IS IT STILL TRUE THAT THERE IS NO SALVATION OUTSIDE THE CHURCH?

There is no doubt that today we do not often hear explicated the classic objection: "no salvation outside the Church." The average informed Christian may not know how to solve the problem exactly, but he has a vague feeling that somehow this principle has faded out of vogue because of Vatican II and the subsequent atmosphere of ecumenism.

However, this does not mean that we can regard the problem as solved. Many tacit difficulties hold back the renewal of the faithful. Even more importantly, this principle still forms part of Christian dogma.

Paradoxically enough, the principle "no salvation outside the Church" is scarcely orthodox in origin. Saint Cyprian of Carthage used it against a papal doctrine which held that heretics who converted to the Church did not have to be rebaptized. Basing himself on the principle of "no salvation outside the Church," Saint Cyprian concluded that baptism administered outside the Church (i.e., in heresy) could not save a person and hence was not valid. Even though the Church did not accept his viewpoint on baptism, professing "one sole baptism for the remission of sins" (the Creed), the principle was retained as valid. There was "no salvation outside the Church."

The profession of faith imposed on the Waldensians by Innocent III (1208) spoke about "the holy Roman Church, catholic and apostolic, outside of which we believe there is no salvation" (Denz. 423). In 1442, the sixteenth ecumenical Council of Florence applied this principle to real sectors of humanity in a very strict and harsh way: The holy Roman Church "firmly believes, professes, and proclaims that no one who lives outside the Church—not only pagans but also Jews, heretics, and schismatics—can share in eternal life. They will go into the eternal fire prepared for the devil and his angels unless they reunite with the Church before they die" (Denz. 714).

The formula itself is repeated in the Bull *Unam Sanctam* (1302) of Boniface VIII, the allocution *Singulari quadam* (1854) of Pius IX, and the first draft of the Constitution on the Church that was to be proposed for definition by Vatican I. This latter schema affirmed: "It is a *de fide* dogma that no one can be saved outside the Church." [8]

So there is no question of denying the principle. Instead we must understand it as the Church understands it. This is what the Holy Office said in a letter[9] to Cardinal Cushing of Boston in 1949: "Among the things which the Church has always preached and will never cease to preach, there is also the infallible declaration which teaches us that there is no salvation outside the Church. But this dogma must be understood in the same sense in which the Church understands it." Going further, the letter explains that this principle holds true for those "who know that the Church has been divinely instituted by Christ." And it affirms that "it is not always necessary that such a person be incorporated *de facto* into the Church as a member; what is required is that he at least be united to her by desire or intention, even though it is not even necessary that this desire be explicit." [10]

Following this line of explanation, contemporary theology developed viewpoints that converge in Vatican II. These views tend to point out the universal scope of this implicit desire, existing wherever there is good will, and the existence of an equally implicit faith in the very gift of self which is love.

On one point contemporary theology had advanced a great deal. Theologians such as Karl Rahner and Edward Schillebeeckx have gone far beyond the facile solution that sets up a visible Church over against an invisible one. The latter solution would say that men within the visible Church are saved by what they do (i.e., faith and the sacraments), and that men within the invisible Church are saved in spite of what they do (i.e., by their good intention). As we have seen in this chapter, the newer theology just referred to teaches us that salvific incorporation into the Church always presupposes that we objectively work at the one common task: the building up of society in love.[11]

When due stress is laid on this brand of reflection, we can understand what Boniface Willems says: "In this [implicit] active faith there exists an *objective* orientation toward the Church, whether one is explicitly conscious of it or not. The principle *no salvation outside the Church* does not mean to concentrate on the boundaries of the Church but rather, on the contrary, it seeks to highlight the universal mediatory role of Christ's Church." [12]

This last phrase brings us to the second part of this CLARIFICATION. It is not enough to understand the principle in a broader sense. We must change the central image in the mental picture that lies hidden behind this formula within many Christians. For they see it as a restrictive condition set down by God with regard to salvation. In other words, they believe that God certainly redeemed all men, but they feel that he made the real redemption of each individual conditional upon their entrance into the Church. However broadly they may interpret this condition, the dominant image does not seem to be that of Paul in the New Testament.

In a previous CLARIFICATION[13] we saw that the revelation of the Law constituted an important, even though incomplete, revolution. It ended up in the discovery of sin rather than in the discovery of redemption. We also saw that to the extent this revelation made Israel the possessor and transmitter of this incomplete mystery, it made her a figure of the Church, the new Israel possessing and transmitting the complete mystery of God's plan. For Paul, the problem of the Galatians with regard to the Law (reiterating Israel's own misunderstanding of the Law) and the problem of the Corinthians with regard to the Church were one and the same problem, requiring one and the same solution.[14] We are no longer under the law because the whole universe has been given to man; neither are we *under the Church* because all things, including celestial realities, have been placed at the service of man.

Now behind this deviation of the Jewish people with regard to the Law, Paul sees a mental image that we should quite logically transpose to the deviation described above with regard to the Church and salvation. That mental image sees some restrictive condition in God's promise.

According to Paul, God made an unconditional promise of righteousness (i.e., of salvation) to Abraham. When the Law came along four centuries later, the Jews interpreted it wrongly. They felt that God had thought over what he did before and had decided to remedy the situation by introducing a new stipulation, that he inserted a restrictive condition in the covenant which once had contained only an unconditional promise. Paul notes that this interpretation is absurd. But this brings him up against a question: If the Law does not restrict or put conditions on the promise of righteousness, then what import does it have? Paul's reply is perfectly logical: If it is not a restrictive condition, it cannot be anything but a helpful instrument, an aid. And the aid it gives is to give us a knowledge (*supergnosis*) of one of the elements involved in righteousness: i.e., sin. The Law then is a slave (the teacher in Roman society) which only appears to rule until we are mature enough to appreciate the reason behind its service (*cf.* Gal. 3:15-29).

In the case of the Church as well there is an *unconditional promise* of salvation made by God. Then, at a specific time, there is the divine manifestation that produces knowledge (*supergnosis*) which is designed to serve as an aid to the promise through the responsible Christians. But in the latter case, the knowledge does not have to do with a transitory, incomplete reality; it has to do with the definitive and total reality of eternal life. That is how Paul presents the matter in his Epistle to Titus:

"From Paul, servant of God and apostle of Jesus Christ, marked as such by faith and knowledge and hope—the faith of God's chosen people, knowledge of the truth as our religion has it and the hope of eternal life. Yes, it is eternal life that God, who cannot lie, promised long ages ago, and now in his own good time he has openly declared himself in the proclamation which was entrusted to me . . ." (Titus 1:1–3).

As we just said, Paul speaks about a promise which is certainly unconditional. It cannot be limited to one people as that of Abraham was. It was made "long ages ago," that is, to the whole of creation[15] which is destined for eternal life by God's gift. Here too the Church arrives on the scene later, limited to its proper time. And by the same logic, it is not meant to restrict the unconditional promise but to help its carrying out. In effect there is a stage in this plan which begins at its own proper time and which requires a new element to be put into play. That element is man's knowledge of the plan that leads to eternal life. In order that this element may truly be present for humanity, God hands down his word, which manifests eternal life to those who have been chosen for the responsibility entrusted to them.

Only by grasping the logic of this whole picture can we understand the absolute necessity of the Church for "those who know," as the letter of the Holy Office to Cardinal Cushing put it. It is necessary for those who know the plan of God and what is required for its carrying out, so that they may be able to avail themselves of this factor which is so decisive for all humanity.

Only in this light can we appreciate the statement of Willems cited earlier: "The principle *no salvation outside the Church* does not propose to concentrate on the boundaries of the Church but rather, on the contrary, it seeks to highlight the universal mediatory role of Christ's Church."

NOTES

1. It should be noted that the effort of some missionaries to study in depth the religion of the peoples they are to evangelize should not be superficially interpreted to mean that Christianity merely serves to complement the insufficiencies of the native religion. Such study prior to evangelization is part of a much broader analysis of the culture through which the faith is to be expressed. Thus, insofar as evangelization is concerned, it has the same value as study of the native language and other aspects of the culture. Evangelizing a new cultural milieu presupposes a tremendous creative effort on the part of the missionary. Such an effort was not intended or carried out at all times, or even in the majority of cases, in the past history of mission work.

2. As the reader may have noticed, the words *religion* and *religious* are used here (and throughout this volume) in their ordinary sociological sense. Within this broader usage, they apply both to primitive religions and more advanced religions, as well as to Christianity. We might use the definition of Robert Bellah here: "Religion is a complex of symbolic forms and actions that relate man to the ultimate conditionings of his existence." In accordance with what has been said, the valuation of this universal phenomenon is ambiguous. Hence many modern theologians prefer to use a different vocabulary to suggest the same distinction we have tried to make in this CLARIFICATION. They main-

tain that Christianity signified a total revolution in the religious world, and only shares superficial externals in common with this world. (Recall what we said in the last chapter, and in the CLARIFICATION dealing with Christian faith and sacraments as opposed to magic.) They would say that, strictly speaking, Christianity is not a *religion*. This more radical use of terminology clashes with current usage even though it clears up the ambiguity. It has a certain truculence that is not too useful for pastoral purposes. In any case, we feel that our remarks and notes clearly indicate our awareness of the distinction, and our position with regard to the whole issue.

3. It should be pointed out that this proclamation will be made only to someone who has in some way questioned us about our faith. Considered in this light, a human experience is properly a precatechesis process when it is motivated by an initial question about what we believe. As its name indicates, precatechesis is a moment in the proclamation of faith; in this sense, it must be distinguished from any other preparation for the gospel.

4. Here it would be worthwhile to inquire among Christians about the principal psychosocial mechanisms that set the precatechesis dialogue in motion. In reality it is lay people more than pastors of souls who are the natural dispensers of precatechesis (*cf*. GS 43). Whom will non-Christians question about the faith, if it is not the laity? Surely it will not be those in charge of the ecclesial community, but those who share the same human, everyday tasks.

This being the case, it is worth noting that in any recognizable form of dialogue the representative of a community assumes a certain role. In other words, his behavior responds to some pre-existing expectation. Thus it would be important to know how Christians generally approach the prospect of precatechesis dialogue, since their manner of approach would reveal a specific conception of the Church and her function. We offer some concrete questions on this problem.

How much time do they feel they must set aside for the task of *listening to* their interlocutor? Do they regard this as something more than gathering information on the real or imagined difficulty that hinders the way to faith? Since such dialogue is regarded as somewhat dangerous for the Christian (GS 21), where will he exercise the prudence demanded? What role is played in this dialogue by the prestige of the Church, which may be open to certain objections?

In the light of what we have said, such questions as these could suggest important revisions and more in-depth study.

5. See CLARIFICATION IV below.

6. See Chapter V in this volume.

7. See CLARIFICATION III of Chapter I.

8. See *La Foi Catholique: Textes doctrinaux du Magistére de l'Eglise*, n. 461.

9. *American Ecclesiastical Review* 127 (1952) 309–311.

10. On the import and causes of this dogmatic evolution, see CLARIFICATION III of Chapter I.

11. See Edward Schillebeeckx, "The Church and Mankind," in *Concilium* 1. And in a more general way, consider the picture of the last judgment on the one hand, and the biblical notion of all things being recapitulated in Christ on the other.

12. Boniface Willems, "Who Belongs to the Church?" *Concilium* 1. The paper by Willems contains an excellent bibliography of modern European works on all the topics discussed in this volume.

13. See CLARIFICATION III of Chapter II.

14. See Appendix II in this volume, II A.

15. On the relationship between creation and redemption, see CLARIFICATION II of Chapter I.

CHAPTER FOUR

Obligations of the Ecclesial Community

CHURCH OF THE MASSES
OR SIGN-COMMUNITY?

What we have seen in the last three chapters would seem to provide an answer, in principle, to the essential question that has to be posed regarding the Church: What is her function and ultimate justification within the human community?

But once we have gotten this far, the consequences of what has already been said crop up as so many new problems. Or, if you prefer to put it another way, they crop up as so many old problems that have been brought back to life by the questions which our present age poses to the Church.

For example, we need only take a cursory glance at the present-day reality of the Church to be confronted with a question: If the function of the Church is what we have described in the preceding chapters, are there people in the Church who do or can fulfill this mission? Are there people outside the Church who do not and cannot fulfill such a mission?

In other words, when we look around us we see a disturbing situation, especially in so-called Christian countries. People are recruited for this community called the Church through social media that have nothing to do with the function described in the preceding chapters. And we quite logically ask ourselves whether such a manner of belonging to the Church is *in fact* the best way, whether there might not be a better way that could be envisioned and sought after.

Do we not find the lower classes alienated from the Church in many traditionally Christian countries? With the desacralization of public institutions, doesn't Christianity tend to become a luxury item? The Council itself makes this admission: "A more critical ability to distinguish religion from a magical view of the world . . . purifies religion and exacts day by day a more personal and explicit adherence to faith" (GS 7). Even though it does not say so, does this not come down to accepting the fact that it is reducing membership in the Church to an aristocracy based on interior qualities if not on money? For, after saying that, it quite logically goes on to say: "On the other hand, growing numbers of people are abandoning religion in practice" (GS 7).

78

To put it more plainly, the Church today must ask herself if all her so-called members truly belong to her and if some nonmembers might not truly belong to her. This was a question which even the primitive Church had to ask herself (*cf.* 1 John 2:19 and Rev. 2 and 3). Indeed such a question cannot be avoided by a Church which claims to be the salt, leaven, and light, which feels obligated to contribute something of decisive importance to the fashioning of human history if she is to justify her existence.

For this reason we feel it would be quite useful to see how Paul resolved one concrete case that came up in the Church at Corinth (1 Cor. 5). By examining his response we will see whether his attitude confirms the basic principles we formulated in the preceding chapters.

The case in question is clear enough. A new Christian, undoubtedly confused by Paul's preaching on the new law of liberty, understood that he was empowered to have sexual relations with his stepmother. The context of the letter shows clearly that neither the Corinthians nor Paul nor even the party in question saw this as a passing frailty. It was not a case where someone was caught in the toils of passion for a moment, later recognized the incompatibility of his conduct with Christ's message, and then sought pardon from God and the community. The person in question here persisted in believing that his continuing behavior pattern was compatible with the Christian name he bore, with the Christian community to which he belonged.

There was the problem, and Paul's letter to the Corinthians indicates that he had already bade them to separate this man from the community in a previous communication. This man could not be allowed to corrupt the whole community (*cf.* 1 Cor. 5:6). But the Corinthians, following this bit of advice to what seemed to be the logical conclusion, had interpreted it to mean that they were to keep away from all human intercourse. For there was no lack of potential contagion in the pagan world, particularly in a place like Corinth!

In response to this problematic situation, Paul has three things to say. In them we will glimpse his picture of the Church.

Firstly he tells them that he never meant to imply that they should separate themselves from *pagan* sinners, or as Pauline terminology puts it, from sinners "in this world." If that were his advice, they "would have to get out of the world altogether" (1 Cor. 5:10). And neither Christ nor Paul would envision such a defensive strategy (*cf.* John 17:15–19).

Secondly, he explains that what he bade them do was to separate themselves from the sinner who is a brother Christian, i.e., who is a representative of the Christian community. In reality every Christian involves the name and import of the Church in his own actions. His very attitudes carries a message. So when the signification that the Church should have is incompatible with the deliberate conduct of some member, Paul demands that the Church prefer her sign-bearing function. And to show that this option is not restricted to exceptional cases, Paul extends the principle to anyone who is a fornicator or idolater or is guilty of adultery, thievery, drunkenness, slander, swindling, and so forth.

Thirdly, Paul writes off the one objection that might be logically raised against this pastoral approach: namely, that he is sacrificing people to the function of the Church. For in Paul's mind the purpose of excluding the person from the community is "so that his spirit *may be saved* on the Day of the Lord" (1 Cor. 5:5). Thus his exclusion from the community is in line with Paul's concern for his salvation rather than opposed to it. Paul is not thinking about his eventual return to the community, even though he does not deny that possibility either. He is rather feeling that the new situation will favor the man's salvation.

Now there can be no doubt that behind these three recommendations lies a full-fledged notion of the Church and her function among men. But before we examine that notion, we might do well to realize that our recommendations would probably have been quite the opposite.

Firstly, the vast majority of Christians, shaped or kept in line by the pressures of the surrounding environment, are weak. In many cases they do not possess what the Council calls a "more personal and explicit adherence to faith" (GS 7). Thus keeping them Christians is presumed to mean safeguarding them from danger and maintaining them in various environments where it is easy to foster their loyalty to the Church. If the Church is supposed to include everyone, then it seems apparent that we must recognize right off that we cannot turn everyone into heralds of her sign-bearing function. Only a small minority can carry this message to other opposed or pluralistic environments. The majority are only capable of accepting this message when they are supported by a majority environment around them.

Secondly, it would undoubtedly be our tendency to accept and praise efforts at improving the witness or sign-bearing function of the Church only to the extent that these efforts did not imprudently jeopardize the seemingly essential thing: namely, ensuring the salvation of the majority by keeping them inside the Church (*cf.* LG 38). We are not at all disposed to subordinate mass membership in the Church to her sign-bearing function, for that would seem to be subordinating the essential to the secondary. For us the Church should have as much of a sign-bearing function as it can while keeping within it those who can only accept a minimum of obligations.

Thirdly, there is an emotional basis behind the foregoing presumptions that is hardly debated at all. It is our conviction that the Church represents the ideal situation for winning salvation for those who are lucky enough to be acquainted with her. So when problems do come up, we are inclined to exclude a person from the Church only if failure to do so might induce many other people to give up their membership in the Church.

Now what could Paul's idea of the Church be when he makes three decisions so opposed to the attitudes we are wont to see and maintain?

Actually Paul simply draws logical conclusions from the central idea that the Church is, essentially and primarily, a *sign*. It has been placed here precisely and exclusively to pass on to men a certain signification, i.e., a message, something that is to be grasped, comprehended, and incorporated to a greater or lesser degree into the fashioning of history and the world. If *the very existence* of the Church is meant to be leaven in the dough, salt in the meal, and light for all those who dwell in the human household, then the ecclesial community must accept the obligations that derive from its essential function.

Following this imperious logic, Paul reaches the following practical and general conclusions. And they serve as the basis for his concrete decisions with regard to the Church at Corinth.

1. The primary preoccupation of the Church is not directed toward her own inner life but toward people outside. Unlike other organizations founded for the benefit of its own members, the Church is a community sent to those who live, act, and work outside her own narrow limits.[1]

So whom is Paul concerned about primarily in resolving the problem faced by the Corinthians? He is concerned about the non-Christian, who is supposed to receive a sign-bearing message attached to the Christian community. It is certainly obvious that the sinfulness of the pagan world can be a danger for the Christian who has been sent into the world. But as Paul sees it, it is equally evident that the Christian is meant to run this risk. To be a Christian is to belong to a community that has been sent into the world. Not to go would be a contradiction in Paul's eyes, a contradiction of far greater riskiness than facing up to the danger inherent in the Christian vocation.

The prevailing attitude today, which we mentioned earlier, suggests that our scale of values has been turned inside out. The Church shows concern for non-Christians to the extent that this is permitted by her primary concern, which is to keep the mass of professed Christians inside the Church. For Paul, by contrast, prudence involves safeguarding the essential thing; we must make sure that the message of the ecclesial community truly reaches the human community, for that is what it is meant to do.

2. Thus the first concern of the Church is the non-Christian, and from this springs her second concern. What should the Christian be if the non-Christian is to receive from the ecclesial community that which God is trying to send him? In other words, the first interior concern of the Church, which must always keep her attention focused on the rest of humanity, is the clarity and transparency of her sign-function.

For Paul it makes no sense to subordinate this transparency to mere numbers. If a person has grasped the function of the Church with regard to humanity, then he must be in accord with it. That is why it is so critically important, in trying to frame the Church in its proper context, to begin by asking the meaning of its insertion in the history of the human race to whom God's universal plan is directed.

A conquering Church and a sign-bearing Church are not two relatively compatible realities in Paul's mind. A faith, a moral code, and a sacramental practice reduced to minimum essentials makes no sense. Why? Because, as we shall see more clearly, the sign-function unceasingly calls for creative dialogue, inventive love, and real disinterestedness. And these qualities are poles apart from any conditions that would ensure minimum standards.[2]

But someone might ask: Doesn't this minimum have something to do with salvation?

3. Here is where Paul's logic goes right to the core of the matter. If the obligations flowing from this sign-bearing function call for the purification of the Church's witness in one way or another—gently or roughly, by one's own decision or another's, by decree or by disinterestedness—then some people who bear the Christian name and who would like to continue in the community will find themselves excluded from it. Far from endangering their salvation, it may serve as the means of ensuring it in Paul's eyes. And if this is true, then we must conclude that at least in some cases the Church (i.e., visible membership in the Christian community) is not always and everywhere the ideal situation with respect to salvation for all men.[3]

This point is of major importance. It shows us that the Church only aids the salvation of those who belong to her when their membership corresponds with the function that the Church is called upon to exercise with regard to the rest of the human race.

In other words, membership in the ecclesial community saves people when it is shouldered as a new and more profound responsibility. And this fact is simply the ultimate consequence of something we already know: that the Church is an undreamed of possibility for love. Insofar as all the elements of the Church point the way to this love, membership in the Church will likewise point the way to salvation. But as soon as these new elements, which are meant to bolster love, are detached from this responsibility and are lived for the benefit of those who have availed themselves of them, then membership in the Church becomes a backward step on the road to salvation. It becomes another form of egotism.[4]

In Paul's mind, then, the Church cannot escape the law that underlies all love. Every potential instrument of love—be it a loaf of bread, a glass of water, a program for establishing justice or communicating a revelation—can be turned into an instrument of egotism. And the greatest imprudence of all, for the human community which enjoys the greatest spiritual richness, would be to overlook the colossal opportunities for egotism offered by the things which God has given it so that it might shoulder responsibility for human history.

We have already considered the true import of faith and the sacraments. We have seen that they differ from love only insofar as they combine man's potentialities for love with actual possession of its mystery. So there is a real danger to be considered here. If this possibility for love is turned back in upon itself by mistake, if it is considered to be an instrument and guarantee of salvation itself framed within a context of hallowed efficaciousness, if its formulas are considered to be salvific when they are utilized with material exactitude, then we get a brand of egotism that is elevated to the level of the sacred. We need not even mention how these elements can be distorted in the pious practices of the people.

We may well be amazed on the day of judgment to find that countless Christians are saved *in spite of* their faith and their sacraments. That thought should make us stop and think about our desire to find a minimum number of obligations to impose on people, so that those who are incapable of self-giving and assuming responsibility toward others might be kept inside the Church. In trying to find such a minimum are we not doing wrong to the salvation process as well as to humanity, insofar as our wrong interpretation of faith and the sacraments tends to bolster the egotism we all nurture within ourselves?

So we are finally confronted with the fundamental dilemma. If the community called Church wanted to be the community of all mankind, or at least of the majority of mankind, it would have to take the line of least resistance and make it as easy as possible for people. In reality, however, the Church will always be selective. The line of least resistance is an egotistical tack, and the Church would have to cater to egotism if she chose to become the community of the majority. And the great danger is that she may give in to that temptation. Indeed it may be more than just a danger!

It is certainly obvious that some of the barriers presently separating many people from the Church are illegitimate ones which run counter to the gospel message. They relate membership in the Church to money, education, and power. But even when we sweep these false barriers away, one barrier will still remain. It is the harsh and selective criterion of personal self-giving assumed as a real responsibility.

When this barrier is felt to be a painful one which we are ashamed to accept, when we argue against it by saying that the Church must be a Church of the "lowly," meaning those who cannot get beyond this barrier, then in reality we are paying tribute to an aristocratic conception of Christianity in the bad sense of that word. If we are driven by a desire to expand the boundaries of the ecclesial community by eliminating this responsibility of self-giving, we are actually living as if membership in it were a *privilege* that *always* betters the situation of those who possess it. Cherishing a shameful aristocratic outlook, we seek to excuse our seeming prerogatives by sharing them as widely as possible.

No one would complain about people being left outside the Church if membership in the Church were regarded as a risk. Consider how much work is involved in building a city. Would anyone complain if some people were left out of that project? Would people accuse the work force of being an aristocracy because its members pursue specialized studies and possess certain protective elements that others lack?

Now some might feel that such examples are beside the point here. But that only proves they have not read the Gospel. For our example is merely a modern interpretation of a conversation presented in the synoptic Gospels: "The mother of Zebedee's sons then came before him, with her sons. She bowed low and begged a favour. 'What is it you wish?' asked Jesus. 'I want you,' she said, 'to give orders that in your kingdom my two sons here may sit next to you, one at your right, and the other at your left.' Jesus turned to the brothers and said, 'You do not understand what you are asking. Can you drink the cup that I am to drink?' 'We can,' they replied" (Matt. 20:20–22).

The person who makes such a request of the Church does not know what he is asking for either. He is asking for an aristocratic privilege. And the only aristocracy he will get, if he really wants it, is an aristocracy of self-giving and love that may even entail death. Surely this is one of the most critical aspects of Christian life today. Because of the false conception of the Church that they have, many people do not know what they are asking for by belonging to the Church. If they are to think and speak and act in the right framework here, there must be a twofold change in the prevailing notion of Christian *risk*.

First of all, when the Church is presented to the vast multitude of human beings, it must be associated with the notion of risk. Because the Church is a risk. The proper outlook to guide us here is one provided by the gospel; it combines various elements already known to us. We have already seen that the Christian is the person whose mission is tied up with the gift God has given him: i.e., wisdom to understand fully the mystery (*cf.* Eph. 1:9). And now we can look at the somewhat jesting remark of Jesus which really makes the picture clear for us: "The servant who knew his master's wishes, yet made no attempt to carry them out, will be flogged severely. But one who did not know them and earned a beating will be flogged less severely. Where a man has been given much, much will be expected of him; and the more a man has had entrusted to him the more he will be required to repay" (Luke 12:47–48).

Speaking in pastoral terms, we might well ask ourselves whether we really take seriously these words of Saint Paul: "If anyone does not make provision for his own relations, and especially for members of his own household, he has denied the faith and is worse than an unbeliever" (1 Tim. 5:8).

Secondly, the multitude is in greater danger if the Church, in receiving them, loses its sign-bearing function than if it receives the Church's message with all its import from outside the Church. Here again we must remember what really keeps a person internally alienated, even if he is within the reality called the Church. It is the condition of mass membership and egotism that refuses the task of self-giving. What is the one and only way in which he can be helped? We cannot do it by confirming him in his egotism. We must summon him to self-giving, even if that is only one part of his existence, and inspire him to shoulder responsibility for others. Only this can help him to salvation, whether he is inside or outside the visible community of the Church. In other words, the basic aid that the Church offers to human beings does not involve introducing them into the Church in an improper way, exposing them to her risk without removing the obstacle to salvation posed by selfishness. The basic help she offers comes through her sign-bearing function; for in this function they hear resonances of the message that can change their existence even though it may not convert them into Christians. If it does not resonate through her sign-bearing function, the message will not reach them even if they are physically within the Church.

Here again the change in mental outlook and our scale of values must be grounded in a changed way of picturing the Church. And here again the Gospel offers us the authentic images. We all know them but we may not yet truly understand them. The images involved relate to the Church as *leaven* and *salt*.

In one parable Jesus explains how the kingdom is like a small bit of leaven buried in the dough. It produces a change, turning the whole mixture into something else: not into leaven, but into a loaf of bread.

The seasoning work of salt is the same. The savor of the pinch of salt permeates the whole dish of food, not turning it into salt but making it edible. But in this parable Jesus adds another note: the salt may lose its savor and fail to enliven the dish as it should. It ceases to be real salt, just as the Church may cease to be truly salvific. It is of no use if it turns into an arid lump that people will throw out.

We must take these images seriously and change our outlook accordingly. Such a process can more readily and profoundly revitalize the ecclesial community than many lengthy pastoral discussions.

NOTES TO CHAPTER FOUR

1. "She serves as a leaven and as a kind of soul for human society" (GS 40).
2. "For it is the function of the Church, led by the Holy Spirit who renews and purifies her ceaselessly, to make God the Father and His Incarnate Son present and in a sense visible. This result is achieved chiefly by the witness of a living and mature faith, namely, one trained to see difficulties clearly and to master them" (GS 21).
3. "All the sons of the Church should remember that their exalted status is to be attributed not to their own merits but to the special grace of Christ. If they fail moreover to respond to that grace in thought, word, and deed, not only will they not be saved but they will be the more severely judged" (LG 14). It is this grace of Christ that allows the Church to carry out her *raison d'être,* to be a leaven.
4. "He is not saved, however, who, though he is part of the body of the Church, does not persevere in charity. He remains indeed in the bosom of the Church, but, as it were, only in a 'bodily' manner and not 'in his heart'" (LG 14).

CLARIFICATIONS

I. THE RELEVANCE OF THE GRAND INQUISITOR TODAY

In studying these topics concerning the Church, we could benefit greatly from exploring their resonances in modern literature, particularly in the literature of our own nations. Contact with the most powerful expressions of the modern spirit could greatly help the Church to reach the maturity she must have in her dealings with the world (*cf.* GS 43).

We cannot undertake such an exploration here. But we should like to examine a few passages in *The Brothers Karamazov,* where Dostoievski presents us with the confrontation between Christ and the Grand Inquisitor. The "Legend of the Grand Inquisitor" has had a profound impact on many Christian thinkers. It is an important piece in Western culture which relates to our present discussion.

We all recall the fearsome "dialogue" between the Inquisitor and Christ, the latter having returned to earth. The Inquisitor is supposed to be someone continuing Christ's work on earth, but actually he is radically opposed to its spirit. He does all the talking, explaining his views passionately and in great detail. And he eventually reveals his profound separation from Christ and his commitment to the forces of Satan.

The Inquisitor begins by re-examining Christ's dialogue with Satan during the temptations in the desert. As the Inquisitor sees it, the three propositions put forward by Satan were not temptations at all. They would have given Christ the means to reach the great mass of mankind with his message. And he asks Christ to think them over with him again and see who was really right.

As the Inquisitor sees it, the first proposition comes down to something like this. Christ is planning to go into the world empty-handed, offering people a gift of freedom. Being naive and dull-witted, they could not possibly appreciate this gift; indeed they would be terrified by it. How could the "bread from heaven" possibly compare with earthly bread in the eyes of these weak people? Even if thousands and tens of thousands came to him for this bread, what would they be in comparison with the millions and tens of millions who could not part with earthly bread for the sake of his bread? The Inquisitor feels that Christ has a predilection only for those who are great and powerful, that he showed no concern for the countless millions who might indeed love him but would not be capable of this, that he was content to let them be tools in the hands of the great and the strong. *The Inquisitor, by contrast, loves those millions too.*

In refusing Satan's offer of bread, Christ closed the door on any possibility of a numerically universal Church, which would open its portals *effectively* to all men. In the eyes of the Inquisitor, this revealed great lack of love on Christ's part. Freedom of conscience is a very seductive idea to human beings, to be sure, but it also entails great pain. Instead of accepting Satan's offer, which would have guaranteed tranquillity for man's conscience, Christ offered man an enigmatic and uncertain reality to which he was not accustomed. He, who had supposedly come to give his life for men, lived and acted as if he did not love men at all.

The second "temptation" brings the Inquisitor to the same conclusion. In order to ensure liberty, Christ refused to ground his Church firmly on a miracle even as he had already refused to ground it on earthly bread. The same thing happened on the cross, when he might have won over his persecutors by coming down from it. But he refused to conquer people with miracles, demanding freely chosen faith from them. Here again he overrated human beings, in the opinion of the Grand Inquisitor, and therefore demanded too much of them. In so doing, he failed to have real effective compassion for them. If he had not rated them highly, he would not have demanded so much of them. That would be more like real love. Sure, he could show select souls how to exercise freedom and love, but what about the countless weak souls that are not capable of this? Did Christ come only to offer a select pathway to a small elite? The question goes right to the heart of the whole problem we have been discussing, the human condition and the obligations of the Christian, and the Inquisitor feels that Christ opted for an elite.

Now the Grand Inquisitor, who is the representative of the Church in Dostoievski's eyes, confesses his terrible secret. Out of love for human beings, he and his cohorts have decided that Satan was right and fashioned the Church accordingly. They are not on Christ's side but the devil's, and they have been since the Church acquired direct temporal power under Charlemagne.[1] At that point in time they accepted from Satan the gift that Jesus refused in the desert.

But even then Christ could have accepted temporal power, if he had accepted Satan's third proposition. Why did he refuse it? If he had accepted Satan's offer, he would have been able to give human beings everything they really look for on earth: someone to adore, someone to entrust their thinking to, someone to unite meekly under as so many ants in an anthill. Wouldn't that have been the right way to help the weak and show love for the lowly? The Inquisitor once followed Christ's footsteps into the desert, but then he thought it over and chose not to follow such a foolish pathway. He is one of the many people who have tried to correct Christ's mistakes, to shed overweening pride in liberty and freely chosen love out of concern for frail human beings.[2]

Only an authentic notion of the Church can resolve the dilemma posed by Dostoievski's Grand Inquisitor. We try to tackle it in the main text of this chapter and CLARIFICATION II. But this passage in Dostoievski shows how far the objection can be pushed against any such solution.

II. DOES THE CHURCH CONSTITUTE AN ARISTOCRACY?

The reader will recall that in Chapter I of this volume we presented the Church as a reality incarnated in history and striving hopefully toward a goal. By this very fact, it will always face limitations in its journey through time.

Now this fact gives rise to two problems, one of them quite serious and the other less so. As we have just seen, the desire to make the Church universal in numerical terms clearly leads many Christians into tendencies that are contradictory to the very essence of the Church and sometimes contradictory in themselves. Since any radical form of self-commitment is a clearly aristocratic attitude proper to strong personalities, they would like to have a Church without any message or, at most, with a general and abstract message. They realize that any concrete message is open to rejection. Even more importantly, comprehension of this message presupposes a minimum degree of intellectual and truly human life—something that was certainly not possessed by Neanderthal man long ago and that is not possessed today by a vast proportion of human beings who lack education, food, and peace. On the other hand, an abstract non-existential message lacks the allure that could make it universal; so people try to formulate some kind of seemingly concrete abstraction: Christianity is food, peace, justice, development, or whatever. Unfortunately the label does not stick too well in reality, with the result that the identification of Christianity with some human ideal ends up as one more form of mystification.

In looking for a Church that is totally "of the people," i.e., one that is capable of being a Church for even the most primitive and lowly types of human beings, people rail against any and every form of "intellectualism." By this term they mean any attempt to turn Christian truths into truths that are truly comprehended and that operate creatively in real life. They see such an attempt as an obligation above and beyond most people, for the vast majority of human beings do not think for themselves but follow readymade formulas. They rail against "elitism" which would try to effect the revolution implied in Christ's message, because it would restrict Christianity to the few who would be willing to shoulder this revolutionary task.

What is more, if they do not rail against the larger fact that the Church left a million years of human history outside its ken, it is only because this would force them to accuse Christ himself of the same intellectualism and elitism. After all, Christ allowed humanity to go through its darker eons and only then founded the Church in a more developed phase of history. Some might even propose to correct Christ's course of action if they could, for the sake of the masses, even as the Grand Inquisitor of Dostoievski claimed to do.

Such tendencies often reveal an underlying anxiety over human beings that dominates the logic of finding the best way to help them. But leaving such tendencies aside, we must ask quite seriously whether the obligations involved in bearing the Christian name do not indeed convert the Church community, bent upon being a sign-bearing one, into an *aristocratic* community.

The word aristocracy, like other words such as intellectualism and elitism, is capable of exercising a type of verbal terrorism over people. No one wants to be tainted with such a label, and people are ready to give up essential aspects of Christianity to avoid this. So we must analyze the word more closely to free ourselves from its emotional overtones.

Now the very assumption of responsibility for others constitutes those who assume it into a type of aristocracy vis-à-vis those toward whom they assume responsibility. To shoulder responsibility is to feel obligated for something that does not oblige others: *Noblesse oblige*. And along with this goes all the inherent dangers in this additional obligation that inevitably separates one from others.

This process is not peculiar to the ruling classes. The industrial worker himself is quite familiar with it. The union activist shoulders a responsibility which makes him distinct, for he chooses to risk more. His position is different in this respect and in others too. The greater risk he runs is compensated for by the greater solidarity he encounters in cases of dispute. The common laborer outside the unions does not have the risk nor the solidarity. Here we see a typical case of aristocracy in the proper sense of the word.

What is more, union responsibility demands some degree of liberation from the worker's own condition, precisely so that the labor leader may render better service to the common welfare of the working class. Herein lies a danger facing any union. It may be taken over by an aristocratic minority that becomes more and more separated from the labor masses, that gradually tends to forget the aspect of service and to stress its own privileges until it drops its original function.

It would be utopian to dream of a responsibility that did not constitute an aristocracy, both in the proper sense of the term and in terms of its potential deviation. Any such responsibility can coopt the facilities essential to its authentic function and convert them to its own selfish use. Money, education, prestige, power, and free time can be distorted in this way. That is a norm underlying all societal life.

Now it is quite obvious that the Church is subject to this same norm. However much the word "aristocracy" may frighten us, we cannot deny that the Christian community was summoned by Christ to shoulder a difficult responsibility right from the start. If anything that places demands on people necessarily leaves the masses outside, then following Christ could not constitute an ideal for the multitude: "If anyone wishes to be a follower of mine, he must leave self behind; day after day he must take up his cross, and come with me" (Luke 9:23).

If anyone reads the program of Jesus outlined in the gospel today, he will be struck by the same thought that came to his disciples when they heard it from his lips: "Then who can be saved?" (Mark 10:26). And as we shall see immediately, the noteworthy thing is that this program did not represent the highest level of perfection. It was not fashioned of lower grades of perfection underneath, for it represented the minimum level of perfection required for salvation. Jesus certainly did not present a pastoral program for the masses in his teaching.

In line with this teaching, the primitive Christian community maintained characteristic obligations that made it an exceptional entity and that set it in opposition to the law of least resistance which prevailed in worldly society and its mass mechanisms. Consider Paul's exhortation to the Corinthians: "Must brother go to law with brother—and before unbelievers? Indeed, you already fall below your standard in going to law with one another at all. Why not rather suffer injury? Why not rather let yourself be robbed?" (1 Cor. 6:6–7). Now any community which feels obligated to pursue this outlook to its logical consequences is clearly aristocratic in the sense described above.

Thus it is that when Christianity became the religion of the masses in the West, it necessarily had to introduce a distinction here. It distinguished between the commandments and the evangelical counsels. The former were the same precepts as those of the Old Testament decalogue. They applied to all, but now they were considered with greater scrupulosity and a greater concern for sins of intention (cf. Matt. 5:17–49). The latter counsels were for religious people who aspired to perfection.

Thus the daily obligations of the primitive Church now showed up as a form of monastic utopianism. The harsher demands of the gospel are seen to be directed toward those who live a "spiritual life" in the world—or more logically, outside the world.

The whole thrust of spiritual and theological renewal in the modern Church represents a reaction against this separation. When Jesus said to the rich young man, "If you wish to go the whole way, sell your possessions and give to the poor . . . come, follow me" (Matt. 19:21), he was not inviting him to be a monk or a religious. When he said, "If you wish to go the whole way," he meant, "If you want to be a Christian." Because being a Christian involves giving up one's life for others—nothing more and nothing less.

The whole thrust of modern ecclesial renewal converges toward this comment of Vatican II: "In the Church, everyone belonging to the hierarchy, or being cared for by it, is called to holiness . . . Thus it is evident to everyone that all the faithful of Christ, of whatever rank or status are called to the fullness of the Christian life and to the perfection of charity" (LG 39–40). And this perfection of love is nothing else but that which Christ described: "There is no greater love than this, that a man should lay down his life for his friends" (John 15:13).

A few pages earlier we briefly alluded to the origin of the pejorative connotations ascribed to the word "aristocracy." But if the latter signifies shouldering the demands and risks of responsibility for others, then the means of carrying out this obligation should not logically seem to be a privilege for those who accept this risk, even though it may separate them from the multitude. However, if these means are then detached from the responsibility and turned into ends in themselves, then the "aristocracy" has become a degenerate reality, an elite grounded on its own privileges. Like the Church community itself, the word "aristocracy" is ambiguous; it can have two different meanings. And this two-way possibility is open to the Church as well.

III. THE CHURCH AND POLITICAL POWER

1. We have tried to show that the Church is a sacramental community with a mission among men, not a closed circle in which the Christian

lives out his faith and ensures his own salvation. Why, then, is it more likely to appear as a dominion rather than as a form of service? Why does it present itself as a maternalistic entity committed to outdated systems rather than as a fraternal, friendly entity transcending specific civilizations? Considering its actual cast, is it surprising that other religions and even governments see it as a rival or an enemy? What aspect does it wear in Latin America, for example?

These questions prompt us to analyze some of the temporal consequences of the errors into which the Church is drawn by the lure of power rather than the obligation of service. Here we wish to examine the matter of political power, but not the question of the Church's relations with other religions nor the whole problem of church–state relations.

2. When we compare various definitions of the Church, we can see how much the historical context influenced both their elaboration and their interpretation. And we can ask what image evoked each definition.

The encyclical *Immortale Dei* (Leo XIII, 1885) points out that the Church

> is composed of human beings in the same way that the civil community is. Nevertheless, considering the aim it seeks and the means it uses to achieve this aim, it is supernatural and spiritual. Hence it is distinct and different from the political power. What is even more important, it is complete in its own way and juridically perfect. Thanks to the will and grace of its founder, it contains within itself and for itself all the elements and facilities necessary for its activity and integrity. And since the aim envisioned by the Church is the loftiest aim imaginable, incapable of further enrichment, *so too is its power above and beyond any other power;* it cannot in any way be subordinate or subject to the civil power.

By contrast, Vatican II has this to say: "The assembly of those who, in faith, look on Jesus as the author of salvation and the source of unity and peace was summoned together by God and established as a Church, so that it might be the visible sacrament of this salvific unity for each and every person" (LG 9).

What was the historical current underlying *Immortale Dei?* In Chapter II, we traced some of the basic features of that whole period (CLARIFICATION IV). In general, access to the Church came more by birth than by conversion. Emphasis was placed on stability, thus impeding the flexibility needed to adopt new forms of Christian living. There was a tendency to identify Christianity with Western civilization. Neither the encounter with other age-old cultures nor the force of contemporary events broke down the fortress. Faith became a matter of routine, shored up by a spiritual power that was exercised ambiguously in the temporal order. In a word, the institution prevailed over the charisms.

What *image* of the Church informs the definition provided by *Immortale Dei?* More than sixty years later we find that image in another book: "The Church is a supernatural, visible, perfect, and independent society, founded by Christ and governed by his vicar the pope, for the direct care of religion and the eternal salvation of men." [3] As a result, the author concludes that total separation between Church and state cannot exist because "civil society is obliged to render Catholic worship to

God, in the actual order we are in." And he also adds that "it is up to the Church to order public authorities and officials to attend religious ceremonies."

The historical context of *Lumen gentium* is quite different. The Church moves between two poles: charism and institution. In its effort to update the Church, Vatican II shifts the stress closer to the charismatic pole and moves it away from the institutional pole. The sociocultural trend toward ever greater pluralism in the last few centuries seems irreversible. Even though the mentality of institutionalized Christendom subsists nostalgically in many sectors, the historical situation of Christendom has disappeared once and for all or is fast on the way to disappearing.

What impression do we get from this new attitude in the Church? It seems that the Church has recovered her former alacrity and flexibility, the same features she displayed in moving from the Semitic world to the Greek world and from the Greek world to the Roman world. Once again the Church seems to be relating faith to human history, thus re-establishing the tension between faith and its objectivation. Only by recognizing the fact of a pluralistic society will the Christian realize once again that he is to function as a *sign*. Only by meeting the non-Christians of his day will he be able to undertake a mature consideration of the objective formulations of his faith, so that he may make the authentic Good News accessible to his contemporaries.[4]

3. Political analysis cannot be left on the abstract level. But in order to proceed further, we must establish some determining facts.

Firstly, throughout the world we find a growing and logical secularization of the public sectors. This is also true in Latin America, especially in urbanized regions. This process is not the result of any ideological conspiracy but the inevitable byproduct of the spread of the mass communications media. For these media provide each individual with the possibility of opting for different systems of thought and different lifestyles. The logical consequence of this is also clear. The more people make decisions democratically and the more authority tries to satisfy its obligations to the majority, the more public institutions come to reflect the pluralism existing in society and to preserve the least common denominator of shared ideology. This is especially true in underdeveloped countries where such institutions cannot be multiplied too readily.

Here a second element is added to the picture. Due to the process just described, civil institutions that had been wholly Christian, that had ensured the power and permanence of Christendom and fostered an environment maintaining people's allegiance to Christianity, are now in danger of being transformed from public institutions into private institutions or objects of a personal decision. To take one example: due to the pressure of pluralistic majorities, the public Christian schools are now tending to be transformed into laicist public schools, with the result that the wholly Christian school is obliged to turn itself into a private school. Matrimony, whose indissolubility was once sanctioned by public law, now tends to become a personal and private decision insofar as the law reflects the pluralism of society itself.

Confronted with these two facts, those charged with the task of watching over the Christian community reach some appraisal of the situation. In general, it is clear to them that Christianity, more than any other ideology, must be supported by the pressure of the surrounding environment if it is not to turn into a purely personal, heroic, reflexive conviction. And one does not have to be a sociologist to realize what a diminution of the Christian world this would bring about.

Now if these leaders cherish the first picture of the Church mentioned above in connection with *Immortale Dei,* we should not be surprised to find that they will use all their pastoral influence over the faithful to involve them in the political scene and to block the change which would make Christianity a private matter. This indeed has been the principal tack of the Latin American hierarchy over the past century or so. It has operated as a political pressure group on the continent.

Now various consequences flow from all this. To begin with, it is trying to oppose a movement of secularization which is growing more and more popular, more and more the thrust of the majority. This fact means that the Church, as a pressure group in politics, frequently resembles one of those small parties whose only power lies in serving as a means to form a majority through a coalition of various minority parties. And presumably it will be able to bargain for certain advantages in the process. In other words, the support of the Church is usually sought after by persons and parties who do not have sufficient support among the people or who have not gained it as yet. This is not a fiction invented by us here. Politicians are well aware of it, as one nonbeliever points out: "In Latin America it is impossible to carry out any revolutionary program without having the collaboration [?] or the consent of the Church; to ensure such support, one must guarantee all the demands she makes with regard to legislation concerning religious worship, religious education on the three levels of schooling, the prohibition of divorce, etc." [5]

As one can see, the comment does not lodge a simplistic accusation against the Church. It does not accuse the Church of siding with dictators or the ruling classes for the sake of power or financial support. Instead it accuses the Church of being indifferent to the political program of persons and parties, of being concerned solely about maintaining the dominion of Christian civil institutions in the sphere of public interests.

Perhaps the clearest and most explicit example of this policy was the pastoral letter of the Argentinian episcopate when Juan Perón ran for election the first time in 1945. Perón was unsure of his political power insofar as it was grounded in his program for social reform, but he was not unaware of the tactic just described. He noticed that the other political parties had subscribed to the modern process of secularizing various institutions, advocating laicized schools, separation of Church and state, and laws permitting divorce. In his platform, by contrast, Perón promised to maintain the status quo, that is, the religious character of those public institutions. In their pastoral letter, the bishops began by explaining that every person had an obligation to use his vote, and that this vote should favor the greater good or, in its absence, the lesser evil. But then it pinpointed one decisive point that was not to involve any weighing or balancing against any other factor: "No Catholic can vote for candidates whose platform includes" one or more of the measures that would undermine the public status of Christian institutions (i.e., laicized schools, separation of Church and state, laws permitting divorce).[6] In other words, this pastoral letter turned Christian institutions into the absolute criterion of any political program, so that the Christian would even have to vote for the worst candidate if he were the only one who did not attack these institutions. For this very same reason, when Perón did not fulfill his promise on this point, the Argentinian Church did not weigh the overall effect of his political and social program. It turned from support to opposition.

The case may not always be this clear and explicit, but the basic approach has been implemented with the same effectiveness all over the Latin American continent. It accounts for most of the positions adopted by the Church in the political arena. The Church has not worshipped power, nor canonized Trujillo and other Latin American dictators. She has used them, believing that she was thereby fulfilling her obligation toward the Christian masses. In so doing, she was caught up in the framework of an older image of the Church, an image which Vatican II has sought to correct.

4. On a much smaller scale we do find other types of political attitudes associated with the Church, particularly in recent days.

One incident may serve as an example and introduce us to the problem. In July 1966, twenty Brazilian bishops wrote a joint pastoral letter in which they expressed support for the impoverished common laborers who lived and worked in the Northeast province of the country. The central figure in this episode was Dom Helder Camara, archbishop of Recife-Olinda. Since his diocese was located in this region, he was in a good position to appreciate the miseries of one-crop labor and the imperialism of the large sugarcane planters.

The manifesto of the bishops urged the workers to "be strong and intrepid, the leaven of the gospel in the world of labor." A great political uproar ensued. On one side the military authorities accused Dom Helder of being an agent of "Communist subversion." On the other side, some members of the clergy and the laity vigorously supported Dom Helder's stand. The president of the Catholic fraternities in Rio de Janeiro declared: "If it is a choice between the sword and the cross, we will always choose the cross."

Finally it was the government faction that conceded. General Gouveia, chief of the tenth military district, was removed. On the same day his replacement, General Aguiar, announced a program of war against the wretched conditions of country life, General Gouveia and two thousand of his troops received Communion in the cathedral at Recife. On the following day, in the presence of Bishop Camara, members of the regional government, and garrison troops, General Aguiar declared that the manifesto of the bishops had "great spiritual and human value." [7]

But declarations have not been the only activity of the Church. In various countries it is the episcopate that is, for all practical purposes, entrusted with the task of promoting human betterment in their cities and towns. They do this through the large amount of aid they receive (from Germany and the United States in particular), and through the political guarantees they offer.

In all the cases cited in this CLARIFICATION, the institutional Church has used political power as an instrument. But in the latter case, as opposed to the former ones, the use of this power is dedicated exclusively to the service of human beings rather than to the enhancement of Christianity.

A question does remain. When such aid is to benefit human beings in general, who should be in charge of handling it: the hierarchical Church, the human community as a whole, or the representative political structure? This task does not seem to be in accord with the function of the Church, and particularly not in accord with the conception of the Church held by Vatican II (see for example, GS 43), unless we are talking solely about a *substitutive* effort. By this we mean that the Church and its officials would shoulder this task only when there is a lack of personnel or institutions to handle imperative needs.

But more careful scrutiny is required in any case. The Church must see at what point her substitute effort may unwittingly turn into an indirect use of power designed to preserve the Christian masses from the options offered by pluralism.

In judging the authenticity of the Church's substitute effort in individual cases, one might well consider such questions as these:

a) Is the Church really the only group that can offer this aid? We cannot answer this question with a yes, if by that we mean that only the Church is allowed by the government to offer such aid. For such an answer would indicate that it is not a matter of substitution but of official designation. And this may even come down to opposition to the government.

b) Does the aid doled out by the Church truly reach everyone? Here again we cannot really answer yes, if by that we mean simply that the Church offers it to everyone. As a person gains more respect for himself, he is less and less inclined to ask aid from some institution whose opinions he does not share.

c) Whether the Church has resources of her own or gets them from sources in Europe and North America, could not these resources be handed over directly to responsible officials in each and every community? We cannot answer no here, if by that we mean to imply that there are no responsible people in the community. First of all, when social welfare organisms are involved, it is always possible to obtain some sort of guarantee and to dole out the aid judiciously. Secondly, and even more importantly, if the local leaders do not act responsibly, then the way to solve the problem is not to sweep it under the rug but to fight it with political tactics from within the community itself.

d) Couldn't the laity take charge of matters which are now in the hands of the hierarchy in this realm? We cannot answer no, if by that we mean to imply that there is always a danger of the issue being turned into a political one by the laity. When a problem is political, the hope of a radical solution lies in making it a political issue. Foreign aid can be shrouded in the same atmosphere of colonialism and paternalism that may envelop the religious domain.

e) Would the Church continue to make a contribution if the aid institution were guided by an ideology other than her own? We cannot answer no here, from the viewpoint we are considering, if we justify our answer by saying that the Church would then be helping to propagate ideas she does not share. For in saying this, we are admitting that the Church's effort is not just a substitute one but also a means of preventing the spread of other ideas.

5. What *image* of the Church would accord with her nature as a sacramental community having a mission of service to mankind such as we have already described? It seems to us that she would appear to be faithful to her rationale and mission if she evinced a clear commitment to collaborate in the work of authentic human development, without getting mixed up in the political government of the state; or even if she reacted strongly against political regimes that violate man. This aspect will be appreciated even more clearly and concretely if people see Christians, as individuals and fellow citizens, assuming personal responsibility in this area; if they see them supporting regimes that foster human betterment and rebelling against those which do the opposite.

Both on the individual and the communal level, relations between the Church and political authority should be framed in terms of *service* rather than in terms of jurisdiction: "The Church and the world are not two wholly distinct realities that confront each other and thereby come into conflict. Instead they are two distinct aspects of an indivisible unity. The Church is the conscious awareness and visible presence of the gift which God makes of himself to a world open to the plentitude of his communication." [8]

NOTES

1. This was the second stage in the formation of Christendom. The first took shape when Constantine declared Christianity to be the state religion.

2. F. M. Dostoievski, "The Legend of the Grand Inquisitor," in *The Brothers Karamazov.*

3. González Moral, *Philosophia Moralis* (Santander: Sal Terrae, 1948).

4. Ricardo Cetrulo, "Problemas post-conciliares," *Diálogo* (Montevideo), No. 11, pp. 10–16.

5. Ramón Alcalde, "La Iglesia Argentina: Instrucciones para su uso," *Cuadernos de Contorno* (Buenos Aires), July 1957.

6. *Cf. Criterio* (Buenos Aires), November 22, 1945, p. 497.

7. A report on this event can be found, for example, in *Le Monde*, August 21–31 1966, and in ICI No. 271 (Sept. 1, 1966), p. 30. See also José de Broucker, *Dom Helder Camara: The Violence of a Peacemaker* (Maryknoll, N.Y.: Orbis Books, 1970), pp. 43 ff.

8. Ricardo Cetrulo, "El Concilio ¿libera a la Iglesia de equivocos?" *Diálogo*, No. 6, p. 1.

CHAPTER FIVE

Church-World Interdependence

HOW DO THEY DIALOGUE TODAY?

How do we carry out this dialogue in which the Church offers its contribution to the human community? And specifically, how is it carried out today? Dialogue really presupposes concrete interlocutors, and the world in general is not a concrete interlocutor. The concrete participant here is precisely this world in which we live; a world which only recently discovered it had the power to annihilate itself; a world which is rushing pell-mell along a crazy course that is alienating more and more of mankind from the benefits that a minority enjoy; a world of great metropolises, bureaucracies, and mass communications media; a world of poverty and hunger; a world that must have a reduced birthrate.

We are concerned here to move from the basic principles that informed the start of our inquiry into the concrete reality of the world. Such a concern is not merely a didactic one; it is theological to the core.

When we said that the Church was supposed to be a *sign* of salvation in the midst of humanity, the term remained ambiguous from several points of view. It might seem to imply that the Church could do this by herself, that she could enlighten the world so long as she had a focal source of light.

We are often led toward this interpretation by the habit of viewing the Church as a perfect society, in the sense that she had within herself all the elements she needs to effectively carry out her mission and need not go outside herself for help: That is why some find an element of strangeness in such conciliar passages as the following: "Thus the Church, at once a visible assembly and a spiritual community, goes forward together with humanity and experiences the same earthly lot which the world does. She serves as a leaven and as a kind of soul for human society." (GS 40). There is also a passage which goes even further and explains that this leaven and soul are not already prepared beforehand and then simply offered to the world, that they are but one element in a whole complex of interdependent elements: "People are waiting for an answer to these questions. From the answers it will be increasingly clear that the People of God and the human race in whose midst it lives render service to each other" (GS 11). In dialogue, mutual service means that both contribute truth. If it is to be converted into truth that will effectively help man's progress within the plan of God, even the absolute truth of the Church must grow and receive nourishment: "In a wonderful manner conscience reveals that law which is fulfilled by love of God and neighbor. In fidelity to conscience, Christians are joined with the rest of men in the search for truth, and for a genuine solution to the numerous problems which arise in the life of individuals and from social relationships" (GS 16). And finally, it is not always the world which is at fault when this dialogue is not carried out or when it is carried out with less depth and scope than it should: "The Church also realizes that in working out her relationship with the world she always has great need of the maturity which comes with the experience of the centuries" (GS 43).

This outlook should not surprise the reader after what we have said in preceding chapters on the contribution of the Church to humanity in history. There we presented the church-world relationship as a dialogue that matures on both sides under the influence of grace. It continually stimulates an encounter between faith that is beginning and faith that already knows God's response, so that from these two there may emerge the concrete historical truth that corresponds with God's salvific plan for all men and all ages.

What may not have been brought out so clearly is the extent to which the formulation of faith-inspired questions is essential for dialogue and the degree to which our faith-inspired response may be restricted interiorly if it is not related to the questions raised by human history in a given epoch and situation. We shall try to tackle those points now, reflecting on two correlative points: (1) what the world gives the Church and (2) what the world asks from the Church.

Let us begin by considering what today's world gives to the Church. Among the many typical traits that would seem to sum up the "modern world," we are going to focus on just a few—those which are least bound up with specific or particular situations. This obviously means that we are choosing to neglect some of the most interesting and perhaps critical traits of today's world. But our main concern here is not such major problems themselves but the nature of the Church, so we are more interested in the overall characteristics of the modern world.

Let us try to focus on the most solid feature of present-day history, that feature which is clearly gathering weight in it and which is not subject to human whim. This feature may well be the ever growing and accelerating store of energy which man has at his disposal for solving and satisfying his needs. As man moves and operates in history, he is as it were impelled by some basic drive to move from readily available sources of energy to hidden ones. In this sense the world is becoming more and more artificial, more and more human (i.e., more and more dependent on man), and hence more and more demanding on man himself. These new sources of energy harass man. His foothold in nature becomes smaller and smaller. Like a child who leaves his feet to mount a bicycle, man is finding that his balance is based on a process of movement.

One of the consequent features of this balance-in-motion is the need for ever greater communication. It is not a whim or a passing fad or an ideological thrust; if man is to have balance in a world-in-motion, then all men must be permanently present to each other. For the first time in human history, people scattered all over the world can be the object of our love because now they are no longer faceless entities. We know how they live, how they think, how they suffer.

Does this situation offer anything of importance to the Church? Yes indeed! For the first time since Christ enunciated his command of love twenty centuries ago, it is no longer an abstract principle but a concrete guideline. It is as concrete as the daily news that reaches us from all over the world, as concrete as the face of starvation that appears on our television screens.[1]

The Gospel tells us about a man who was journeying from Jerusalem to Jericho. He was assaulted by robbers and left for dead. A priest and a Levite passed close by him and continued on their way without stopping to help him. Today we find ourselves close by, without journeying. The vast majority of mankind barely ekes out a living, and their cries come to us through all our media of communication. We may try to hide from this invasion of upsetting information, insisting on our virtues and our moral attitudes. But the once hushed sentiment of the Gospel explodes in our ears: "Anything you did for one of my brothers here, however humble, you did for me." There is no escape.

But that is not all. It is not just that men have drawn closer together and become definitively present to each other. The thrust of man's proper balance in the future is more and more placing the fate of all in the hands of all. And here again this thrust is not based on arbitrary choice or on ideological tenets. Indeed it is taking place despite the efforts of some to place the fate of mankind in the hands of a few or to judge it according to a few simplistic ideas. Man's very effort to survive on this planet is inexorably placing more and more decision-making factors in the hands of all.

When we attempt to solve any problem within too limited bounds of reality, the problem causes even greater unbalance and is not solved at all. We must continually seek broader and more global solutions just to survive.

A few centuries from now, when the still fresh picture of the atom bomb exploding among human beings is erased from man's memory, he may well celebrate the day on which man acquired this dreadful power to destroy himself. Why? Because from that day on, even though we may not have realized it then, no spot on this planet could be disregarded and no facet of mankind could be overlooked without danger of igniting the spark that could destroy the whole world.

Men may not love each other any more than they did before. But when any spot on the globe or any creature can become the fuse for such an absolute force, then we glimpse a curious analogy with the absolute power and value of God's love for "our brothers, however humble."

However, the picture evoked by nightmarish potentialities for destruction is only the surface image. This world divided into watertight compartments based on geography, culture, race, nationality, and territory is inevitably giving way to a world of interconnections rooted in the economic realities of its growing energy sources. This economic network is putting the fate of all into the hands of all. Why? Because the basic structure taking shape is stronger and more decisive than any attempts to perpetuate the gap between rich and poor, and it will eventually supersede these attempts in one way or another.

A random example will make this clear. Suppose that the problem of overpopulation in Japan reaches the point where hundreds of thousands of children will not be born unless the economy can support them. At that point my choice of a particular car may well decide, to some extent at least, whether these children are born or not. My choice of a Japanese car may allow a child to be born, while the choice of an American or German car may simply increase one of the highest per capita incomes in the world by a slight margin.

The example may seem crude and simplistic. It is only an example But there is some reality behind it. And the world in which we live may give an unexpected twist to the words which Christ spoke. How surprised we may be on the last day to hear Christ say: "You have my Father's blessing; come and possess the kingdom, for you chose to live and let me be born too . . . the curse is upon you; go from my sight . . . for you chose to live but denied me life!"

When we hear Christians saying that they are on good terms with God because they do not kill people or rob their neighbor, we cannot doubt their sincerity. But we can wonder at their words. In what kind of world will they be able to live with such shortsighted perspectives?

A third feature of the modern world is the growing thrust of socialization. It too is inevitable and independent of human ideologies and choices. Earlier we said that man has constructed a world which is further and further removed from nature. We could call the latter the original world of nature, because we are in fact living in a second world of nature that is growing and becoming more and more inevitable. It is composed of a whole system of human relationships which must grow in number and complexity if we are to solve the basic problems of survival: hunger, lack of education, violence, etc.

In short, we hardly ever find the individual operating alone against nature any more. When we do see an instance that seems to be of this sort, it is usually a societal activity in disguise because it is made possible and limited by a growing web of societal relationships. Everything about our life—our security, our nourishment, our leisure—depends upon the maintenance of a social order which we may not see but which has become as close and as indispensable to us as the air we breathe.

Unlike the air, however, the social order is never neutral. Precisely because this order determines the fate of all men, it inevitably makes us collaborators or accomplices—not only by what we do but also by what we fail to do. To sit quietly at home is to adopt a public stance which can mean life or death, nourishment or hunger, justice or exploitation for other human beings. And if we are Christians, it means something to God too.[2]

A person may claim that he has never killed anyone. But in a world of ever growing socialization, he must be aware of what he is doing at the other end of the chain from which he derives sustenance, education, and perhaps even religion. Only then will he appreciate the terrible weight of these words: "The man who does not love is still in the realm of death, for everyone who hates his brother is a murderer, and no murderer, as you know, has eternal life dwelling in him" (1 John 3:15).

What does the world give to the Church today? The answer is now clear to us. It gives to the Church a sense of urgency and deep relevance that she never had before. The situation of the world and the message of the Church converge. If man's response must flow from what he has received, and if holiness and salvation are measured in terms of this response rather than in terms of what he has received, then it is a wondrous epoch for the Church.[3] We do not measure the holiness of the individual but the growth of Christ to full measure in the world. Today our Church, with all its crises and problems, is two thousand years more adult than the early Church. If a twentieth-century Christian lives his life with open eyes and heart, he will not be called upon to bear witness once. He will be called upon to bear witness over and over again, in every action that he performs. Despite our deficiencies and cowardly failings, we stand before a lofty challenge!

To put it another way, Christ is fulfilling the promise he made long ago: "I shall draw all men to myself, when I am lifted up from the earth" (John 13:32). More and more Christ is taking the center stage in history, even if only to judge it. Whether human beings realize it or not, the world itself is moving us all toward the judgment which God chose to effect by placing the destiny of all things in our hands.

What, then, does the world of today give to the Church? It offers to the Church a wondrous and terrifying presence of Christ, one that is far more suitable for the universe than his continuing physical presence on earth (John 16:7). Why? Because it represents the deepening universalization and recapitulation of the Word made incarnate in our history.

We have just seen examples of what the world gives the Church. But the gift is only such insofar as there is a job attached to it. There is no pure privilege in the Church, and nothing is a gift in that sense. Everything that the Christian receives is immediately turned into a responsibility. Now we have already seen that the responsibility of the Church, her very rationale, is her sign function. Everything that the Sign-Church receives is immediately turned into a new sign-bearing obligation. Thus the growing presence of Christ in our world today is not just a source of joy; it also presents us with a deeper obligation. We must adopt a deeper moral attitude to face up to his deeper summons.

As we noted above, some of the basic things which Christ said seem to relate specifically to our epoch, insofar as they are now clearly pertinent and obvious. The same can be said about some of the moral obligations which Paul laid down for Christians; today they seem very necessary if we are to measure up to Christ's summons. Let us take a look at them.

1. Some of the first questions raised by the churches which Paul founded had to do with moral matters. The Church in Corinth, for example, raised questions which ranged from specific issues (such as the lawfulness of eating meat sacrificed to idols) to general principles (such as the lawfulness of impure acts).

On both issues Paul replies in an insistent and shocking way: " 'I am free to do anything, you say' . . . no doubt I am free" (1 Cor. 6:12 twice; 1 Cor. 10:23 twice). To us it is a strange reply, particularly when we note that in one case he is talking about fornication! He obviously is not talking about some special privilege he enjoys, even though he uses the word "I" here. It is his way of enunciating a general principle, even as we say: *"You* can do what you like . . . but . . ."

The *but* is important. Paul is not saying that the actions in question are indifferent. One need only read other passages in the same letter to see how he chastises people for their failings and sins, even going so far as to urge excommunication (1 Cor. 5). And what is more, there is a *but* after each enunciation of the general principles: "Yes, but not everything is for my good"; I am free to do anything, but I will not let myself be enslaved by anything. "Yes, but is everything good for us? . . . Yes, but does everything help the building of the community?" So Paul is not equating good deeds and bad deeds or saying that all deeds are good.[4]

As we can see, Paul contrasts what we are free to do with what is good or advantageous for the Christian. The superficial reader might then conclude that he is minimizing the difference between the two courses of action. Our spontaneous reaction might well be: "So it is *only* a question of being advantageous or good for a person?

Again we would be on the wrong track, because in Paul's eyes this matter of being advantageous is a matter of life or death for the Christian: "Surely you know that the unjust will never come into possession of the kingdom of God. Make no mistake: no fornicator or idolater, none who are guilty of adultery . . . will inherit God's kingdom" (1 Cor. 6:9–10).

The phrase, "I am free to do anything," is a key item here; it has been misunderstood and misinterpreted in many manuals of moral theology, even though it is one of the central points in Paul's gospel.

The import of the formula is nevertheless clear. Paul intends to analyze the morality of the cases presented to him, but he begins by correcting the way in which they have been formulated by the Corinthians. Both those who were formed by the Old Testament and the adherents of mystery religions (not to mention ourselves today[5]) examined such questions in terms of the lawfulness or unlawfulness of the deeds involved. It was as if God had set up some catalogue against which they were to be measured, each type of deed being neatly arranged by genus and species. If one knew the type of deed involved (e.g., eating meat sacrificed to idols), one could presumably tabulate the morality of the action.

Now one may rightly ask how this outlook is corrected by considering the "advantageousness" of the deed rather than its lawfulness. In real life the difference between the two approaches is considerable. In itself lawfulness or unlawfulness is something that comes into the picture prior to or independent of the person performing the act. Advantageousness, however, can only be examined with respect to the person involved. Advantageousness presupposes and suggests a personal involvement. Actions catalogued on some *a priori* list are not moral; they are useful or harmful to some personal plan. When Paul is examining the same type of problem in another letter, he writes this: "I am absolutely convinced, as a Christian, that nothing is impure *in itself*" (Rom. 14:14).

Two things in this text should be noted. While it may appear that Paul is dealing concretely with ritual or legal purity and impurity, and not with morality in general terms, the context shows that he wanted to give an example of something that was much broader in scope. It is not just that legal purity and impurity cannot be established in terms of the act alone; the point is that any moral judgment on an act must take account of the overall project within which the act is performed.[6] Here Paul alludes to something that will become even clearer further on, and he does so by using the solemn formula with which he distinguished the essentials of Christ's message from his own interpretation or opinion: "I am absolutely convinced, as a Christian."

Now what is the central principle of Paul's gospel that relates to the case already presented? The answer to this question is clearly interwoven in the passage cited earlier. After Paul has pointed out that everything is lawful and that the Corinthians can eat whatever kind of meat is offered to them, he then explains why: "The earth is the Lord's and everything in it" (1 Cor. 10:26).

Quite obviously Paul leaves one step of this argument implicit, and without that step we might not understand what he is saying: Eat everything because the earth belongs to the Lord *and the Lord has given it to you.* If the last phrase were not implied, Paul's talk about the earth belonging to the Lord might only provide a reason for "being careful."

Here we have a central point in Paul's gospel. We are no longer under the law because now, joined with Christ, we have reached adulthood and have taken possession of our inheritance. The Father has given the universe to his children come of age. A minor may legitimately ask his tutors what he is permitted to do. But a person would be disowning his father if he asked the same question after he had come of age and received his inheritance, that inheritance being "the earth and everything in it." As Paul puts it: "So long as an heir is a minor, he is no better off than a slave, even though the whole estate is his; he is under guardians and trustees until the date fixed by his father. And so it was with us. During our minority we were slaves to the elemental spirits of the universe, but when the term was completed, God sent his own Son . . . to purchase freedom for the subjects under the law, in order that we might attain the status of sons. To prove that we are sons, God has sent into our hearts the Spirit of his Son, crying 'Abba! Father!' " (Gal. 4:1–6).

Here Paul goes so far as to sum up the mission of the Son and the mission of the Spirit in the liberty of the Christian, i.e., in a whole new attitude toward the moral question. And it is so important in his eyes that he regards one's failure to understand this change as equivalent to making the process of evangelization null and void (*cf.* Gal. 4:11).[7]

That still leaves us with much to grasp and explicate, to be sure, but the basic fact is that Paul proposes a morality based, not on submission to the law, but on *creative* activity. We are not to be ordered about by things; they are at our disposal: "For though everything belongs to you . . . yet you belong to Christ, and Christ to God" (1 Cor. 3:22–23).

2. Having reached this point, we must avoid the temptation to go back and worry about the unsettling breadth of the moral outlook presented by Paul. It is certainly not a relativistic morality, as we can see from Paul's application of it to concrete cases. On the contrary, his application of it to concrete cases opens up into an even more demanding moral rigorousness.

The logical question that arises here is this: Within what framework do we operate in analyzing what is "good for us" or "advantageous"? If we have a filial attitude toward God, does this mean that we have absolute freedom in choosing what we want to do? Are all our plans and projects equivalent on the moral plane?

Certainly not. Paul sums up the Christian program in these terms: "He who loves his neighbor has satisfied every claim of the law. For the commandments, 'You shall not commit adultery, you shall not murder, you shall not steal, you shall not covet,' and any other commandment there may be, are all summed up in the one rule: 'Love your neighbor as yourself.' Love cannot wrong a neighbor; therefore the whole law is summed up in love" (Rom. 13:8–10).[8]

Here we are told the point of departure: the new law. As Paul told the Galatians, we have been liberated from the law. But we have not been liberated from it to live any way we choose; we have been liberated to follow a *new law,* one which is not hanging over us but is rather the very embodiment of our free being: the law of love.[9]

Thus what justifies a man's actions in principle is the fact that he performs them within and for a program of love. When a Christian couple is getting married, they should not ask themselves: What has been prescribed and commanded in connection with this state? For in reality only one thing is prescribed: "He who loves his neighbor has satisfied every claim of the law."

Now this love is actually more complex than it might seem at first glance. It is more complicated than the ecstatic and fulfilling emotion of the couple in love. All human love within history is a creation, a continuing creation along an unforeseen road. In concrete reality no two persons are alike, and no particular set of circumstances lasts a whole lifetime. The pathways of love are not interchangeable. They cannot be learned from books, and very few generalities can be laid down about them.

It is certain that love is the one and only thing demanded of us. But to love is to build something up, and no one can take our place in this unique and progressive task. In order to set out on this road, we must start by liberating ourselves from a servile moral outlook that questions the lawfulness of things. So when Paul says that love satisfies every claim of the law, he does not mean that it is simply a summing up of the commandments. He also means that it involves an authentic revolution which turns morality into a *dynamic* reality that is ever on the move. And it is so not only because we fulfill it step by step but also because we *discover* it step by step.

That is why Paul completes the passage cited above with this phrase: "I am absolutely convinced, as a Christian, that nothing is impure in itself; only, if a man considers a thing impure, then to him it is impure" (Rom. 14:14). Saint Augustine's words are true: "Love and do what you will." But we do well to add the remark of De Lubac: "But don't be too quick to think you know what love is."

To get back to our example of the two lovers, it is certainly true that they need only have true love for each other to approach marriage in a Christian way. But it is just as certain that they do not yet know what the further fashioning of this love is going to demand from them. Gradually they will learn that they cannot effectively love one another in their personal depths without fashioning ever broader horizons: children, society. Gradually any sincere and clear-eyed love will demand that other interests, persons, and values enter the picture and become an integral part of the union, even though at the beginning it seemed that love for each other was enough to effect it.

For example, we can examine this same marriage reality from the outside, as it were: i.e., in terms of the universe as a whole or the welfare of humanity, of which this couple is but one part. If we do, then we see that this union of man and woman is the necessary and perduring condition for the survival and progress of the human race. And the universal importance of this particular value will logically and rightly lead us to say that the principal aim of this union is the transmission of life. But even though man is subject to this order of things, it does not mean that the problem of morality should be presented concretely in terms of this order. If the Christian knows what Paul knew, if he or she knows that the world is theirs because they have inherited with Christ, then they need not be afraid to give first place to their love. To give first place to the transmission of life would be to falsify their marriage and their love.

Even though they may know in theory the decisive importance of opening up to a new life, they will come to appreciate and live it existentially if their love first acquires fuller depth and scope. Hence it becomes obvious that true Christian moral awareness is a pathway that runs through the realities of concrete existence. Step by step we discover the obligations of love, which become more numerous and more demanding all the time. And no general catalogue can replace this process.[10]

If one tells a person that going to Mass on Sunday and not killing people are equally grave obligations, then one deforms his moral conscience even though it may be true. For going to Mass acquires its authentic moral value only after a person has come to understand the elemental obligations of love and their connection with our communitarian participation in the Eucharist. If a person goes to Mass only because he is commanded to, he does not have a Christian moral outlook in Paul's eyes.

Of course this does not mean that "after" must be taken in a strictly chronological sense. Love is a delicate thing when it involves mortal men who have only one life to live, who go through certain stages of growth and capability only once. Such love cannot be left to chance. Like everything worthwhile that man achieves, it must be prepared for in advance. There is a proper place for reasoned explanation, which generalizes and arranges things and which, to some extent, precedes actual experience. No one can say sincerely that he is following the law of love, if he takes chances with love out of haste, disinterest, or whim.

Thus moral progress in this framework, which means discovering experientially the ever-expanding scope and depth of love's demands, does not involve moving from one uncertainty to another. It involves moving from one set of convictions to another set of convictions that are ever more open, more solid, and more fecund. Christian moral life grows in the same way faith does: "If a man is weak in faith, you must accept him without attempting to settle doubtful points. For instance, one man will have faith enough to eat all kinds of food, while a weaker man eats only vegetables. The man who eats must not hold in contempt the man who does not, and he who does not eat must not pass judgment on one who does; for God has accepted him . . . everyone should have reached conviction in his own mind. . . . For no one of us lives . . . for himself alone" (Rom. 14:1–7).

The earnestness with which we plot out our love, studying its possibilities and the laws governing its performance, will indicate whether we truly love or are only self-seeking. It will show whether we have fallen into the snare which Paul warns us against: "You, my friends, were called to be free men; only do not turn your freedom into licence for your lower nature, but be servants to one another in love" (Gal. 5:13).

For Saint Paul, then, Christian morality is not only creative but also progressive.

3. Now at this point some might feel that what we have said implies that the end justifies the means.

To be sure, in the personal history of each human individual we must expect to find a progressive moral purification of the means employed. A morality grounded on means is not Christian, as we have already seen. Since love can begin so simply and naively, putting the emphasis on the ends intended (i.e., on love's program) could lead people to use foolish means (e.g., killing, robbing, defying society, etc.) to carry it out. When two people are passionately in love, it is not always possible to show them the importance of the laws which society has laid down for the concrete carrying out of their love. They may quite readily disregard valid and meaningful prohibitions. Would it be better, then, to tone down the importance of their love in order to stress the importance of those means? The Christian response is no!

But the Christian response also involves something else. From the very start it offers them the best means of morally purifying all the means they use in love. How? By showing them the intimate relationship between these means and love itself. It is true that we are not enslaved to means, to the things of this world. But if we are to be truly free, we must see to it that dubious means do not destroy what we are trying to fashion. If a person uses things capriciously and thereby destroys his intended program, he is not free. The free man is he who uses means which help him to carry out his program. The danger is not that the end may justify the means. The danger is that we may use means which only seem to bring us to our goal but actually block us from it in the long run.

What the Christian message does is this. From the very beginning it sheds light on the relationship of love to hope: i.e., to the long-range goal. It sheds light on the relationship of love to humanity as a whole, on the relationship of love to the power of man's heart when we do not have the means to physically carry out our love. Thus the Christian message puts the Christian in the best possible position to effect the continuing moral purification of the means he is employing. Here the reader might want to look again at Chapter III of this book.

Now let us follow Paul to his conclusions. When he wrote that "everyone should have reached conviction in his own mind," he went on to add that "none of us lives for himself alone." And when he said that favoring the "lower nature" must not be the end result of Christian freedom, he went on to note that the true end result should be "service to one another." And when he offers a solution to one of the problems posed by the Corinthians he speaks of freedom, as we have seen, but freedom qualified by what is good and constructive, and he adds, "Each of you must regard, not his own interests, but the other man's" (1 Cor. 10:24).

In the preceding paragraphs we examined the point of departure on the pathway of Christian morality. In the foregoing words of Paul we find the driving force behind this journey.

If a person is concerned about what is permitted and what is prohibited, he is implicitly trying to acquire "morality." In other words, he is trying to get some qualifying property that will bring positive or negative judgment on him by its presence or absence. In one way or another, a morality based on lawfulness or unlawfulness is oriented around one's own self.[11] By contrast, the moral life about which Paul speaks is based on the interests of our neighbor. We are "moral," if we can use that term, not insofar as we don some quality, but insofar as we express and carry out our intention to build up the existence of our neighbor. Hence we can take Paul's words as our own: "We are free to do anything, but does everything help to build the community?" (1 Cor. 10:23).

This calls for a thoroughgoing revolution in our inmost being, because our current moral outlook is pre-Christian.[12] Even God's judgment, such as it is described in Matthew's Gospel (Matt. 25), is understood by us in a childish way. Paul teaches us that we must grow up, that we must connect our conception of judgment with a morality centered around the constructive fashioning of the world: i.e., around our neighbor's interests. Our concern must shift from wanting to know how we will be judged to finding out what we have done to help construct a world for our fellowmen:

> "I am like a skilled master-builder who by God's grace laid the foundations, and someone else is putting up the building. Let each take care how he builds. There can be no other foundation beyond that which is already laid; I mean Jesus Christ himself. If anyone builds on that foundation with gold, silver, and fine stone, or with wood, hay, and straw, the work that each man does will at last be brought to light; the day of judgment will expose it. For that day dawns in fire, and the fire will test each man's work. If a man's building stands, he will be rewarded; if it burns, he will have to bear the loss; and yet he will escape with his life, as one might from a fire" (1 Cor. 3:10–15).[13]

In other words: the morality which Paul teaches us as a consequence of Christ's message is not only creative and progressive but also social.[14]

4. It is social in a specific way, however, with a focus of attention that is so to speak typically Christian. Paul does not cease to draw the logical and direct consequences of Christ's mandate, and to insist upon this obligation: in a creative moral life, our love-based attitudes must flow from the concrete needs of those around us. Thus the liberty of the Christian, as a creative force, is in the service of the needs of those who are nearby: i.e., *our neighbors*. It would make no sense in Christian terms to speak about some brand of liberty that left our neighbors out of account: "Certainly food will not bring us into God's presence; if we do not eat, we are none the worse, and if we eat we are none the better. But be careful that this liberty of yours does not become a pitfall for the weak" (1 Cor. 8:8–9).

But there is more. The Christian is creative, as every human being can be, but he has an element that is peculiarly his own for the work of creating: *what he knows*. As we have said over and over again, the Christian is he who knows. And what he knows has been given to him precisely so that he might build up man's world out of love. Hence in the Christian moral outlook, where our concern is directed toward others, special attention is focused on one of man's major needs: the questions which are formulated sooner or later by love. We have discussed this matter before, noting that God placed the Church on earth to provide an answer to these questions. So it should not surprise us that Christian morality is essentially a morality of *dialogue*.

It was in the context of the Corinthians' problem in regard to meat already offered to idols that Paul was speaking in chapter 10 of freedom and its relation to what is good and constructive and in the interest of our neighbor. He goes on to specific directives: "You may eat anything sold in the meat-market without raising questions of conscience; for the earth is the Lord's and everything in it. If an unbeliever invites you to a meal and you care to go, eat whatever is put before you, without raising questions of conscience. But if somebody says to you, 'This food has been offered in sacrifice,' then, out of consideration for him, and for conscience' sake, do not eat it" (1 Cor. 10:25–29).

There are two unsettling things in this response. First of all, we are inclined to regard it as a rather twisted moral outlook. Why should the presence of another human being change the lawfulness or unlawfulness of something? That is the question which rises in our mind, and it shows how tenaciously we cling to a moral code based on lawfulness. Something is either permitted or not permitted for us. It is a morality for us as individuals, and the presence of our neighbor seems to be an intrusion.

The second thing which strikes us the wrong way would also have done that to the Corinthians, so Paul anticipates it. He had already said that when someone has an implicit question about what the Christian is doing, the Christian should refrain from eating the meat both for the sake of the one who called attention to it and on account of the conscience issue. The first part is clear enough: one refrains for his neighbor's sake. But why should one refrain "for conscience' sake"? Paul clears up the expected problem at once: "Not your own conscience, I mean, but the other man's" (1 Cor. 10:29).

Right here we have an essential point. When we hear the word "conscience," we do exactly what the Corinthians probably did: we immediately focus on the moral conscience of the person performing the deed. And we do so precisely because we see the moral law as something centered around the doer. But when Paul is talking about conscience as a determining element in Christian morality, he has his eye on the conscience of the person in front of the doer. We are placed here for that person's salvation. We are supposed to help introduce into his mind a message that he may already be seeking unwittingly. Christian morality is precisely this: with our attitudes and our whole way of living we are to create a response to that question. For the Christian, to speak of creative morality is to speak of a *sign-bearing* morality. And to live as a sign is to live a life of continuous dialogue—not only by our words but also by our attitudes.

How easy, by comparison, is a morality which distinguishes the realm of the permitted from the realm of the prohibited! Such a morality hands the former realm, already neatly plotted out, over to the free will of the doer as if it were his own private property; there he is presumably free to do what he feels like doing. This other morality, by contrast, demands that we be inventive in every new circumstance and with every person we meet. On every such occasion we must fashion anew the attitude that will allow us to dialogue with him. We must be totally available and at his disposal, in a way that is truly life-giving.

If we reflect once again on what today's world gives to the Church, we will realize soon enough that only a creative, progressive, social signbearing morality can answer the demands of our age. By the same token, we have just seen that the Christian morality which flows from the New Testament is such a morality. So we may begin to sense the convergence that is taking place between a proper understanding of Christianity and the gathering tide of time in our era.

NOTES TO CHAPTER FIVE

1. "Thanks primarily to increased opportunities for many kinds of interchange among nations, the human family is gradually recognizing that it comprises a single world community and is making itself so" (GS 33).

2. "Sacred Scripture . . . teaches us that the love of God cannot be separated from love of neighbor: 'If there is any other commandment, it is summed up in this saying: Thou shalt love thy neighbor as thyself. . . . Love therefore is the fulfillment of the Law' (Rom. 13:9–10; cf. 1 John 4:20). To men growing daily more dependent on one another, and to a world becoming more unified every day, this truth proves to be of paramount importance" (GS 24).

3. "The promotion of unity belongs to the innermost nature of the Church, since she is 'by her relationship with Christ, both a sacramental sign and an instrument of intimate union with God, and of the unity of all mankind' " (GS 42).

4. Cf. Karl Rahner, *Theological Investigations*, Vol. II, *Man in the Church*, (London: Darton, Longman & Todd; Baltimore: Helicon, 1963), p. 101.

5. One need only recall the catalogue of questions for a person's examination of conscience.

6. Christ himself alluded to this morality in a phrase that is not always given the theological weight it should have: "Do you not see that nothing that goes from outside into a man can defile him. . . . It is what comes out of a man that defiles him . . . these evil things all come from inside, and they all defile the man" (Mark 7:18–20).

7. "He did not spare his own Son, but gave him up for us all; and with this gift how can he fail to lavish upon us all he has to give?" (Rom. 8:32).

8. Seeing this text and others like it, we might properly ask what Paul understands by the law. It is not just the law of Moses carried to the legalism of the Pharisees (see, for example Rom. 7:7). Nor is it just the law of the decalogue. It is everything that man does not choose: "Thus the law was a kind of tutor in charge of us . . . and now that faith has come, the tutor's charge is at an end. . . . There is no such thing as Jew and Greek, slave and freeman, male and female" (Gal. 3:24–28). Thus Christian morality involves desacralizing not only the so-called "moral" law but all physical laws as well, in order to put everything that a man does not choose under his free will, first of all, and then in the service of love.

9. By this very fact, liberty as well as love can show up as the definition of Christian morality, according to Saint Paul: " 'I am free to do anything,' you say. Yes, but not everything is for my good. No doubt I am free to do anything, but I for one will not let anything make free with me." And he adds an example: " 'Food is for the belly and the belly for food,' you say. True; and one day God will put an end to both. But it is not true that the body is for lust; it is for the Lord—and the Lord for the body" (1 Cor. 6:12–13). In other words, Paul distinguishes the relative and the perishable from the personal and absolute; the digestive and sexual functions belong to the former. Man must not be enslaved to that which is supposed to be in his service. But in the last analysis all of this, even the body, is man; and it is not a spiritualistic morality. God himself does not relativize bodily man, and he expects man to follow his lead (cf. GS 24).

10. "Let everyone consider it his sacred obligation to count social necessities among the primary duties of modern man, and to pay heed to them. For the more unified the world becomes, the more plainly do the offices of men extend

beyond particular groups and spread by degrees to the whole world." This conciliar comment is preceded by examples: "It grows increasingly true that the obligations of justice and love are fulfilled only if each person, contributing to the common good, according to his own abilities and the needs of others, also promotes and assists the public and private institutions dedicated to bettering the conditions of human life. . . . Many in various places even make light of social laws and precepts, and do not hesitate to resort to various frauds and deceptions in avoiding just taxes or other debts to society. Others think little of certain norms of social life, for example those designed for the protection of health, or laws establishing speed limits" (GS 30). Here we find new duties that have been discovered by constructive love.

11. And by that very fact it is opposed to that feature of faith which, according to Paul, frees man from preoccupations with fashioning his own salvation and engenders in him an altruistic attitude: the further edification of his brother. Thus if a person uses Christian "faith" solely as a measuring rod for judging what he may or may not do, without worrying about his brother, he in fact does not have faith at all. In short, he does not have the capacity to give up self-preoccupation and be truly moral. This may help us to understand a passage in Paul's epistles which might otherwise seem to be a meaningless digression. He is talking about our conduct in the presence of those who are weak, and he interjects the following: "If you have a clear conviction, apply it to yourself in the sight of God. Happy is the man who can make his decision with a clear conscience! But a man who has doubts is guilty if he eats, because his action does not arise from his conviction, and anything which does not arise from conviction is sin (i.e., is not moral for the Christian)" (Rom. 14:22–23). See Max Zerwick, S.J., *Analysis Philologica Novi Testamenti* (Rome: Biblical Institute, 1953), p. 359.

12. "Profound and rapid changes make it particularly urgent that no one, ignoring the trend of events or drugged by laziness, content himself with a merely individualistic morality" (GS 30).

13. We are at a new start: "Always speak and act as men who are to be judged under a law of freedom" (James 2:12). "But the man who looks closely into the perfect law, the law that makes us free, and who lives in its company . . . that is the man who by acting will find happiness" (James 1:25).

14. "Thus, with the needed help of divine grace, men who are truly new and *artisans of a new humanity* can be forthcoming" (GS 30).

CLARIFICATIONS

I. THE LONG HIATUS IN DIALOGUE

In her relations with the world the Church has not always conducted herself in accordance with the principles set forth by Vatican II in *Gaudium et spes.*

The last few centuries of church history provide ample proof of this. She has tended to withdraw into herself when she could not gain her presumed rights. Her pastoral approach has been to create another world within the world, fashioning her own institutions that isolated the Christian from the rest of humanity. These attitudes hindered church-world dialogue and produced a divorce between religion and everyday life in the consciousness of Christians. Today we are quite familiar with the theology of history and a theology of terrestrial realities; but we must remember that these are recent items.

For a long time theology showed no interest in the new dimensions and potentialities of man; it took no account of the new conception of the universe that was being fashioned by the more privileged sector of humanity. One example will suffice. Cardinal Billuart, an authoritative theological thinker, devoted all his efforts to commenting on the theology of Saint Thomas Aquinas, which came from the thirteenth century; but he did not attempt any dialogue with his own contemporary, Rousseau. Theologians expended their energy in interminable controversies over grace, turning their backs on science and industrialism, which were reshaping the world, and disregarding capitalism and Marxism, which were transforming the social order.

This theological attitude was underscored by the magisterium, which issued unfriendly condemnations of progressive cultural currents in the world. There was the *Syllabus* and many other documents that sought to restore the old regime.

It was not until the advent of Leo XIII that the doors of the Church were thrown open. It was he who gave impetus to the attitude of encounter and dialogue with the world that culminated at Vatican II.

We should not wonder, then, that the whole revolutionary thrust of the modern age has been elaborated without the help of the Church, that it has taken up arms against the Church and pointed to her as a sign opposed to the progress of man in history.

This being the historical fact, we should try to find some explanation for it. What were the roots of this lack of encounter between the Church and the world?

To reply to this question, we must start with the fortuitous but privileged situation of the Church in the Middle Ages. The attempted synthesis of Saint Augustine was perfected by the genius of Saint Thomas Aquinas with the help of Aristotelian categories. What was the end result of this intellectual synthesis? In the first place, his philosophical vision of existence and of the world in particular served as a perfect framework and vehicle for revelation. Philosophy was the handmaid, the slave, of theology.

Secondly, through this synthesis we attained the perfect unity of knowledge, which was neatly arranged in hierarchical form. In man the soul ruled the body; the passions were subject to the will, the will to the intellect, and the intellect was ruled by faith. Nature for man was the epiphany of God. Its different realms were hierarchically arranged to serve man and to enable him to dialogue with God. Human relationships formed concentric circles, moving out from the family circle to social classes to political society; ultimately, through the Church, they were all subordinate to God. Man saw the historical process as so many preparatory steps for salvation. One age succeeded the next, moving toward an encounter with Christ. We lived in the final age, awaiting the parousia. The human adventure was seen as a journey out of the dark shadows cast by the fall into the light of Christ, where all our partial truths would find their full expression, where profane realities were a prelude to religious realities, and where religious expression sought the truth of the Christian religion. The latter was the goal sought by paganism.

This cosmic vision provided a synthesis of human thought. Each element had its place and was properly arranged to lead man to God. Never had such a harmony existed between heaven and earth, time and eternity, individual and society, state and Church, reason and faith. In this synthesis the world lost its autonomy by being integrated into a religious view. And this view was definitive, because once these structures and institutions became part of the divine order, they also became rigid and static.

In short, this synthesis of knowledge and this hierarchical structuring of reality gave rise to a strong temptation toward immobilism. Acknowledgment of this ideal state of affairs tended to look with horror on any element of unrest or curious seeking. Inquiry tended to be anesthetized by the fear that it would break this magic spell of peace and order in society, knowledge and religious practice.[1]

When a religious outlook sacralizes structures and institutions, they tend to become rigid. The end result is that any nonconformist must see himself, to some extent, as a heretic, a desacralizer. This same attitude was applied to all those who went out to seek for truth, such as happened in the Renaissance. As Pomponazzi wrote in his book, *Quaestiones de remanentia elementorum*: "The person who desires to seek out truth must be a heretic." He maintained that even though Aristotle showed unequaled wisdom, philosophizing meant something more than "repeating"; that even the common man could explore further horizons of truth.

Or, as Campanella put it, arguing *ad hominem:* "If a person is afraid to be contradicted by natural realities, then he is aware of his own falsity. Hence if a person tries to restrict the sciences in the name of Christian laws, then he thinks ill of Christianity or causes others to be suspicious of it." [2]

The truth can bring about a change in our image of the world, but it does not entail unbelief nor does it make it impossible for us to synthesize human thought with Christian revelation.

The Church had a backward attitude toward the new image of the world that was being shaped. It was rooted in the fact that she had inextricably tied faith to a specific and static image of the world. As Schmaus puts it: "It was a grave and disastrous error when many Christians and non-Christians maintained that faith and our picture of the world were tied to each other hard and fast. One of the truly tragic facts of the modern age is that various believers felt they had to hold on to an outdated picture of the world in order to maintain their faith; and that those who discovered and fashioned new pictures of the world often felt obliged to reject the faith in order to affirm their discoveries and free them from the authority erroneously attributed to faith."

To reach the old synthesis of human thought and revelation, theologians had known enough to read the "signs of the times." Theologians lost this knack when confronted with the new historical situation and the new horizons of human thought. What they had already acquired became a temptation for them. To be sure, the political and religious crisis which raised doubts about the faith influenced them in no small measure. So the chasm between the Church and the world grew wider. The world was now characterized by a process of mobility and progress, and new images replaced the old. The cosmic world of Ptolemy gave way to that of Copernicus; the physics of Newton gave way to that of Einstein; the static description of living phyla (Linnaeus) gave way to the evolutionary description of Darwin; the classic picture of man gave way to that of depth psychology and sociology. As all this took place, the Church seemed to grow more and more distrustful of the sense and thrust of history.

This mistrust prevented her from seeing that the sense and thrust of history is a permanent category of salvation history; and it also prevented her from dialoguing with the world, whose thought became more and more bound up with the process of historical becoming. All this was a calamity for the Church, because her essence and function is defined in terms of dialogue and service to the world. And we must realize, as Vatican II points out (GS 44), that the Church has received much from her enemies in recognizing and backing the autonomy of the profane world.

Now that the Church is picking up her dialogue with the world, now that she is embracing anew the Christian ideas which had left their mother's home like the prodigal son (but which also were the true impetus behind world progress), she is gaining a clearer awareness of her true function in history. The assaults on her have liberated her from the temptations of "Christendom." These assaults may not have been well-intentioned in every respect, but with the passage of time they have turned into a "happy fault."

There was a long hiatus in church-world dialogue. Vatican II ended that hiatus *in principle*. It is now up to us to end it in deed.

II. ECONOMIC DEVELOPMENT CHALLENGES THE CHURCH

The world situation and the Church's message are converging toward each other. The Church and the world offer each other mutual service.[3] Fidelity to the basic commandment to love God and our neighbors as ourselves is uniting Christians with the rest of mankind in a common search for truth and solutions to our problems. In this union, the Church acts as a leaven and the world helps the Church to mature.

What does today's world ask from the Church? In trying to answer this question at the start of this chapter, we began by focusing on the ever increasing and accelerating store of energy that man has at his disposal for solving his problems and needs. It drives man to communicate with other men and to make contacts outside the narrow circle of the family. It makes every human being ever more responsible for his fellow men, be they near or far away. And we summed up this line of thought by saying that the world gives to the Church a fearsome and wondrous presence of Christ. The impact of human realities allows the Church to deepen, universalize, and recapitulate the Word-made-Flesh in every moment of human history.

Here we shall simply try to illustrate some of the economic aspects of the increased store of energy which is now at man's disposal. The economic expansion of the last few decades provides us with a concrete base. More scholarly analyses carry this study back to the beginnings of the industrial revolution at the end of the eighteenth century.[4] The phenomenon is evident in both the industrialized and the nonindustrialized nations.[5]

People generally recognize three components in this economic expansion: population growth, technological progress, and human organization together with geographic expansion.

Population growth has had both static and dynamic repercussions on economic expansion in the last century.[6] Among the dynamic repercussions are the expansion of production and consumption (exploitation of new lands, new factories, new countries, etc.) and the development of new activities to satisfy the new individuals. There are also derived repercussions: a greater need for production means (e.g., tractors, trains, etc.) to produce more goods or transport them from one place to another.[7]

Population growth also has static repercussions: the division of labor, organization of production facilities, arrangement of communications and markets, etc.[8] We shall examine them again when we consider the third component, human organization.

The second component is technological progress.[9] The function of the business entrepreneur becomes quite obvious. In his search for profits, he takes risks, makes decisions, and introduces innovations in the business he runs.[10]

Older forms of conveyance are replaced by steam, then the locomotive, then electrical energy, then nuclear energy. The gas lamp is replaced by the carbon filament and then by the neon light. All these technological advances bring in their wake a widespread redistribution of production forces both in advanced and backward areas.[11]

The third component is human organization together with geographical expansion. On the one hand, large-scale migrations transform the underlying conditions for economic exploitation. They also affect the mounting costs of production for the world's primary resources, which are determined by the physical and economic limits on the availability of nonreproducible mineral resources.[12] An acre of land ceases to be an obsession for the Irishman when he reaches Patagonia, and mutton is now measured by the head rather than by the pound.

On the other hand, human economic efforts clearly seek to bring about industrial reorganization, division of labor, business conglomerates, and indirect methods of production so as to get more benefit from so-called secondary resources. By means of investment, and particularly during periods of business decline, they try to get as much profit per capital unit out of the means of production (e.g., factories) and thus to extend their markets.

This overall recovery is the result of whole-scale planning and re-organization, usually backed up by the government.[13] But contrary to what some pessimists believed, it need not necessarily bring about the breakup of the system.[14]

Put briefly, these three components (population growth, technological progress, and human organization with geographical expansion) produce an irreversible economic expansion. Man has available more goods and more factors to meet his needs. At the same time he has an increased responsibility to himself and to his fellow men. He is more dependent on other men, and he must communicate more with them in order to keep the road open to a more humane life for all.

Has the Church always understood this worldly idiom? It certainly is not an idiom sanctioned by some theological school, and when we read it in the newspaper we are not inclined to call it "the Word of God." But it is the idiom of man's economic realities, and it too belongs to the economy of grace.[15]

What might the attitude of the Christian have been in past decades, if he had understood what was going on? If he had realized that the growth in population obligated him to work harder and better, to get more out of his patch of land or his factory, to collaborate with other men so that tractors would produce more, and means of transportation and communication would be more efficient? If he had realized that all these were meant to give more jobs and opportunities to his fellow men, not just to produce personal comfort and to give him a chance to practice philanthropy in an overly affluent society?

What might the attitude of the Christian have been if he had seen technological progress as a means of distributing greater benefits to himself and his fellow men? If he had seen it as a means of making man's life more human and less primitive? Would he have been more willing to make decisions and take risks, to invest in manufacturing enterprises that produce collective benefits rather than in secure real-estate ventures that provide him with rental income?

What might the attitude of the Christian have been if he had realized that the massive influx of immigrants to the American continents called for something more than the steadfast maintenance of old religious frameworks? That it would not be enough to send chaplains to these groups? That the conditions of daily life would have to be profoundly transformed? What if he had realized that he, as a Christian, possessed a store of human experience that could have exploited these new riches even more fruitfully? That his contribution would have profound repercussions throughout the world, totally reordering the patterns of production and consumption on both sides of the Atlantic? That he could have brought about an economic reorganization and a division of labor on a worldwide scale, opening new sources of primary resources and creating new stores of secondary resources?

What face would the Church present to the world today, if Christians had realized all that? We will never know. But in the decade between 1950 and 1960, the population growth rate in Latin America was 27.5 percent. Today's industry operates with atomic energy and automation. The European Common Market, the Central American Common Market, and the Latin American Free Trade Association offer new guidelines for human organization, industrial plant sites, and commercial and financial groupings. They indicate that more and better production means not only to have more but to be more human, that profit is not the fundamental driving force behind economic progress, that laissez-faire competition is not the supreme law of economics, and that private property is not an absolutely unconditional right for the individual.

Will the Church be able to deepen, universalize, and recapitulate the Word-made-Flesh in this present moment of human history? The analysis we have just made is grounded on every human being alive today: free or imprisoned, fellow countryman or outsider, healthy or sick, hungry, thirsty, or cold. Will these hard facts give to the Church the fearsome presence of Christ in today's humanity? Schillebeeckx's words make us reticent,[16] but the words of *Populorum progressio* give us reason to think that we can say yes.

III. THE CHURCH AND THE THRUST OF EVOLUTION

How shall we characterize our age within the framework of cosmic development? The thought of Teilhard de Chardin offers interesting and useful pointers, without obliging us to get into disputed areas.

As we know, the essential thrust of Teilhard's world vision is drawn from the domain of the sciences. It consists in applying analogically to all empirical reality the evolutionary perspective that paleontology used as the hypothesis for its own proper work.

To give an example: this approach signifies that the transition from the anthropoids to man is analogous to the transition from primitive life to sentient life and from inert matter to living things.

But it is not just a matter of analogy; it is also a matter of evolution. Each threshold not only reproduces but goes beyond the previous thresholds, in accordance with a specific position in time and the order of perfection. It is a line that points toward man, that is, the being whose threshold consists precisely in being able to assume the evolution of the universe.

This notwithstanding, man himself needed a million years of preparation so that he might be able to realize this potentiality. And now is the moment when he is beginning to do it. It is only within the last hundred years or so that he has begun to glimpse this destiny.

Teilhard de Chardin uses a marvelous image to describe this reality:

> Up to now human beings have lived apart from each other, scattered around the world and closed in upon themselves. They have been like passengers who accidentally met in the hold of a ship, not even suspecting the ship's motion. Clustered together on the earth, they found nothing better to do than to fight or amuse themselves. Now, by chance, or better, as a natural result of organization, our eyes are beginning to open. The most daring among us have climbed to the bridge. They have seen the ship that carries us all. They have glimpsed the ship's prow cutting the waves. They have noticed that a boiler keeps the ship going and a rudder keeps it on course. And, most important of all, they have seen clouds floating above and caught the scent of distant islands on the horizon. It is no longer agitation down in the hold, just drifting along; the time has come to pilot the ship. It is inevitable that a different humanity must emerge from this vision.[17]

The reader will readily see that the age about which Teilhard de Chardin speaks can be identified with the world we have spoken about in this chapter. His words may also help the reader to understand various things that have been said in the course of this book.

1. It is not surprising that Christianity did not reveal all its potentialities while humanity was preparing for this piloting work, or even that Christianity did not adopt the creative perspective for which it was in fact created. Just as the human spirit needed a long period of preparation to develop all its potentialities, often seeming to be tongue-tied and primitive, so too did the Church.

As Teilhard de Chardin sees it: "At the core of the social phenomenon there is coming to a head a form of ultra-socialization. Through it the Church is gradually taking shape, vivifying all the spiritual energies of the noosphere under her influence and fashioning them into their sublimest form. The Church is the reflectively Christified portion of the world, the principal focal point of interhuman affinities for super-charity, the central axis of universal convergence." [18]

While the language is different, the reader will note the radical similarity between Teilhard de Chardin's formulations and our comments on the essence and function of the Church. The Church is not the "Christified portion" of the universe but the *reflectively* Christified portion. In other words, she not only lives out charity under the influence of Christ's grace but is also capable of super-charity: i.e., love when it reaches (revealed) awareness of its own mystery.

2. When we consider the Church as an element in this process, we are dealing precisely with the breakthrough to superabundant awareness which takes place when divine revelation completes and balances the reflective element already present in evolution with the apparance of the human stage. Thus the Church performs a necessary function for hu-

manity. The latter keeps advancing, and it would perish if it did not: "The more man opens up to the notion of man's universal function and appreciates the decisive role of consciousness and free choice in the world, the more he will realize that the appearance of reflective thinking on earth necessarily calls for something else to balance and complete it. This something else is the reflection of the whole on the monad (subsequent to the reflection of the monad on itself): i.e., a revelation." [19]

3. So the Church fulfills an essential function in evolution. One might say that she constitutes its ultimate cycle. For Teilhard de Chardin as for us: "Christianity in the world does not just represent the religious aspect of a transitory civilization, as it might seem to do at times . . . It is much more . . . It is a phenomenon of universal scope, attesting to the appearance of a *new vital order* within the human situation." [20]

But this new cycle or vital order follows a universal law whereby the perceptible differentiation becomes smaller and smaller on the upper thresholds. It does not introduce any "morphological" separation between human beings; it is in the realm of consciousness. "When [the Christian phylum] is framed in an evolution that is interpreted as the rise of consciousness, it becomes evident that it moves precisely in the presumed direction of the thrust of biogenesis." [21]

Some might object that if this change is only in the realm of consciousness, it is merely a secondary change. The whole thrust of Teilhard's systematic thought would violently challenge such an outlook, posing quite another view of the matter. Since it is grounded on the reflection which man has acquired about his own existence in the world, the reflection which allows for Christian revelation is the only element capable of enabling humanity to make a radical advance. Like Saint Paul, Teilhard calls this reflection "true *gnosis*." [22] And we already know that only a dynamic equilibrium, i.e., one based on the future, can prevent the ruin of what evolution has been trying to achieve: "Even as the lure of the future is gradually replacing the simple effort to survive within us, we begin to glimpse that an unfinished ideal is gradually taking over a greater portion of our ideas and personal feelings." [23]

Only a way of knowing that comes from Totality can serve as a support for a humanity that is being transformed. It must enlighten us about that which still lies outside our experience but which is truly the goal and balancing rod of our lives: "Starting with man, the activation of energy necessary for maintaining and advancing evolution is achieved by stimulating a focal point of attraction situated ever higher and farther away in time. In other words, more and more this activation takes on the characteristics and dimensions of a *faith*." [24] Or to put it another way: "The world cannot continue to progress toward greater complexity and consciousness, once it has become a human world, unless it also opens up an ever more explicit place for the spiritual forces of hope." [25]

4. Here too the Church abides by the law governing the successive thresholds of evolution. Not only do they become less and less perceptible from the outside at each turn; they also become more and more a minority and yet, despite that, more and more universal. Why? Precisely because universality continues to change in nature with each evolutionary change. The universality within the reach of matter is one thing; the

universality of living things is another thing; the universality of human effort still another.

Thus one can say of the Church—only to an even higher degree—what one could say of the change in universality which took place with the appearance of life: "Life appears as a fragile and miniscule phenomenon amid the sidereal realms, a speck of moss on a grain of dust, an improbable anomaly . . . Yet it is in fact the end point which, in a far superior way, specifies and typifies the universal evolutionary phenomenon. What matters the scantiness of the living substance, when its quality is extreme?" [26]

Here we see how life achieves its universality, as opposed to the universality of inert matter. And this will be even more true and certain of the appearance of man: "Evolution is a cosmic process of personalization. Seemingly a joke by comparison with thermodynamic forces, the quantity of hominized energy nevertheless represents the hope of the world." [27]

Into this process of personalization the Church introduces the mystery of love, now made conscious, which is the ultimate and decisive personalizing leaven of the universe. Its fragility and meagerness, even within the "sum of hominized energy," are no obstacles to the universality concentrated within it.

5. Teilhard de Chardin's thought goes even further, offering an explanation for this *smallness-universality* phenomenon which characterizes the higher and decisive syntheses of evolution.

The law of least effort, translated into statistics, applies to the simplest syntheses at the lower end of the evolutionary scale. By this very fact its universality is quantitative; and the energy which is accumulated thereby is minimal and subject to the loss of unavailable energy in a closed system which is known as entropy.

To obtain something like atomic energy, for example, it was necessary to overcome the law of least effort at a terrible price, and to get back to difficult syntheses which were statistically improbable and ultimately minority ones in themselves.

But life itself is an example of this struggle: "Life is framed in the prolongation of that last tendency. A minority force in the universe yet a majority force in its own order, it represents a victory for organized structure, diversity, variation, and the re-gradation of energy. As Schrödinger puts it, it is a *negative entropy:* something that *negates entropy*." [28] Commenting on Teilhard de Chardin's thought, Rideau explicates this last thought that a theology of the Church should make its own "analogically": "As a biological specialist, Teilhard de Chardin did not fail to point out the distinctive features of living beings and the originality of life: its capacity for invention and additiveness, its vector running counter to that of material energy, its thrust toward the improbable . . . Even more importantly, there is the number, relative simplicity, and almost identicalness of elemental material entries, which means they can only be the object of statistical laws. By contrast, the living being must be considered, first and foremost, in its individuality." [29]

It is certainly clear that in human history the process is the same: "Mutations do not become operative except at the price of a revolution against degraded forms of the human." [30] The slight substance of the Church, at its deepest roots, is nothing else but its opposition to that which is not love but uniformity, not a creation of higher energy forms but a compromise with the principle of least effort. In short, it is her condition as a leaven.

Only within this perspective do we see the Church as "the central axis of universal convergence and the precise emerging point of an encounter between the universe and the Omega Point." [31]

IV. THE SIGNS OF THE TIMES AND THE CAPACITY FOR DIALOGUE

The reader might well be asking himself another question. Since the Christian possesses a revelation, a dogma, a doctrine, doesn't this very fact constitute a barrier to the dialogue we seek to establish?

1. In reality every mature human being possesses a doctrine: i.e., a system of coherent ideas and values through which he receives, analyzes, and judges his experiences. Does that constitute a barrier to dialogue?

To be sure, any doctrine is a barrier when it is turned into an absolute, when it becomes something that cannot be touched or changed and thus divides humanity into factions. This vehement attachment to a specific conception of life is what turns a person into a *fanatic;* he tries to bring his ideas and values into the temple (*fanum*), to sacralize them. Whatever it may appear to be on the surface, this attitude has its fundamental roots in the insecurity of one's personality.

Obviously a fanatic doctrine is impervious to dialogue with others. Contemporary history offers us abundant examples of the sorry consequences. But not every doctrine is fanatical. There are open-ended doctrines which, *by their very structure,* admit of being questioned. Just as there are persons who do not need a closed world to maintain their consistency. When a doctrine is lived out in this way, it does not divide people; it enriches them.

The problem becomes more pointed if we ask whether Christian doctrine may not be *in itself* a closed doctrine. Aside from some less essential features, there are certain things that would suggest an affirmative answer to this question.

Since Christianity is a revealed message, it is obvious enough that there is something unalterable and untouchable in Christian doctrine. Why, then, do we maintain that it is not a hindrance to dialogue? For two fundamental reasons.

Firstly, because what has been revealed is not something capable of modifying real-life experience. It confronts the same tasks of human life that we all encounter in our "quest for truth," as Vatican II puts it. Secondly, because we believe that what God has revealed is not a recipe book of solutions for concrete problems. Even though the Christian may find his inspiration in it, he cannot maintain that a given solution is *the* Christian solution (GS 43).

Knowing that Jesus Christ is God is something that will serve as an inspiration for all the decisions of the Christian, but it will not wholly determine any one of them. There will always be an irreducible element that comes from his experience in history, which he shares with other human beings. In the concrete, the jump from the stated belief ("Jesus Christ is God") to a concrete decision may seem to be a short and quick one. It was so for the crusader, for example, who readily slew pagans in order to gain the reward of heaven. Even then, however, the concrete face of the man he was to slay must have raised some mute question about this seemingly fundamental duty. And as Christianity has matured, the step from stated belief to concrete action has stretched out greatly, requiring the Christian to face up to all man's questionings. Knowing that Jesus Christ is God will still shed light on our actions, but man's questions will become more and more important—not only for what we choose to do but also for appreciating what the formulas of our faith mean. In this way the Christian adult will move from fanaticism to dialogue without denying the immutability of his faith.

We find these two elements united in the notion of the signs of the times, which we believe to be fundamental in the task of dialogue.

The theological conception of the signs of the times has its point of departure in the *de fide* belief that God's merciful activity is present in the history of all humanity, that man's history is a sacred history.

The Church does not have a monopoly on God's activity. She is a servant of this activity which goes well beyond her. By virtue of his prophetic vocation, the Christian is supposed to discern in history (in *his* history) the places and events which in themselves are a preparation for the gospel. This means that a "human happening" is not just an "occasion" for the believer to exercise his "charity" or interject his "doctrine"; this happening possesses an interior act of grace and hence its own proper summons to the gospel. These happenings take quite different forms, some of them seeming to be quite distant from the doctrine of the Church.

From our point of view, the interior attitude of the Christian is not that of a "superior being" armed with a doctrine; it is that of one who serves concrete man because he is a servant of the Word. The Christian knows that *there* in the nonbeliever and the world God's loving activity is effectively at work and is moving toward the illumination of the gospel.

Thus before everything else, and *by virtue of his doctrine,* the Christian is open, benevolent, well disposed, and receptive to every human activity, every human unrest, every human quest. He is not summoned to pass judgment on the basis of certain principles; he is summoned to enlighten, to proclaim the Good News. His attitude in dialogue with the nonbeliever is one of "sincere searching." The world has much to teach him about God. It will oblige him to purify his faith and to continually repudiate certain byproducts that will inevitably get into the mix. And then it will pose the "real questions" to which his faith must offer a response.

At the same time, however, his attitude will not be one of inferiority. The world does not shatter his faith, it opens up unsuspected horizons to it. And within these horizons he will understand the enormous importance of his mission and exclaim serenely: "Woe to me if I do not preach the gospel!"

In the light of this interpretation we can now read a passage in *Gaudium et spes*: "To carry out such a task, the Church has always had the duty of scrutinizing the signs of the times and of interpreting them in the light of the gospel. Thus, in language intelligible to each generation, she can respond to the perennial questions which men ask about this present life and the life to come, and about the relationship of the one to the other. We must therefore recognize and understand the world in which we live, its expectations, its longings, and its often dramatic characteristics. Some of the main features of the modern world can be sketched as follows" (GS 4).

If we read this text closely, we will see that it is worlds apart from the attitude of the fanatic.

The Church has the *duty* of scrutinizing the signs of the times in order to "be able" to reply in a suitable way. And every concrete form of response is, in turn, kept under control by the signs of the times that appear: "Even against the intentions of their proponents, however, solutions proposed on one side or another may be easily confused by many people with the gospel message. Hence it is necessary for people to remember that no one is allowed in the aforementioned situations to appropriate the Church's authority for his opinion" (GS 43). In other words, the believer does not approach the nonbeliever with a prefabricated response. His response will be forged in their joint effort.

Fidelity to the Word includes fidelity to the moment of history, that is, to the hidden action of God in our world. It is from this angle that one should read Part II of *Gaudium et spes*. It enumerates some of the signs of our times, but it is not engaged in sociology. The Council Fathers glimpse the activity of God in our world, the Christian graces that inhabit it.

This attitude of mind, created by reflective comprehension of the notion of signs of the times, leads us to distinguish two levels in our interlocutor: (1) the level of intellectual or doctrinal formulation and (2) a much deeper existential level that can only be imperfectly expressed by intellectual categories. Thus the Christian will often be able to discern the work of the Spirit underneath so-called atheistic or materialistic formulas: "It is perfectly legitimate to make a clear distinction between a false philosophy . . . and economic, social, cultural, and political undertakings, even when such undertakings draw their origin and inspiration from that philosophy. True, the philosophic formula does not change once it has been set down in precise terms, but the undertakings clearly cannot avoid being influenced by the changing conditions in which they have to operate." [32]

Between doctrine and doctrine dialogue would be impossible. But the Christian, as the servant of God's activity in the world, must by virtue of his doctrine go beyond doctrine and intellectual formulations. He overcomes the initial clash between two fundamentally different mentalities by having "radical confidence" in the perennial activity of God's love in men.

2. This brings us to a problem of great moment on the Latin American continent. We said above that "there are open-ended doctrines which, *by their very structure,* admit of being questioned." And by alluding to principles and documents we tried to show that Christianity is

such a doctrine. Now if Christianity is a doctrine that admits of being questioned by its very structure, how can it be made the defining basis of a labor union or a political faction?

The reader will see that we are alluding to such things as Christian Democratic parties, that is, to any party (be it confessional or not) that describes itself as desiring to put into practice the doctrine or inspiration of Christianity.

This theme can readily wound deep sensibilities, so we want to be as precise as possible. In what follows we do not intend to discuss or debate the merits or political necessity of such groups. Nor are we debating the reasons of a political nature that may make it advisable and possible in the concrete for a Christian to work in such groups.

The basis of our considerations here is this fact: the attempt to somehow define the group in terms of Christian social doctrine. Here, for example, is a passage in the declaration of principles of CLASC (*Confederación Latinoamericana Sindical Cristiana*): "*In its aims and methods CLASC finds its inspiration in Christian social doctrine*" (our italics).

Now this definition may or may not have much practical importance and certain advantages for the group. But we believe that it gives rise to serious *church problems*. That does not settle the question of its right to exist, but it should be kept in mind in any attempt at evaluation.

In reality any political faction or labor union of an ideological inspiration is in the concrete the result of two forces. On the one hand, there is operative some ideological content or inspiration that serves as its guiding spirit. On the other hand, a need for power is operative. The need to acquire power or to use it or to maintain it requires a reduction of this ideological content (which in itself is capable of embracing many different solutions) to one or more concrete solutions.

In other words, the ideological amplitude and flexibility permitted by the system or underlying inspiration perdures at the level where a small handful of leaders discuss various options; on the level of the masses, however, there tends to be a simplistic identification of the ideology with the solutions that are required by a compromise with reality. And note that we are not saying the latter level is evil or negligible; it is in fact indispensable.

Hence when we examine the religious impact or the ecclesial consequences of a phenomenon such as the Christian Democratic Party, it is quite erroneous to consider the problem in terms of the clear-mindedness, sagacity, and flexibility of its political leaders. That is not where the problem lies. Even the whole system of Christendom did not preclude or rule out freedom, sanity, and flexibility on the part of those who were capable of making profound decisions despite the surrounding mass ambience. The obstacle embodied in Christendom, and thus hypothetically in the groups we are discussing here, crops up on the level of the masses. It relates to those people who find themselves in a situation where problems are considered solved without any personal decision on their part.

Some people tend to pose the question in these terms: "I have firm, open-ended convictions and I am ready for dialogue. What is to stop me from joining with others like me to find solutions for our country that accord with our convictions?" But posing the question in this way falsifies the socioreligious problem, presenting it as a moral decision. For the real question is the absence of a moral decision on the level of the masses.

And this is precisely what happens when the label of Christian inspiration is identified, in the eyes of the masses, with a given solution that in itself is no more Christian than any other solution.

Sociologically speaking, this gives rise to a twofold rigidity. The ideology hardens because of its combat with other possible solutions proposed by outsiders or insiders. Political in-fighting takes place to justify *this specific* decision that has been adopted. Secondly, the political triumph of the solution adopted appears to be the helpful ally of the underlying ideology (in this case, Christianity), using for this purpose a power that is alien to it.

In these circumstances it will take an effort to dialogue with other possibilities that may be just as Christian in principle as the one upheld by the group which goes under a Christian name (or by the majority of them). They will have to fight the same tendency toward simplification and adaptation to the masses that appeared during the centuries of Christendom and that opposed what it considered to be "non-Christian" ideas.

In other words, no matter how clear-eyed their leaders may be and no matter how nonsectarian they may claim to be, such groups have a strong tendency to move in the same direction as the regime of Christendom did long ago. They tend to set themselves up in opposition to the Christian's vocation and obligation to dialogue with the signs of the times.

And this is true, even though other reasons may make it seem necessary to adopt this course as the lesser evil.

V. WAS THE CHURCH'S SOCIAL DOCTRINE A PRELUDE TO DIALOGUE?

Let us explain the meaning of this question first. We have been talking about an encounter between the Church and the world in dialogue. Now is this something new in Christian awareness that finds its official expression in Vatican II? Or do we find this same attitude in the social doctrine that the Church has been elaborating since *Rerum novarum?*

When we consider the concern of the Church for the problems having to do with the social, political, and economic organization of the earthly city, we might be inclined to answer yes to the last question. The Church has made a serious effort to reflect on the problems posed by the industrial revolution over the last century. She has taken pains to see to it that Christian principles would be given a place in the new order. She has taken a strong stand against social injustice and in favor of man's dignity. She has kept a close eye on the evolution of socialist doctrines,[33] and the Russian revolution.[34] All this would seem to represent dialogue with the world already, so that Vatican II merely provides us with a more general formulation of it.

But it would be anachronistic to view the matter this way. We would be overlooking the reason behind her concern with social questions and the scope of her involvement here. We can get somewhere with our initial question if we consider how the Church justified her right to speak authoritatively on temporal matters, despite her supernatural orientation. Indeed the very fact that she felt a need to justify this right is significant.

Throughout the preconciliar period that runs from Leo XIII to Pius XII inclusively, the involvement of the magisterium in social problems was dominated by an unquestioned affirmation: the Church has the right and the duty to speak out on these problems. Leo XIII: "With earnestness and with a right that is clearly ours, we undertake a discussion of this matter." [35] Pius XI: "Before going into these matters, We set forth as Our basic principle . . . the right and the duty that oblige us to judge with supreme authority these social and economic questions . . . Both in the social and the economic order, they are subject to Our supreme judgment." [36]

Here we want to analyze the basis for claiming this right. One basis of a pragmatic nature, which is alluded to in the papal documents, goes back to an old idea of Saint Thomas: Under certain minimal social and economic conditions, religious life cannot be lived at all unless a person is exceptionally heroic. Pius XII talks in this vein: "The growth and strengthening of religious life presupposes a certain measure of sound economic and social conditions." [37] It is obvious that unhealthy living conditions, promiscuity, inadequate food, and insecurity can polarize man's energy to such an extent that his preoccupation with religion can fade away. It is certainly obvious, but it is not enough to serve as a foundation for the right of the Church to intervene in social matters.

So the magisterium offers a deeper reason, relating the present social unrest and conflict with man's abandonment of the moral law and presenting moral principles as the best solution to the "social question." [38] If in the last analysis social and economic problems imply specific forms of human relations, then morality will be the key to overcoming conflicts. But there is an added note involved. As the structure of economic transactions becomes more complex and as older forms of craftsmanship give way to more complex industrial setups, human relationships lose their face-to-face quality. It is not so easy in these new circumstances to discern the moral implications of man's activity in the socioeconomic sphere.

It is here that one finds justification for the intervention of the Church into matters that are apparently outside her jurisdiction. Insofar as she is the "guardian of the moral law," [39] and has the function of "mother and teacher" (a phrase picked up by John XXIII), she has the right and the duty to enlighten the conscience of her children on the moral implications of their temporal activities within the new historical context.

The end result was the gradual elaboration of a corpus of social moral doctrine. It was the fruit of a confrontation between "the principles derived from right reason and the treasury of revelation"[40] and the changing historical situations. The task of the Church is to *animate* the social order with the principles of social morality thus elaborated.

That brings us back to our initial question. Was not this activity of the Church a dialogue with the world, as Vatican II meant the term? The answer is no. Throughout the period of time that runs from Leo XIII to Pius XII, the elaboration of the Church's social doctrine was governed by a conception of the universe and theological principles that differ from those which underlay some isolated positions of John XXIII, which were explicitly formulated by Vatican II, and which were later embodied in *Populorum progressio*.

Let us consider the general conception of the universe underlying the social doctrine of the Church in this earlier period. This conception totally lacked an evolutionary perspective. To be sure, there is an awareness that changes are taking place. Pius XI evinced such awareness in relating his encyclical to that of Leo XIII,[41] and Pius XII evinced it in his many radio messages. It was precisely this awareness of change that gave rise to new documents, which were meant to explicate and develop the Church's social doctrine. An evolutionary perspective, however, means something more than just an awareness of change. It implies an awareness of the direction in which this change is moving. It implies a certain faith in the progress of humanity toward greater maturity. It implies a certain optimism, which we do find in some comments of John XXIII,[42] and which is clearly evident in conciliar passages that suggest a whole new perspective: "Therefore, by virtue of the gospel committed to her, the Church . . . acknowledges and greatly esteems the dynamic movements of today . . ." (GS 41).

In other words, social conflicts are something more than a symptom of moral decay which the Church must denounce and then correct by offering guidelines.[43] They are symptoms of a growth crisis for the human race. Mankind is testing new forms of living, experiencing the difficulties of the road he is already on, and deciding whether there is need to revise things. And this growth and maturation are not alien to, but in accordance with, the evangelizing mission of the Church. Only within this outlook can what is taking place in humanity be regarded as signs of the times; only then can they induce the Church to dialogue authentically with the world. In saying that this perspective was absent from the social doctrine of the Church in an earlier period, we are simply saying that Christian awareness had not yet reached that deeper stage which made possible the basic outlook and orientation of Vatican II.

In addition to this lack of an evolutionary perspective, the elaboration of the social doctrine of the Church took place in a different theological context. This theological context was prior to, or contemporaneous with, the whole polemic about the notion of the supernatural and its relationship to the natural (see CLARIFICATION II, Chapter I).[44]

In the idiom of the Church's social doctrine, the temporal is conceived to be a natural structure in which man operates; it has value for the Christian only because of the relationship existing between respectful observance of the natural law and our striving toward a supernatural end.[45] Or, as Pius XI might put it, we seek our supreme (supernatural) end through the particular ends that are proper to our activity in its different domains; and these natural ends are transposed into another order by their subordination to the supreme end: "If we faithfully observe the moral law, the particular ends we seek in our economic and social life will readily become a part of the universal order of ends; mounting step by step through these ends, we will attain the ultimate end of all things which is God." [46]

If one reads these texts attentively, he will readily see that this social doctrine was elaborated in a dualistic context. The world, as it were, acquired its value from something outside itself: that is, from the moral connotations of every human action.

Now real church-world dialogue presupposes, first of all, a positive evaluation of the world (by which we mean precisely: of non-Christian humanity) and of its process of evolution and maturation. Secondly, this valuation must be such that the Church (or Christians) not only seek to "animate" man's economic and social life with moral principles but also receive a real contribution from the non-Christian world.[47] Such an evaluation can only exist within a theological conception that affirms man's historical vocation (every man's) to be a supernatural vocation; that does not see grace as a privilege exclusive to Christians but as the gratuitous communication of a God who gives himself to every man, a communication which man chooses to accept or reject in every human relationship whether or not he is aware of the deeper significance of his option.

This brings us to the second theological presupposition that dominated the elaboration of the Church's social doctrine: its conception of the Church and its relationship with the world.

The most explicit formulation of this outlook is undoubtedly Leo XIII's *Inmortale Dei,* an encyclical which discusses the Christian constitution of the state. In it he defines the Church as "a supernatural and spiritual society . . . complete in its own order and juridically perfect" (n. 9). She assumes an authority over all men, who in reality belong to her or by vocation are called to her. This power, being supernatural in its goal, is above any temporal authority (n. 9). Her subjects are also subjects of the civil authority (n. 11). Should there be a conflict, it should be remembered that this runs counter to the wisdom of God: "In the physical world he has so regulated the forces of nature with wondrous harmony and balance . . . that they do not run counter to each other but rather work together to bring about the wondrous beauty and perfection of the universe" (n. 11). The Church sees her relationship with civil authority as something analogous to the relationship between soul and body. "To judge the extent and quality of this union, one must consider the nature of the two related powers. One must also take account of the excellence and nobility of the objects for which they exist. One has as its proximate and principal aim the care and protection of man's transitory and fleeting interests; the other seeks to procure for him the eternal riches of heaven" (n. 12).[48]

This language does not permit us to interpret the social doctrine of the Church (which was elaborated within this theological context) in terms of dialogue. A Church which dialogues and works with the rest of mankind is a Church that knows she is part of humanity; a Church that knows she is the conscious portion of the deeper mystery that is being worked out in every human life, and in all of humanity taken together in its process of historical becoming. A Church that dialogues is a Church that knows she is, by definition, in the service of humanity. On this we would insist, for our whole book is a development of that conception.

The analysis we have made here forces us to one conclusion. By virtue of the conception of the universe underlying these documents, and by virtue of the theological presuppositions from which it stemmed, the social doctrine of the Church prior to Vatican II (except for scattered passages in the writings of John XXIII, which we have not examined here) cannot be considered as the start of authentic church-world dialogue —even though this doctrine showed a positive interest in the world. Our analysis is not at all meant to be a judgment on the past. It is meant rather to point up the originality of the change in perspective we have today, from an angle of vision that we had not used in the earlier part of this book. To ignore the process involved would be to ignore the fact that Christian awareness progresses as humanity matures, that it reaches new levels of profundity in its work of receiving and comprehending the Word of God. It would also be to ignore the fact that Vatican II, despite some ambiguities in its formulations, represents the original expression and embodiment of the arrival of Christian awareness at this new threshold: its definitive entry into dialogue with the world.

NOTES

1. Other social factors intervened to bolster these institutions and a monolithic doctrine, as we saw in CLARIFICATION IV of Chapter II. Here we want to stress the temptation to intellectual stagnation in the face of such an ideal and seemingly perfect outlook.

2. Tommaso Campanella, *Apologia pro Galileo* (1622).

3. See CLARIFICATION III of Chapter III.

4. León H. Dupriez, *Des mouvements économiques généraux* (Louvain: Nauwelaerts, 1951); Joseph A. Schumpeter, *Theorie der Wirtschaftlichen Entwicklung* (Berlin: Dunker and Humboldt, 1952).

5. To confirm this, one need only compare the expansion indices for decades for Great Britain, Germany, and the United States (Dupriez, *op. cit.*, p. 246) and the production indices for cereal grains and wool, for Argentina and Canada, from 1880 to 1939 (*cf.* G. Grandau, *Ernteschwankungen und wirtschaftliche Wechsellagen, 1875–1913* (Jena, 1939).

6. Joseph A. Schumpeter, *Capitalism, Socialism and Democracy* (New York: Harper & Row, 1960), pp. 111–120.

7. E. C. Snow, "The Limits of Industrial Employment," *Journal of the Royal Statistics Society,* II (1953) 259.

8. I. Ferenczi, *L'optimum synthétique de peuplement* (Paris: Institut international de coopération intellectuale, 1938).

9. Schumpeter, both books cited above.

10. Philippe de Woot, *La fonction d'entreprise* (Louvain: Nauwelaerts, 1962).

11. W. Bowden, "Wages, Hours and Productivity of Industrial Labor: 1909 to 1939," *Monthly Labor Review* (September 1940), p. 531.

12. Ferenczi, *op. cit.*

13. Dupriez, *op. cit.*

14. Karl Marx, *Das Kapital*; Joseph A. Schumpeter, *Capitalism . . . , op. cit.*

15. See CLARIFICATION II of Chapter I.

16. Edward Schillebeeckx, Press Conference on Schema XIII, Rome, September 17, 1964, especially the conclusions.

17. Pierre Teilhard de Chardin, *L'activation de l'energie* (Paris: Editions du Seuil, 1963), p. 80; "The Rise of the Other," *Activation of Energy* (New York: Harcourt, Brace, 1971), pp. 73–74.

18. Teilhard de Chardin, *Comment je vois*, cited by Emile Rideau, *La Pensée du Père Teilhard de Chardin* (Paris: du Seuil, 1965), p. 498. English editions: *The Thought of Teilhard de Chardin* (New York: Harper & Row, 1967); *Teilhard de Chardin: A Guide to His Thought* (London: William Collins Sons, 1967). Most of the texts cited here are taken from *La Pensée* . . . , which contains much unpublished material.

19. *Le sens humain*, Rideau, *ibid.*, p. 402. By *monad* Teilhard de Chardin does not mean a unity closed in upon itself; he means the person, the unique creature whom God loves for its own sake and who, like God, finds fulfillment only in self-giving (*cf.* GS 24).

20. *Le Christianisme dans le monde*, Rideau, *ibid.*, p. 534.

21. *Le phénomène humain*, p. 3321. Rideau, *ibid.*, p. 152.

22. *Génèse d'une pensée*, p. 334. Rideau, *ibid.*, p. 271.

23. *L'activation de l'énergie*, pp. 387–88. Rideau, *ibid.*, p. 304.

24. Rideau, *ibid.*, p. 306.

25. *La vision du passé*, p. 324. Rideau, *ibid.*, p. 386.

26. Rideau, *ibid.*, p. 161.

27. *Ibid.*, p. 223.

28. *Ibid.*, p. 172.

29. *Ibid.*, p. 166.

30. *Ibid.*, pp. 253–254.

31. *Comment je vois*, Rideau, *ibid.*, p. 498.

32. John XXIII, *Pacem in terris*, n. 160.

33. Leo XIII, encyclical *Rerum novarum*, n. 4; Pius XI, *Quadragesimo anno.*

34. Pius XI, *ibid.*, n. 43.

35. Leo XIII, *op. cit.*, n. 11.

36. Pius XI, *op. cit.*, n. 14.

37. Pius XII, Address to Italian Catholic Action Group, May 3, 1951; AAS 43 (1951), p. 377.

38. Leo XIII, *op. cit.*, n. 13: "This question will find no acceptable solution if one does not have recourse to religion and the Church . . . Because the Church is the one which draws doctrines from the gospel that are either able to resolve the dispute completely or at least take the harsh edge off it" (*ibid.*, n. 11). "We feel it is the right time . . . to diligently explore the modern economic setup and socialism in order to discover the roots of the present unrest and to point out the one and only road to saving restoration: i.e., Christian reform of social customs" (Pius XI, *op. cit.*, n. 3).

39. The expression is that of Pius X: "Since religion is the guardian of the moral law, the foundation of social order, it follows that to re-establish order in a wholly changed society, nothing is more necessary than giving due honor to religious principles" (Letter to the directors of the Social and Economic Association for the Catholics of Italy, January 18, 1901; AAS 33 (1901), p. 389.

40. Pius XI, *op. cit.*, n. 3.

41. In Part III of *Quadragesimo anno*, Pius XI describes the changes that took place in the capitalist economic system and in socialist doctrine from the time of Leo XIII to his own encyclical. Note also this passage in Part I of the encyclical: "Moreover, the new needs of our era and the changed condition of things call for a more careful application of Leo XIII's doctrine and even some additions to it" (*op. cit.*, n. 13).

42. John XXIII, Allocution at the opening session of Vatican II, October 11, 1962, n. 14.

43. Leo XIII, *op. cit.*, n. 11.

44. The encyclical *Humani generis* bears witness to a moment of theological crisis that has not yet been resolved. In n. 13 it alludes to the debate in progress; "Others denigrate the notion of the gratuitousness of the supernatural order, maintaining that God could not create a being with intelligence without ordaining such beings to the beatific vision." It is not without significance that various theologians seriously affected by *Humani generis* took an active part in Vatican II and are cited by Paul VI in *Populorum progressio*.

45. "By divine ordination, there is a relationship between observance of the natural law and the route which man must follow to reach his supernatural end" (Pius XII, Address to the Cardinals and Bishops, November 2, 1954).

46. Pius XI, *Quaragesimo anno*, n. 14.

47. *Cf.* GS 44, 25, etc.

48. One might object that the language of Pius XII in *Mystici Corporis* is quite different from that of Leo XIII. It is certain that Pius XII gives us a much richer vision of the inner life of the Church that goes beyond the juridical tone of Leo XIII. But even though it comes 59 years after *Immortale Dei*, *Mystici Corporis* does not bring us one step forward with regard to the relationship of the Church to the world. The problem was still outside the conscious attention of the Church.

Conclusion

Two different feelings tend to arise when we attempt to probe the mystery of the Church as we have done in this volume. Since they are quite different feelings, it is not unusual that they may manifest themselves separately in groups of people that are different. But neither is it unusual for both to show up in one and the same person.

One feeling is a feeling of *liberation*. This is particularly evident among lay people. If they are conscious of their mission, they feel an obligation to dialogue with nonbelievers and to focus the eye of faith on the events taking place in present-day human history. But at the same time they have often felt suffocated by attitudes which shocked them but which they considered to be an inherent part of their faith. They may have regarded them as essential for their personal salvation. Or, on a higher level, they may have been disgusted by them but accepted them, in self-surrender to Christ, as conceptions that were inextricably associated with the Christian way of life.

When they are shown that this association is simply the result of oversimplification, mass Christianity, and a religion kept at the infantile level, they feel quite liberated. Then can now live a more authentic and coherent life, obeying the summons to be creative and constructive. They feel a sense of liberation and joy.

The second feeling is one of *insecurity*. When the Church was aiming primarily to preserve the faith of people who never underwent a serious conversion, who therefore never had to go through the essential process, the life of the Church wore a different aspect. There were certain things to do. Faith was easy to understand. It could stand firm against all objections and it had solutions for every problem. To move from such a brand of Christianity to the one offered here is to have a certain feeling of anxiety. Now Christianity must be lived as a creative principle; open to dialogue, sensitive to new problems, obliged to offer new formulations. Such anxiety is a necessary partner for any and all liberation.

Gérard Huyghe, bishop of Arras, had this to say about the transition to an adult Christian morality: "For many years we have offered a teaching that was clearcut, easy, and filled with formal categories which told people what venial and mortal sin was. But if we want Christians to be truly adult and to take their spiritual and moral life into their own hands, we can no longer give them such crutches. We must offer them a dynamic principle that will operate in their own hearts. What is the primary thing in Christian morality if it is not love? Love is far more demanding than any moral norms we could spell out. But it is obvious that there will *inevitably* be a period of uncertainty between the time people leave their crutches and the time they feel truly capable of acting out of love. It is a time of growth." * Here we have the second feeling, which is simply the other side of liberation.

This anxiety is necessary, but it is also compatible with joy. One person who shared this discussion process with us had this to say: "I came with many problems, and now I leave with many more. But the problems that haunt me now are not the ones I came with."

If the reader has experienced this same thing, then we have achieved our objective. God willing, we shall examine his new problems in the volumes that follow this one, and that touch upon other great themes of the Christian life.

---

* ICI, No. 231 (January 1, 1965), p. 11.

Appendices

Pertinent Conciliar Texts

Throughout the various chapters of this volume, we have often cited conciliar passages promulgated by Vatican II. Many are presented in the notes.

It seemed advisable and useful to gather these conciliar passages together and present them in the same order in which they appeared in the preceding chapters. This will help the reader in two ways. First of all, he will get a summary of the main ideas developed earlier, a summary based on the supreme ecclesial magisterium. These texts will also provide him with study themes for a deeper intellectual exploration of the doctrinal wealth contained in many conciliar passages. These passages often get lost in the welter of conciliar documents, thus failing to have the real impact they should have.

On the whole, we have been content to organize these texts under chapters and subheadings without adding any detailed commentary. The headings themselves will refer the reader back to the pertinent sections of this volume. There the reader will find the best commentary we could possibly offer.

Chapter One

A. THE CHURCH: A PARTICULAR COMMUNITY

Just as Christ carried out the work of redemption in poverty and under oppression, so the Church is called to follow that same path in communicating to men the fruits of salvation (LG 8).

"Like a pilgrim," the Church "presses forward amid the persecutions of the world and the consolations of God," announcing the cross and death of the Lord until He comes (LG 8).

However, until there is a new heaven and a new earth where justice dwells (*cf.* 2 Peter 3:13), the pilgrim Church in her sacraments and institutions, which pertain to this present time, takes on the appearance of this passing world (LG 48).

For a monumental struggle against the powers of darkness pervades the whole history of man. The battle was joined from the very origins of the world and will continue until the last day, as the Lord has attested (GS 37).

B. THE CHURCH: A UNIVERSAL REALITY

All men are called to belong to the new People of God. Wherefore this People, while remaining one and unique, is to be spread throughout the whole world and must exist in all ages, so that the purpose of God's will may be fulfilled. In the beginning God made human nature one. After His children were scattered, He decreed that they should at length be unified again (cf. John 11:52). It was for this reason that God sent His Son, whom He appointed heir of all things (cf. Hebrews 1:2), that He might be Teacher, King, and Priest of all, the Head of the new and universal people of the sons of God (LG 13).

C. SOLUTION TO THE ANTINOMY: GOD'S GIFT OF LOVE

1) in which all men participate

God, who has fatherly concern for everyone, has willed that all men should constitute one family and treat one another in a spirit of brotherhood. For having been created in the image of God, who "from one man has created the whole human race and made them live all over the face of the earth" (Acts 17:26), all men are called to one and the same goal, namely God Himself (GS 24).

This likeness reveals that man, who is the only creature on earth that God willed for its own sake, cannot fully find himself except through sincere self-giving (GS 24).

2) and which Christians come to know through revelation

The Christian man, conformed to the likeness of that Son who is the first-born of many brothers, receives "the first-fruits of the Spirit" (Rom. 8:23) by which he becomes capable of discharging the new law of love. Through this Spirit, who is "the pledge of our inheritance" (Eph. 1:14), the whole man is renewed from within, even to the achievement of "the redemption of the body" (Rom. 8:23): "If the Spirit of him who raised Jesus from the dead dwells in you, then he who raised Jesus Christ from the dead will also bring to life your mortal bodies because of his Spirit who dwells in you" (Rom. 8:11). Pressing upon the Christian, certainly, are the need and duty to battle against evil through many trials, and even to suffer death. But, linked with the paschal mystery and patterned on the dying Christ, he will hasten forward to resurrection in the strength which comes from hope.

All this holds true not only for Christians, but for all men of good will in whose hearts grace works in an unseen way. For, since Christ died for all men, and since the ultimate vocation of man is in fact one, and divine, we ought to believe that the Holy Spirit, in a manner known only to God, offers to every man the possibility of being associated with this paschal mystery.

Such is the mystery of man, and it is a great one, as seen by believers in the light of Christian revelation (GS 22).

Chapter Two

A. FAITH IS RECOGNITION OF THE MYSTERY

It is, finally, through the gift of the Holy Spirit that man comes by faith to the contemplation and appreciation of the divine plan (GS 15).

For faith throws a new light on everything, manifests God's design for man's total vocation, and thus directs the mind to solutions which are fully human (GS 11).

For God has called man and still calls him so that with his entire being he might be joined to Him in an endless sharing of a divine life beyond all corruption (GS 18).

An outstanding cause of human dignity lies in man's call to communion with God. From the very circumstance of his origin, man is already invited to converse with God (GS 19).

All this holds true not only for Christians, but for all men of good will in whose hearts grace works in an unseen way. For, since Christ died for all men, and since the ultimate vocation of man is in fact one, and divine, we ought to believe that the Holy Spirit, in a manner known only to God, offers to every man the possibility of being associated with this paschal mystery.
Such is the mystery of man, and it is a great one, as seen by believers in the light of Christian revelation. Through Christ and in Christ, the riddles of sorrow and death grow meaningful (GS 22).

The truth is that only in the mystery of the incarnate Word does the mystery of man take on light. For Adam, the first man, was a figure of Him who was to come, namely Christ the Lord. Christ, the final Adam, by the revelation of the mystery of the Father and His love, fully reveals man to man himself and makes his supreme calling clear (GS 22).

B. THE SACRAMENTS ARE PARTICIPATION IN THE MYSTERY

For, since Christ died for all men, and since the ultimate vocation of man is in fact one, and divine, we ought to believe that the Holy Spirit, in a manner known only to God, offers to every man the possibility of being associated with this paschal mystery (GS 22).

The wonders wrought by God among the people of the Old Testament were but a prelude to the work of Christ the Lord in redeeming mankind and giving perfect glory to God. He achieved His task principally by the paschal mystery of His blessed passion, resurrection from the dead, and glorious ascension, whereby "dying, he destroyed our death and, rising, he restored our life." For it was from the side of Christ as He slept the sleep of death upon the cross that there came forth "the wondrous sacrament of the whole Church" (SC 5).

The purpose of the sacraments is to sanctify men, to build up the body of Christ and, finally, to give worship to God. Because they are signs they also instruct. They not only presuppose faith, but by words and objects they also nourish, strengthen, and express it; that is why they are called "sacraments of faith" (SC 59).

With the passage of time, however, there have crept into the rites of the sacraments and sacramentals certain features which have rendered their nature and purpose far less clear to the people of today; and hence to that extent the need arises to adjust certain aspects of these rites to the requirements of our own times. For this reason the sacred Council decrees as follows concerning their revision (SC 62): The roles of parents and godparents, and also their duties, should be brought out more sharply in the rite itself (SC 67). The rite of confirmation is to be revised and the intimate connection which this sacrament has with the whole of Christian initiation is to be more lucidly set forth (SC 71). The marriage rite now found in the

Roman Ritual is to be revised and enriched in a way which more clearly expresses the grace of the sacrament (SC 77).

C. THE IMAGE OF THE CHURCH WITHIN THE HUMAN COMMUNITY

Thus the Church, at once a visible assembly and a spiritual community, goes forward together with humanity and experiences the same earthly lot which the world does. She serves as a leaven and as a kind of soul for human society as it is to be renewed in Christ and transformed into God's family. That the earthly and the heavenly city penetrate each other is a fact accessible to faith alone: it remains a mystery of human history, which sin will keep in great disarray until the splendor of God's sons is fully revealed (GS 40).

Chapter Three

A. LOVE FOR HUMAN BEINGS HAS NEED OF THE CHURCH

1. Introduction: only one (objective) pathway of salvation

For God's Word, through whom all things were made, was Himself made flesh and dwelt on the earth of men. Thus he entered the world's history as a perfect man, taking that history up into Himself and summarizing it. He Himself revealed to us that "God is love" (1 John 4:8). At the same time He taught us that the new command of love was the basic law of human perfection and hence of the world's transformation.

To those, therefore, who believe in divine love, He gives assurance that the way of love lies open to all men and that the effort to establish a universal brotherhood is not a hopeless one. He cautions them at the same time that this love is not something to be reserved for important matters, but must be pursued chiefly in the ordinary circumstances of life.

Undergoing death itself for all of us sinners, He taught us by example that we too must shoulder that cross which the world and the flesh inflict upon those who search after peace and justice. Appointed Lord by His resurrection and given plenary power in heaven and on earth, Christ is now at work in the hearts of men through the energy of His Spirit. He arouses not only a desire for the age to come, but, by that very fact, He animates, purifies, and strengthens those noble longings too by which the human family strives to make its life more human and to render the whole earth submissive to this goal (GS 38).

For by His incarnation, the Son of God has united Himself in some fashion with every man. He worked with human hands, He thought with a human mind, acted by human choice, and loved with a human heart (GS 22).

In a wonderful manner conscience reveals that law which is fulfilled by love of God and neighbor. In fidelity to conscience, Christians are joined with the rest of men in the search for truth, and for the genuine solution to the numerous problems which arise in the lives of individuals and from social relationships. Hence the more that a correct conscience holds sway, the more persons and groups turn aside from blind choice and strive to be guided by objective norms of morality. Conscience frequently errs from invincible ignorance without losing its dignity. The same cannot be said of a man who cares but little for truth and goodness, or of a conscience which grows practically sightless as a result of habitual sin (GS 16).

The People of God and the human race in whose midst it lives render service to each other (GS 11).

The People of God believes that it is led by the Spirit of the Lord, who fills the earth. Motivated by this faith, it labors to decipher authentic signs of God's presence and purpose in the happenings, needs, and desires in which this People has a part along with other men of our age (GS 11).

2. Love prepares the way for faith

From the very circumstance of his origin, man is already invited to converse with God. For man would not exist were he not created by God's love and constantly preserved by it. And he cannot live fully according to truth unless he freely acknowledges that love and devotes himself to his Creator (GS 19).

Nor is God Himself far distant from those who in shadows and images seek the Unknown God, for it is He who gives to all men life and breath and every other gift (cf. Acts 17:25–28); and who, as Savior, wills that all men be saved (cf. 1 Tim. 2:4). Those also can attain to everlasting salvation who through no fault of their own do not know the gospel of Christ or His Church, yet sincerely seek God and, moved by grace, strive by their deeds to do His will as it is known to them. Nor does divine Providence deny the help necessary for salvation to those who, without blame on their part, have not yet arrived at an explicit knowledge of God, but who strive to live a good life, thanks to His grace. Whatever goodness or truth is found among them is looked upon by the Church as a preparation for the gospel (LG 16).

Yet believers themselves frequently bear some responsibility for this situation. For taken as a whole, atheism is not a spontaneous development but stems from a variety of causes, including a critical reaction against religious beliefs, and in some places against the Christian religion in particular. Hence believers can have more than a little to do with the birth of atheism. To the extent that they neglect their own training in the faith, or teach erroneous doctrine, or are deficient in their religious, moral, or social life, they must be said to conceal rather than reveal the authentic face of God and religion (GS 19).

3. Faith makes love possible for questioning man

Though mankind today is struck with wonder at its own discoveries and its power, it often raises anxious questions about the current trend of the world, about the place and role of man in the universe, about the meaning of his individual and collective strivings, and about the ultimate destiny of reality and of humanity. Hence, giving witness and voice to the faith of the whole people of God gathered together by Christ, this Council can provide no more eloquent proof of its solidarity with the entire human family with which it is bound up, as well as of its respect and love for that family, than by engaging with it in dialogue about these various problems (GS 3).

Therefore, this sacred Synod proclaims the highest destiny of man and champions the godlike seed which has been sown in him. It offers to mankind the honest assistance of the Church in fostering that brotherhood of all men which corresponds to this destiny of theirs (GS 3).

By contrast, when a divine substructure and the hope of life eternal are wanting, man's dignity is most grievously lacerated, as current events often attest. The riddles of life and death, of guilt and of grief go unsolved, with the frequent result that men succumb to despair (GS 21).

But rather often men, deluded by the Evil One, have became caught up in futile reasoning and have exchanged the truth of God for a lie, serving the creature rather than the Creator (cf. Rom. 1:21–25). Or some there are who, living and dying in a world without God, are subject to utter hopelessness (LG 16).

a) exceeding our hopes

Then, with death overcome, the sons of God will be raised up in Christ. What was sown in weakness and corruption will be clothed with incorruptibility. While charity and its fruits endure, all that creation which God made on man's account will be unchained from the bondage of vanity (GS 39).

For after we have obeyed the Lord, and in His Spirit nurtured on earth the values of human dignity, brotherhood, and freedom, and indeed all the good fruits of our nature and enterprise, we will find them again, but freed of stain, burnished and transfigured. This will be so when Christ hands over to the Father a kingdom eternal and universal: "a kingdom of truth and life, of holiness and grace, of justice, love, and peace." On this earth that kingdom is already present in mystery. When the Lord returns, it will be brought into full flower (GS 39).

b) extending to every man

Since human nature as He assumed it was not annulled, by that very fact it has been raised up to a divine destiny in our respect too. For by His incarnation the Son of God has united Himself in some fashion with every man (GS 22).

Coming down to practical and particularly urgent consequences, this Council lays stress on reverence for man: everyone must consider his every neighbor without exception as another self, taking into account first of all his life and the means necessary to living it with dignity, so as not to imitate the rich man who had no concern for the poor man Lazarus.

In our times a special obligation binds us to make ourselves the neighbor to absolutely every person, and of actively helping him when he comes across our path, whether he be an old person abandoned by all, a foreign laborer unjustly looked down upon, a refugee, a child born of an unlawful union and wrongly suffering for a sin he did not commit, or a hungry person who disturbs our conscience by recalling the voice of the Lord: "As long as you did it for one of these, the least of my brethren, you did it for me" (Matt. 25:40; GS 27).

c) beyond the power of our frail human resources

By thus consenting to the divine utterance, Mary, a daughter of Adam, became the mother of Jesus. Embracing God's saving will with a full heart and impeded by no sin, she devoted herself totally as a handmaid of the Lord to the person and work of her Son. In subordination to Him and along with Him, by the grace of almighty God she served the mystery of redemption. Rightly therefore the Holy Fathers see her as used by God not merely in a passive way, but as cooperating in the work of human salvation through free faith and obedience. St. Irenaeus says she, "being obedient, became the cause of human salvation for herself and for the whole human race" (LG 56).

Chapter Four

A. INTERNAL PURIFICATION IN ORDER TO BE A SIGN

For it is the function of the Church, led by the Holy Spirit who renews and purifies her ceaselessly, to make God the Father and His Incarnate Son present and in a sense visible. This result is achieved chiefly by the witness of a living and mature faith, namely, one trained to see difficulties clearly and to master them. Very many martyrs have given luminous witness to this faith and continue to do so. This faith needs to prove its fruitfulness by penetrating the believer's entire life, including its worldly dimensions, and by activating him toward justice and love, especially regarding the needy. What does most to reveal God's presence, however, is the brotherly charity of the faithful who are united in spirit as they work together for the faith of the gospel and who prove themselves a sign of unity (GS 21).

B. TAKING THE CHURCH AS A RESPONSIBILITY NOT AS A PRIVILEGE

All men are called to this catholic unity of the People of God, a unity which is harbinger of the universal peace it promotes. And there belong to it, or are related to it in various ways, the Catholic faithful as well as all who believe in Christ, and indeed the whole of mankind. For all men are called to salvation by God's grace (LG 13).

He is not saved, however, who, though he is part of the body of the Church, does not persevere in charity. He remains in the bosom of the Church, but, as it were, only in a "bodily" manner and not "in his heart." All the sons of the Church should remember that their exalted status is to be attributed not to their own merits but to the special grace of Christ. If they fail, moreover, to respond to that grace in thought, word, and deed, not only will they not be saved but they will be the more severely judged (LG 14).

Chapter Five

A. WHAT THE WORLD GIVES THE CHURCH

For the Council yearns to explain to everyone how it conceives of the presence and activity of the Church in the world of today. Therefore the Council focuses its attention on the world of men, the whole human family along with the sum of those realities in the midst of which that family lives. It gazes on that world which is the theater of man's history, and carries the marks of his energies, his tragedies, and his triumphs; that world which the Christian sees as created and sustained by its Maker's love, fallen indeed into the bondage of sin, yet emancipated now by Christ. He was crucified and rose again to break the stranglehold of personified Evil, so that the world might be fashioned anew according to God's design and reach its fulfillment (GS 2).

The joys and the hopes, the griefs and the anxieties of the men of this age, especially those who are poor or in any way afflicted, these too are the joys and hopes, the griefs and the anxieties of the followers of Christ. Indeed, nothing genuinely human fails to raise an echo in their hearts. For theirs is a community composed of men. United in Christ, they are led by the Holy Spirit in their journey to the kingdom of their Father and they have welcomed the news of salvation which is meant for every man. That is why this community realizes that it is truly and intimately linked with mankind and its history (GS 1).

The Church also realizes that in working out her relationship with the world she always has great need of the ripening which comes with the experience of the centuries (GS 43).

Thus the Church, at once a visible assembly and a spiritual community, goes forward together with humanity and experiences the same earthly lot which the world does. She serves as a leaven and as a kind of soul for human society as it is to be renewed in Christ and transformed into God's family (GS 40).

People are waiting for an answer to these questions. From the answers it will be increasingly clear that the People of God and the human race in whose midst it lives render service to each other (GS 11).

1. Unity for love

One of the salient features of the modern world is the growing inter-dependence of men one on the other, a development very largely promoted by modern technical advances. Nevertheless, brotherly dialogue among men does not reach its perfection on the level of technical progress, but on the deeper level of interpersonal relationships. These demand a mutual respect for the full spiritual dignity of the person. Christian revelation contributes greatly to the promotion of this communion between persons, and at the same time leads us to a deeper understanding of the laws of social life which the Creator has written into man's spiritual and moral nature (GS 23).

Thanks primarily to increased opportunities for many kinds of interchange among nations, the human family is gradually recognizing itself as a single world community and is making itself so (GS 33).

The promotion of unity belongs to the innermost nature of the Church, since she is, "by her relationship with Christ, both a sacramental sign and an instrument of intimate union with God and of the unity of all mankind" (GS 42).

Sacred Scripture . . . teaches us that the love of God cannot be separated from love of neighbor: "If there is any other commandment, it is summed up in this saying, Thou shalt love thy neighbor as thyself . . ." To men growing daily more dependent on one another, and to a world becoming more unified every day, this truth proves to be of paramount importance (GS 24).

Now, for the first time in human history, all people are convinced that the benefits of culture ought to be and actually can be extended to everyone (GS 9).

2. Interdependence for love

Advances in biology, psychology, and the social sciences not only bring men hope of improved self-knowledge. In conjunction with technical methods, they are also helping to exert a direct influence on the life of social groups (GS 5).

Although the world of today has a very vivid sense of its unity and of how one man depends on another in needful solidarity, it is most grievously torn into opposing camps by conflicting forces (GS 4).

Every day human interdependence grows more tightly drawn and spreads by degrees over the whole world. As a result the common good, that is, the sum of those conditions of social life which allow social groups and their individual members relatively thorough and ready access to their own ful-fillment, today takes on an increasingly universal complexion and conse-quently involves rights and duties with respect to the whole human race. Every social group must take account of the needs and legitimate aspirations of other groups, indeed of the general welfare of the entire human family (GS 26).

For this gospel . . . finally, commends all to the charity of all (GS 41).

3. Creative change for love

History itself speeds along on so rapid a course that an individual can scarcely keep abreast of it. The destiny of the human community has be-come all of a piece, where once the various groups of men had a kind of private history of their own. Thus the human race has passed from a rather static concept of reality to a more dynamic evolutionary one. In consequence, there has arisen a new series of problems, a series as important as can be, calling for new efforts of analysis and synthesis (GS 5).

A change of attitudes and in human structures frequently calls accepted values into question. This is especially true of young people, who have grown impatient on more than one occasion, and indeed become rebels in their distress. Aware of their own influence in the life of society, they want to assume a role in it sooner. As a result, parents and educators frequently experience greater difficulties day by day in discharging their tasks.

The institutions, laws, and modes of thinking and feeling as handed down from previous generations do not always seem to be well adapted to the contemporary state of affairs. Hence arises an upheaval in the manner and even the norms of behavior.

Finally, these new conditions have their impact on religious life itself. On the one hand, a more critical ability to distinguish religion from a magical view of the world and from the superstitions which still circulate purifies religion and exacts day by day a more personal and explicit ad-herence to faith. As a result many persons are achieving a more vivid sense of God (GS 7).

B. WHAT THE WORLD DEMANDS FROM THE CHURCH AS A MORAL RESPONSE

1. In general

Though mankind is struck with wonder at its own discoveries and its power, it often raises anxious questions about the current trend of the world, about the place and role of man in the universe, about the meaning of his in-dividual and collective strivings, and about the ultimate destiny of reality and of humanity. Hence, giving witness and voice to the faith of the whole people of God gathered together by Christ, this Council can provide no more eloquent proof of its solidarity with the entire human family with which it is bound up, as well as of its respect and love for that family, than by engaging with it in dialogue about these various problems (GS 3).

Finally, these new conditions have their impact on religion. On the one hand a more critical ability to distinguish religion from a magical view of the world and from the superstitions which still circulate purifies religion and exacts day by day a more personal and explicit adherence to faith. As a result many persons are achieving a more vivid sense of God. On the other hand, growing numbers of people are abandoning religion in prac-tice (GS 7).

Profound and rapid changes make it particularly urgent that no one, ignoring the trend of events or drugged by laziness, content himself with a merely individualistic morality. It grows increasingly true that the obligations of justice and love are fulfilled only if each person, contributing to the common good according to his own abilities and the needs of others, also promotes and assists the public and private institutions dedicated to bettering the conditions of human life. Yet there are those who, while professing grand and rather noble sentiments, nevertheless in reality live always as if they cared nothing for the needs of society. Many in various places even make light of social laws and precepts, and do not hesitate to resort to various frauds and deceptions in avoiding just taxes or other debts due to society. Others think little of certain norms of social life, for example those designed for the protection of health, or laws establishing speed limits. They do not even advert to the fact that by such indifference they imperil their own life and that of others.

Let everyone consider it his sacred obligation to number social necessities among the primary duties of modern man, and to pay heed to them. For the more unified the world becomes, the more plainly do the duties of men extend beyond particular groups and spread by degrees to the whole world (GS 30).

Thus, with the needed help of divine grace, men who are truly new and artisans of a new humanity can be forthcoming (GS 30).

2. Special function of the laity in this central task

The laity, by their very vocation, seek the kingdom of God by engaging in temporal affairs and by ordering them to the plan of God. They live in the world, that is, in each and in all of the secular professions and occupations. They live in the ordinary circumstances of family and social life, from which the very web of their existence is woven.

They are called there by God so that by exercising their proper function and being led by the spirit of the gospel they can work for the sanctification of the world from within, in the manner of leaven. In this way they can make Christ known to others, especially by the testimony of a life resplendent in faith, hope, and charity (LG 31).

The sacraments of the New Law, by which the life and the apostolate of the faithful are nourished, prefigure a new heaven and a new earth (cf. Apoc. 21:1). So too the laity go forth as powerful heralds of a faith in things to be hoped for (cf. Heb. 11:1) provided they steadfastly join to their profession of faith a life springing from faith. This evangelization, that is, this announcing of Christ by a living testimony as well as by the spoken word, takes on a specific quality and a special force in that it is carried out in the ordinary surroundings of the world (LG 35).

Through the sacraments, especially the Holy Eucharist, there is communicated and nourished that charity toward God and man which is the soul of the apostolate. Now, the laity are called in a special way to make the Church present and operative in those places and circumstances where only through them can she become the salt of the earth. Thus every layman, by virtue of the very gifts bestowed upon him, is at the same time a witness and a living instrument of the mission of the Church herself, "according to the measure of Christ's bestowal" (Eph. 4:7).

Besides this apostolate, which pertains to absolutely every Christian, the laity can also be called in various ways to a more direct form of cooperation in the apostolate of the hierarchy (LG 33).

Laymen should also know that it is generally the function of their well-formed Christian conscience to see that the divine law is inscribed in the life of the earthly city. From priests they may look for spiritual light and nourishment. Let laymen not imagine that his pastors are always such experts, that to every problem which arises, they can readily give him a concrete solution, or even that such is their mission. Rather, enlightened by Christian wisdom and giving close attention to the teaching authority of the Church, let the layman take on his own distinctive role.

Often enough the Christian view of things will itself suggest some specific solution in certain circumstances. Yet it happens rather frequently, and legitimately so, that with equal sincerity some of the faithful will disagree with others on a given matter. Even against the intentions of their proponents, however, solutions proposed on one side or another may be easily confused by many people with the gospel message. Hence it is necessary for people to remember that no one is allowed in the aforementioned situations to appropriate the Church's authority for his opinion (GS 43).

The faithful, therefore, must learn the deepest meaning and value of all creation and how to relate it to the praise of God. They must assist one another to live holier lives even in their daily occupations. In this way the world is permeated by the spirit of Christ and more effectively achieves its purpose in justice, charity, and peace. The laity have the principal role in the universal fulfillment of this purpose (LG 36).

In this manner, through the members of the Church, Christ will progressively illumine the whole of human society with His saving light (LG 36).

APPENDIX II

A Biblical Tapestry

The biblical texts presented here do not follow the thematic order of the chapter discussions in this volume, but they bear an intimate relationship to the whole discussion.

In particular, the three stages marking the preparation of ancient Israel for her transformation into the Church (I; A, B, C) could readily serve as an introduction to our reflections in this volume. They can also serve as an examination of conscience for us, showing us to what extent we still harbor a pre-Christian image of the ecclesial community, at least in some respects.

In presenting the biblical texts within this framework, we do not follow the order of the various books in the present setup of the Bible. Instead we follow the different stages of its redaction. That procedure is indispensable if we are to see how the Spirit went about helping Israel to gradually overcome the obstacles hindering her in her progress toward Church.

I The Old Testament

For Saint Paul, Israel is the figure and the preparation for the Church, the definitive reality:

> Consider the practice of Israel . . . (1 Cor. 10:18; RSV)

> Whoever they are who take this principle for their guide [i.e., the new creation that Christ represents], peace and mercy be upon them, and upon the whole Israel of God [i.e., the whole Church] (Gal. 6:16).

So let us look at the resemblance in order that we may be able to recognize the difference.

A. THE ISRAEL OF THE COVENANT

1. **Twofold election:** Here is a type of creed that the Israelites recited when they brought the first fruits of the harvest into the Temple:

> Then you shall solemnly recite before the Lord your God, "My father was a wandering Aramean who went down to Egypt with a small company and lived there until they became a great, powerful, and numerous nation. But the Egyptians ill-treated us, humiliated us and imposed cruel slavery upon us. Then we cried to the Lord the God of our fathers for help, and he

listened to us and saw our humiliation, our hardship and distress; and so the Lord brought us out of Egypt with a strong hand and outstretched arm, with terrifying deeds, and with signs and portents. He brought us to this place and gave us this land, a land flowing with milk and honey. And now I have brought the firstfruits of the soil which thou, O Lord hast given me" (Deut. 26:5–10).

Worse than not choosing Yahweh is abandoning him after choosing him. Here is the renewal of the promise made before Moses upon their departure from Egypt: this time it was made before the dying Joshua after they had occupied the promised land:

"If it does not please you to worship the Lord, choose here and now whom you will worship: the gods whom your forefathers worshipped beside the Euphrates, or the gods of the Amorites in whose land you are living. But I and my family, we will worship the Lord." The people answered, "God forbid that we should forsake the Lord to worship other gods, for it was the Lord our God who brought us and our fathers up from Egypt, that land of slavery. . . . We too will worship the Lord; he is our God." Joshua answered the people, "You cannot worship the Lord. He is a holy god, a jealous god, and he will not forgive your rebellion and your sins. If you forsake the Lord and worship foreign gods, he will turn and bring adversity upon you and, although he once brought you prosperity, he will make an end of you." The people said to Joshua, "No; we will worship the Lord." He said to them, "You are witnesses against yourselves that you have chosen the Lord and will worship him." "Yes," they answered, "we are witnesses" (Josh. 24:15–22).

Every nation of people has its own gods who protect them. Here are two examples:

When the king of Moab saw that the war had gone against him . . . he took his eldest son, who would have succeeded him, and offered him as a whole-offering upon the city wall. The Israelites were filled with such consternation at this sight that they struck camp and returned to their own land (2 Kings 3:26–27).

Israel then sent messengers to the king of Edom asking him to grant them passage through his country, but the king of Edom would not hear of it. They sent also to the king of Moab, but he was not willing. . . . The Lord the God of Israel drove out the Amorites for the benefit of his people Israel. And do you now propose to take their place? It is for you to possess whatever Kemosh your god gives you; and all that the Lord our God gave us as we advanced is ours (Judg. 11:17–24).

As for the nation of Israel, it decided to keep Yahweh as the sole God of its history:

All the peoples may walk, each in the name of his god, but we will walk in the name of the Lord our God for ever and ever (Mic. 4:5).

2. **The "covenant" signifies "mutual fidelity"**: Yahweh is faithful to Israel, giving the nation what it needs in its history:

Therefore I will block her road with thorn-bushes and obstruct her path with a wall, so that she can no longer follow her old ways. When she pursues her lovers she will not overtake them, when she looks for them she will not find them; then she will say, "I will go back to my husband again; I was better off with him than I am now." . . . I will woo her, I will go with her into the wilderness and comfort her; there I will restore her vineyards . . . On that day she shall call me "My husband" and shall no more call me "My Baal" . . . Then I will make a covenant on behalf of Israel with the wild beasts, the birds of the air, and the things that creep on the earth, and I will break bow and sword and weapon of war and sweep them off the earth, so that all living creatures may lie down without fear. I will betroth you to myself for ever, betroth you in lawful wedlock with unfailing devotion and love; I will betroth you to myself to have and to hold, and you shall know the Lord (Hos. 2:6–20).

Israel's fidelity to Yahweh involves the carrying out of his law. Thus the decalogue appears as a clause of the covenant:

> Moses summoned all Israel and said to them: Listen, O Israel, to the statutes and the laws which I proclaim in your hearing today. Learn them and be careful to observe them. The Lord our God made a covenant with us at Horeb. . . . "I am the Lord your God who brought you out of Egypt, out of the land of slavery. You shall have no other god to set against me . . ." You shall be careful to do as the Lord your God has commanded you; do not turn from it to right or to left. You must conform to all the Lord your God commands you, if you would live and prosper and remain long in the land you are to occupy (Deut. 5:1–7, 32–33).

3. **Applying the covenant in history:** Yahweh's law is a law of justice for Israel, not a purely external cult. This is the preaching of the prophets:

> I hate, I spurn your pilgrim-feasts; I will not delight in your sacred ceremonies. When you present your sacrifices and offerings I will not accept them, nor look on the buffaloes of your shared-offerings. Spare me the sound of your songs; I cannot endure the music of your lutes. Let justice roll on like a river and righteousness like an ever-flowing stream (Amos 5:21–24).

> If the Lord of Hosts had not left us a remnant, we should soon have been like Sodom, no better than Gomorrah. Hear the word of the Lord, you rulers of Sodom; attend, you people of Gomorrah, to the instruction of our God: Your countless sacrifices, what are they to me? says the Lord. I am sated with whole-offerings of rams and the fat of buffaloes; I have no desire for the blood of bulls, of sheep and of he-goats. . . . When you lift your hands outspread in prayer, I will hide my eyes from you. Though you offer countless prayers, I will not listen. There is blood on your hands; wash yourselves and be clean. Put away the evil of your deeds, away out of my sight. Cease to do evil and learn to do right, pursue justice and champion the oppressed; give the orphan his rights, plead the widow's cause (Isa. 1:9–17).

For other nations, on the other hand, it signifies separation and extermination:

> When the Lord your God brings you into the land which you are entering to occupy and drives out many nations before you . . . seven nations more numerous and powerful than you—when the Lord delivers them into your power and you defeat them, you must put them to death. You must not make a treaty with them or spare them. You must not intermarry with

them . . . if you do, they will draw your sons away from the Lord and make them worship other gods. Then the Lord will be angry with you and will quickly destroy you . . . for you are a people holy to the Lord your God; the Lord your God chose you out of all nations on earth to be his special possession. . . . Know then that the Lord your God is God, the faithful God; with those who love him and keep his commandments he keeps covenant and faith for a thousand generations, but those who defy him and show their hatred for him he repays with destruction; he will not be slow to requite any who so hate him . . . If you listen to these laws and are careful to observe them, then the Lord your God will observe the sworn covenant he made with your forefathers and will keep faith with you. He will love you, bless you, and cause you to increase. He will bless the fruit of your body and the fruit of your land, your corn and new wine and oil (Deut. 7:1–13).

Concretely, then, the covenant implies that Israel will use moral means for its part and that Yahweh will guarantee its historical success for his part. The sin of Israel in its history was that it did not respect this division of labor, so to speak:

Ephraim (i.e., Israel) and his aliens make a sorry mixture; Ephraim has become a cake half-baked. Foreigners fed on his strength, but he is unaware. . . . Ephraim is a silly senseless pigeon, now calling upon Egypt, now turning to Assyria for help (Hos. 7:8–11).

Shame upon those who go down to Egypt for help and rely on horses, putting their trust in chariots many in number and in horsemen in their thousands, but do not look to the Holy One of Israel or seek guidance of the Lord! . . . The Egyptians are men, not God, their horses are flesh, not spirit; and, when the Lord stretches out his hand, the helper will stumble and he who is helped will fall, and they will all vanish together (Isa. 31:1–3).

Other readings: The Canticle of Moses (Deut. 32) and the story of Saul (1 Sam. 8–15).

B. THE "FLESHLY" ISRAEL

1. **The notion and meaning of creation:** Israel, now persecuted and exiled, focuses its spirituality on the creative power of Yahweh. The first part of Genesis dates from this epoch. And it begins:

In the beginning of creation, when God made heaven and earth . . .

To give hope to the exiles in Babylon, Deutero-Isaiah insists that they are going to be liberated by the one and only God. He is, before anything else, the Creator:

Comfort, comfort my people—it is the voice of your God . . . You who bring Zion good news, up with you to the mountain-top; lift up your voice and shout . . . cry to the cities of Judah, "Your God is here." . . . Who has gauged the waters in the palm of his hand, or with its span set limits to the heavens? Who has held all the soil of earth in a bushel, or weighed the mountains on a balance and the hills on a pair of scales? (Isa. 40:1–12).

He is transcendent:

Why, to him nations are but drops from a bucket, no more than moisture on the scales . . . All nations dwindle to nothing before him, he reckons them mere nothings, less than nought. . . . Do you not know, have you not heard? The Lord, the everlasting God, creator of the wide world, grows neither weary nor faint; no man can fathom his understanding (Isa. 40:15–17, 28).

He is unique. The other gods are vain idols:

What likeness will you find for God or what form to resemble his? Is it an image which a craftsman sets up, and a goldsmith covers with plate and fits with studs of silver as a costly gift? Or is it mulberry-wood that will not rot which a man chooses, seeking out a skilful craftsman for it, to mount an image that will not fall? . . . Do you not know, have you not heard, were you not told long ago? (Isa. 40:18–21).

2. **The notion and meaning of creature:** Contemporaneous and correlative with the notion of Yahweh as creator, there appears the figurative Hebrew term that will designate "creature." Here is the first narrative about the cause of the flood:

When the Lord saw that man had done much evil on earth and that his thoughts and inclinations were always evil, he was sorry that he had made man on earth, and he was grieved at heart. He said, "This race of men whom I have created, I will wipe them off the face of the earth—man and beast, reptiles and birds. I am sorry that I ever made them" (Gen. 6:5–7).

Now compare that passage with the narrative of the same event that was redacted in the era which we were talking about. Note that the list of the various things to be destroyed is replaced by one term which designates all: *all flesh*. This term is translated according to context in more recent translations of the Bible, such as the New English Bible, the New American Bible, etc. We shall indicate its presence in parentheses:

Now God saw that the whole world was corrupt and full of violence. In his sight the world had become corrupted, for all men (*all flesh*) had lived corrupt lives on earth. God said to Noah . . . "I intend to destroy them, and the earth with them (*all flesh*)" (Gen. 6:11–13).

3. **Religion according to the flesh:** A religion based on this spirituality, that is, on the relationship that should exist between a creature and its Creator, has its own distinctive characteristics.

It is universal:

For, as the new heavens and the new earth which I am making shall endure in my sight, says the Lord, so shall your race and your name endure; and month by month at the new moon, week by week on the sabbath, all mankind (*all flesh*) shall come to bow down before me, says the Lord; and they shall come out and see the dead bodies of those who have rebelled against me; their worm shall not die nor their fire be quenched, and they shall be abhorred by all mankind (*all flesh*) (Isa. 66:22–24).

It is based on the absolute dependence of the creature on the "God of the spirits of all mankind (*all flesh*)" (Num. 16:22; 27:16). It holds true for their physical existence:

All of them look expectantly to thee to give them their food at the proper time; what thou givest them they gather up; when thou openest thy hand, they eat their fill. Then thou hidest thy face, and they are restless and troubled; when thou takest away their breath, they fail and they return to the dust from which they came; but when thou breathest into them, they recover: thou givest new life to the earth (Ps. 104:27–30).

It also holds true for their moral uprightness. Their Creator God cannot be turned aside by any created justice:

Plunderers have swarmed across the high bare places in the wilderness, a sword of the Lord devouring the land from end to end; no creature (*no flesh*) can find peace (Jer. 12:12).

These are the words of the Lord: I am against you; I will draw my sword from the scabbard and cut off from you both righteous and wicked. It is because I would cut off your righteous and your wicked equally that my sword will be drawn against all men (*all flesh*), from the Negeb northwards. All men (*all flesh*) shall know that I the Lord have drawn my sword; it shall never again be sheathed (Ezek. 21:3–5).

And the reason is put well in the Book of Job:

Can mortal man be more righteous than God, or the creature purer than his maker? (Job 4:17).

4. **The problem of the covenant:** Now if that is the case, what has happened to the covenant in history? At first glance, it would seem that everything goes on the same except that success in history has been transposed to the personal level:

Happy is the man who does not take the wicked for his guide nor walk the road that sinners tread . . . He is like a tree planted beside a watercourse, which yields its fruit in season and its leaf never withers: in all that he does he prospers (Ps. 1:1–3).

I have been young and am now grown old, and never have I seen a righteous man forsaken (Ps. 37:25).

And men shall say, "There is after all a reward for the righteous; after all, there is a God that judges on earth" (Ps. 58:11).

But the difference between the public and private reality gives rise to a doubt:

In God have we gloried all day long, and we will praise thy name for ever. But now thou hast rejected and humbled us and dost no longer lead our armies into battle . . . Thou hast sold thy people for next to nothing and had no profit from the sale. Thou hast exposed us to the taunts of our neighbours, to the mockery and contempt of all around . . . All this has befallen us, but we do not forget thee and have not betrayed thy covenant; we have not gone back on our purpose, nor have our feet strayed from thy path . . . Bestir thyself, Lord; why dost thou sleep? (Ps. 44:8–23).

How good God is to the upright! How good to those who are pure in heart! My feet had almost slipped, my foothold had all but given way, because the boasts of sinners roused my envy when I saw how they prosper. No pain, no suffering is theirs; they are sleek and sound in limb. . . . So wicked men talk, yet still they prosper, and rogues amass great wealth. So it was all in vain that I kept my heart pure and washed my hands in innocence. For all day long I suffer torment and am punished every morning.

Yet had I let myself talk on in this fashion, I should have betrayed the family of God. So I set myself to think this out but I found it too hard for me, until I went into God's sacred courts; there I saw clearly what their end would be. How often thou dost set them on slippery ground and drive them headlong into ruin! . . . I would not understand, so brutish was I, I was a mere beast in thy sight, O God. . . . yet God is my possession for ever. They who are far from thee are lost; thou dost destroy all who wantonly forsake thee (Ps. 73:1–27).

To cite an historical example, the Maccabees felt the same way:

Judas said to his men: "Do not be afraid of their great numbers or panic when they charge. Remember how our fathers were saved at the Red Sea, when Pharaoh and his army were pursuing them. Let us cry now to Heaven to favour our cause, to remember the covenant made with our fathers, to crush this army before us today. Then all the Gentiles will know that there is One who saves and liberates Israel" (1 Macc. 4:8–11).

But look what happened to a group of people who chose not to fight on the Sabbath in order to keep the law:

At that time many who wanted to maintain their religion and law went down to the wilds to live there. . . . A large body of men went quickly after them, came up with them, and occupied positions opposite. They prepared to attack them on the Sabbath. . . . Without more ado the attack was launched; but the Israelites did nothing in reply . . . So they were attacked and massacred on the sabbath, men, women, and children, up to a thousand in all, and their cattle with them (1 Macc. 2:29–38).

Thus there gradually developed the notion that God mysteriously directs the course of history without human morality having any influence on his direction:

There is an empty thing found on earth: when the just man gets what is due to the unjust, and the unjust what is due to the just. I maintain that this too is emptiness. . . . I applied my mind to acquire wisdom and to observe the business which goes on upon earth . . . and also I perceived that God has so ordered it that man should not be able to discover what is happening here under the sun. . . . I applied my mind to all this, and I understand that the righteous and the wise and all their doings are under God's control; but is it love or hatred? No man knows. Everything that confronts him, everything is empty, since one and the same fate befalls every one, just and unjust alike, good and bad, clean and unclean, the man who offers sacrifice and the man who does not (Eccles. 8:14, 16–17; 9:1–2).

It is all one; therefore I say, "He destroys blameless and wicked alike." When a sudden flood brings death, he mocks the plight of the innocent (Job 9:22–23).

And the only answer to this complaint is the one that Job himself receives, pointing to the mysterious transcendence of God the Creator:

Then the Lord answered Job out of the tempest: "Who is this whose ignorant words cloud my design in darkness? Brace yourself and stand up like a man; I will ask questions, and you shall answer. Where were you when I laid the earth's foundations? Tell me, if you know and understand. Who settled its dimensions? Surely you should know" (Job 38:1–5).

Then Job answered the Lord: "I know that thou canst do all things and that no purpose is beyond thee. But I have spoken of great things which I have not understood, things too wonderful for me to know. I knew of thee then only by report, but now I see thee with my own eyes. Therefore I melt away; I repent in dust and ashes" (Job 42:1-6).

C. THE REMNANT OF ISRAEL

1. **The new covenant:** Belief in the historical covenant did not disappear with the revelation of God's transcendence; but now it is interiorized. It is no longer the whole nation of Israel (quantitatively) that is destined for it, but a remnant of the nation (qualitatively).

Then those who are left in Zion, who remain in Jerusalem, every one enrolled in the book of life, shall be called holy. If the Lord washes away the filth of the women of Zion and cleanses Jerusalem from the blood that is in it by a spirit of judgement, a consuming spirit, then over every building on Mount Zion and on all her places of assembly the Lord will create a cloud of smoke by day and a bright flame of fire by night (Isa. 4:3-5).

Then I asked, "How long, O Lord?" And he answered, "Until cities fall in ruins and are deserted, houses are left without people, and the land goes to ruin and lies waste, until the Lord has sent all mankind far away, and the whole country is one vast desolation. Even if a tenth part of its people remain there, they too will be exterminated like an oak or a terebinth, a sacred pole thrown out from its place in a hill-shrine" (Isa. 6:11-13).

All this shows that it is no longer a question of a contract but of an election, of a divine initiative. Thus the new covenant will not be the result of moral conduct but the cause of it:

The time is coming, says the Lord, when I will make a new covenant with Israel and Judah. It will not be like the covenant I made with their forefathers when I took them by the hand and led them out of Egypt. Although they broke my covenant, I was patient with them, says the Lord. But this is the covenant which I will make with Israel after those days, says the Lord. I will set my law within them and write it on their hearts; I will become their God and they shall become my people. No longer need they teach one another to know the Lord; all of them, high and low alike, shall know me, says the Lord, for I will forgive their wrongdoing and remember their sin no more (Jer. 31:31-34).

2. **The remnant is a poor and lowly people:** Only such a people can adopt the spiritual dispositions called for by this new covenant:

On that day, Jerusalem, you shall not be put to shame for all your deeds by which you have rebelled against me; for then I will rid you of your proud and arrogant citizens, and never again shall you flaunt your pride on my holy hill. But I will leave in you a people afflicted and poor. The survivors in Israel shall find refuge in the name of the Lord; they shall no longer do wrong or speak lies (Zeph. 3:11-13).

The life-giving inspiration of this people is hope, a hope reserved for them:

Seek the Lord, all in the land who live humbly by his laws, seek righteousness, seek a humble heart; it may be that you will find shelter in the day of the Lord's anger (Zeph. 2:3).

In effect, the life of this people offers a continuing contrast. On the one hand they seem to be abandoned:

> All who see me jeer at me, make mouths at me and wag their heads: "He threw himself on the Lord for rescue; let the Lord deliver him, for he holds him dear!" (Ps. 22:7–8).

> Why stand so far off, Lord, hiding thyself in time of need? The wicked man hunts down the poor. . . . thy judgements are beyond his grasp . . . He says to himself, "I shall never be shaken, no misfortune can check my course." . . . he crouches stealthily, like a lion in its lair crouching to seize his victim. . . . Arise, Lord, set thy hand to the task; do not forget the poor, O God (Ps. 10:1–12).

On the other hand, it is the poor and lowly alone that Yahweh hears:

> The poor victim commits himself to thee; fatherless, he finds in thee his helper. . . . Thou hast heard the lament of the humble, O Lord, and art attentive to their heart's desire, bringing justice to the orphan and the downtrodden (Ps. 10:14–17).

3. **The eternal hope of the poor:** What exactly is the hope-filled world of these lowly people before the proclamation of the gospel? We find it in the Book of Wisdom, which was written in Greek. In the first place, God is a Creator of good only:

> God did not make death, and takes no pleasure in the destruction of any living thing; he created all things that they might have being. The creative forces of the world make for life; there is no deadly poison in them. Death is not king on earth, for justice is immortal (Wis. 1:13–14).

It is man's behavior that produces evil and death:

> Do not stray from the path of life and so court death; do not draw disaster on yourselves by your own actions (Wis. 1:12).

> God created man for immortality, and made him the image of his own eternal self; it was the devil's spite that brought death into the world, and the experience of it is reserved for those who take his side (Wis. 2:23–24).

Hence human existence is a gamble. And the way the wicked play it out, it leads to the definitive triumph of death:

> Godless men by their words and deeds have asked death for his company. Thinking him their friend, they have made a pact with him because they are fit members of his party (Wis. 1:16).

> They said to themselves in their deluded way: "Our life is short and full of trouble, and when a man comes to his end there is no remedy; no man was ever known to return from the grave. By mere chance were we born, and afterwards we shall be as though we had never been" (Wis. 2:1–2).

This explains the moral norm of the wicked:

> "Come, then, let us enjoy the good things while we can, and make full use of the creation, with all the eagerness of youth. . . . Down with the poor and honest man! Let us tread him under foot; let us show no mercy to the widow and no reverence to the grey hairs of old age. For us let might be right! Weakness is proved to be good for nothing" (Wis. 2:6–11).

It also explains why they try to justify themselves by oppressing the just:

> "Let us lay a trap for the just man; he stands in our way, a check to us at every turn; he girds at us as law-breakers, and calls us traitors to our upbringing. . . . he says that the just die happy, and boasts that God is his father. Let us test the truth of his words, let us see what will happen to him in the end . . . Outrage and torment are the means to try him with" (Wis. 2:12–19).

By contrast, the conduct of the just man is based on a different gamble:

> For though in the sight of men they may be punished, they have a sure hope of immortality (Wis. 3:4).

> Honest work bears glorious fruit, and wisdom grows from roots that are imperishable (Wis. 3:15).

The final outcome vindicates the just man and matches the stakes involved:

> Then the just man shall take his stand, full of assurance, to confront those who oppressed him and made light of all his sufferings; at the sight of him there will be terror and confusion, and they will be beside themselves to see him so unexpectedly safe home. Filled with remorse, groaning and gasping for breath, they will say among themselves: "Was not this the man who was once our butt, a target for our contempt? Fools that we were. . . . How far we strayed from the road of truth! . . . What good has our pride done us? . . . All those things have passed by like a shadow . . . like a ship that runs through the surging sea, and when she has passed, not a trace is to be found." . . . The hope of a godless man is like down flying on the wind . . . But the just live for ever; their reward is in the Lord's keeping (Wis. 5:1–15).

This then is the life of the just until the final judgment comes:

> After a little chastisement they will receive great blessings, because God has tested them and found them worthy to be his. Like gold in a crucible he put them to the proof, and found them acceptable like an offering burnt whole upon the altar (Wis. 3:5–6).

4. **The redemptive value of the testing:** This testing of the just does more than ensure their own salvation. Their suffering is also justified in that it has value for the salvation of all. The Old Testament glimpsed this truth and recorded it in the songs or poems that deal with the "Suffering Servant of Yahweh." The themes of *lowliness, remnant,* and *messianic fulfillment* become concrete in the person of this Servant:

> Behold, my servant shall prosper, he shall be lifted up, exalted to the heights. Time was when many were aghast at you, my people; so now many nations recoil at sight of him, and kings curl their lips in disgust. For they see what they had never been told and things unheard before fill their thoughts. Who could have believed what we have heard, and to whom has the power of the Lord been revealed? He grew up before the Lord like a young plant, whose roots are in parched ground; he had no beauty, no majesty to draw our eyes, no grace to make us delight in him; his form, disfigured, lost all the likeness of a man, his beauty changed beyond human semblance. He was despised, he shrank from the sight of men, tormented

and humbled by suffering; we despised him, we held him of no account, a thing from which men turn away their eyes. Yet on himself he bore our sufferings, our torments he endured, while we counted him smitten by God, struck down by disease and misery; but he was pierced for our transgressions, tortured for our iniquities; the chastisement he bore is health for us and by his scourging we are healed. We had all strayed like sheep, each of us had gone his own way; but the Lord laid upon him the guilt of us all. . . . He was assigned a grave with the wicked, a burial-place among the refuse of mankind, though he had done no violence and spoken no word of treachery. Yet the Lord took thought for his tortured servant and healed him who had made himself a sacrifice for sin; so shall he enjoy long life and see his children's children, and in his hand the Lord's cause shall prosper (Isa. 52:13—53:10).

Then comes the promise of Yahweh himself:

After all his pains he shall be bathed in light, after his disgrace he shall be fully vindicated; so shall he, my servant, vindicate many, himself bearing the penalty of their guilt. Therefore I will allot him a portion with the great, and he shall share the spoil with the mighty, because he exposed himself to face death and was reckoned among transgressors, because he bore the sin of many and interceded for their transgressions (Isa. 53:11–12).

Yet even for this Israelite remnant of lowly people, the New Testament will be the "good news," the great innovation.

II The New Testament

One way to approach the New Testament in trying to find out what it has to say about the Church, the Israel of God, would be to read what it has to say about the "apostolic kerygma." In other words, we could see in what way the apostles and first disciples presented the "good news"; i.e., the gospel and its particular community, the Church.

But we can also adopt another approach, which has a more concrete tinge even though it involves more reading between the lines. We can try to grasp the image of the Church that takes shape in the problems confronted by the first ecclesiastical communities. The doctrine goes further than the problems themselves.

A. THE CHURCH AND THE "FLESHLY" OUTLOOK

1. The problem of the Church in Galatia was that some wished to subordinate man to religious factors that would be more in line with the Old Testament. They were preaching a false gospel; that is, a position that was not the Christian one:

I am astonished to find you turning so quickly away from him who called you by grace, and following a different gospel. Not that it is in fact another gospel; only there are persons who unsettle your minds by trying to distort the gospel of Christ. But if anyone, if we ourselves or an angel from heaven, should preach a gospel at variance with the gospel which you received, he shall be held outcast. I now repeat what I have said before: if anyone preaches a gospel at variance with the gospel which you received, let him be outcast! (Gal. 1:6–9).

Peter himself was not free of blame in this respect, and he was admonished severely by Paul for holding an ambiguous position. But the doctrine involved here goes beyond the whole problem of the "Judaizers." There was a whole "fleshly" attitude here, which saw man's justification proceeding from the fulfillment of religious law:

> You stupid Galatians! You must have been bewitched—you before whose eyes Jesus Christ was openly displayed upon his cross! Answer me one question: did you receive the Spirit by keeping the law or by believing the gospel message? Can it be that you are so stupid? You started with the spiritual; do you now look to the material to make you perfect? (Gal. 3:1-3).

This outlook continues that of the Old Testament and, in fact, it denies the novel facet of Christ and makes his cross useless:

> If righteousness comes by law, then Christ died for nothing (Gal. 2:21).

2. The problem of the Church in Corinth was that some tried to apply this mentality to the overall Christian religious law; that is, to the institutional aspects of the Church. The problem of the moment was that the Corinthians were debating the relative merits of being baptized by different disciples and apostles:

> I appeal to you, my brothers, in the name of our Lord Jesus Christ: agree among yourselves, and avoid divisions; be firmly joined in unity of mind and thought. I have been told, my brothers, by Chloe's people that there are quarrels among you. What I mean is this: each of you is saying, "I am Paul's man," or "I am for Apollos"; "I follow Cephas," or "I am Christ's." Surely Christ has not been divided among you! Was it Paul who was crucified for you? Was it in the name of Paul that you were baptized? Thank God, I never baptized one of you—except Crispus and Gaius . . . (1 Cor. 1:10-14).

This outlook too ends up by nullifying the novelty of Christ's cross. Even though it may be a typically "Christian" attitude in sociological terms, it must be combatted "so that the fact of Christ on his cross might have its full weight" (1 Cor. 1:17). It too is a *fleshly* attitude; it does not go beyond the natural, human level:

> This is the Spirit that we have received from God, and not the spirit of the world, so that we may know all that God of his own grace has given us; and, because we are interpreting spiritual truths to those who have the Spirit, we speak of these gifts of God in words found for us not by our human wisdom but by the Spirit. . . . For my part, my brothers, I could not speak to you as I should speak to people who have the Spirit. I had to deal with you on a merely natural plane, as infants of Christ. And so I gave you milk to drink, instead of solid food, for which you were not yet ready. Indeed, you are still not ready for it, for you are still on the merely natural plane. Can you not see that while there is jealousy and strife among you, you are living on the purely human level of your lower nature? When one says, "I am Paul's man," and another, "I am for Apollos," are you not all too human? (1 Cor. 2:12-3:4).

3. To live the Church in a "spiritual" way (insofar as its visible and institutional elements are concerned, we might add), we must frame it in its authentic place. And its authentic place can only be understood in terms of the gospel. Religious law is not an end but a means:

> So never make mere men a cause for pride. For though everything belongs
> to you—Paul, Apollos, and Cephas, the world, life, and death, the present
> and the future, all of them belong to you—yet you belong to Christ, and
> Christ to God (1 Cor. 3:21–23).

What Christ did precisely was to change the former status that these
things held in religion "according to the flesh." They were once regarded
as elements of some kind of contract whereby man reached God, and
man was enslaved to these elements:

> My brothers, let me give you an illustration. Even in ordinary life, when a
> man's will and testament has been duly executed, no one else can set it
> aside or add a codicil. Now the promises were pronounced to Abraham . . .
> What I am saying is this; a testament, or covenant, had already been
> validated by God; it cannot be invalidated, and its promises rendered in-
> effective, by a law made four hundred and thirty years later. If the in-
> heritance is by legal right, then it is not by promise; but it was by promise
> that God bestowed it as a free gift on Abraham (Gal. 3:15–18).

It is this discovery of the gratuitousness that is the novel feature of Christianity vis-à-vis older religion:

> This is what I mean: so long as the heir is a minor, he is no better off than
> a slave, even though the whole estate is his; he is under guardians and
> trustees until the date fixed by his father. And so it was with us. During
> our minority we were slaves to the elemental spirits of the universe, but
> when the term was completed, God sent his own Son, born of a woman,
> born under the law, to purchase freedom for the subjects of the law, in
> order that we might attain the status of sons. To prove that you are sons,
> God has sent into our hearts the Spirit of his Son, crying "Abba! Father!"
> You are therefore no longer a slave but a son, and if a son, then also by
> God's own act an heir (Gal. 4:1–7).

We are traitors to this "new" situation when we go back and restore a
religious universe *over* ourselves, for God has decreed it for our sakes:

> Now that you do acknowledge God—or rather, now that he has acknowl-
> edged you—how can you turn back to the mean and beggarly spirits of the
> elements? Why do you propose to enter their service all over again? You
> keep special days and months and seasons and years. You make me fear
> that all the pains I spent on you may prove to be labour lost (Gal. 4:9–11).

B. THE CHURCH AND ITS EXPECTATION
OF THE PAROUSIA

1. The problem of the Thessalonians was to know how to wait for
the second coming of Christ. In his first epistle to them, Paul gave them
this general overview:

> May the Lord make your love mount and overflow towards one another
> and towards all, as our love does towards you. May he make your hearts
> firm, so that you may stand before our God and Father holy and faultless
> when our Lord Jesus comes with all those who are his own (1 Thess.
> 3:12–13).

This day seemed to be near at hand:

> This we tell you as the Lord's word: we who are left alive until the Lord
> comes shall not forestall those who have died; because at the word of com-
> mand, at the sound of the archangel's voice and God's trumpet-call, the
> Lord himself will descend from heaven; first the Christian dead will rise,
> then we who are left alive shall join them, caught up in clouds to meet
> the Lord in the air. Thus we shall always be with the Lord (1 Thess.
> 4:15–17).

The consequences of this belief were mentioned by Paul in his second
epistle to them:

> We hear that some of your number are idling their time away, minding
> everybody's business but their own (2 Thess. 3:11).

> And now, brothers, about the coming of our Lord Jesus Christ and his
> gathering of us to himself: I beg you, do not suddenly lose your heads or
> alarm yourselves, whether at some oracular utterance, or pronouncement,
> or some letter purporting to come from us, alleging that the Day of the Lord
> is already here (2 Thess. 2:1–2).

Paul issues strict orders to them:

> To all such we give these orders, and we appeal to them in the name of the
> Lord Jesus Christ to work quietly for their living (2 Thess. 3:12).

> Even during our stay with you we laid down the rule: the man who will
> not work shall not eat (2 Thess. 3:10).

One of Paul's recommendations to the Philippians fits in here too:

> And now, my friends, all that is true, all that is noble, all that is just and
> pure, all that is lovable and gracious, whatever is excellent and admirable
> —fill all your thoughts with these things . . . and the God of peace will be
> with you (Phil. 4:8–9).

2. The problem goes deeper when we consider three basic facts in
the life of primitive Christians. They were not simply passing time in
good pursuits while they waited for the second coming. A real vision of
history was involved here.

First of all, certain important aspects of history were yet to take place:

> Let no one deceive you in any way whatever. That day cannot come before
> the final rebellion against God, when wickedness will be revealed in human
> form, the man doomed to perdition. He is the Enemy. . . . For already the
> secret power of wickedness is at work, secret only for the present until the
> Restrainer disappears from the scene (2 Thess. 2:3–7).

So there does exist a *mystery*. It is a plan for history which also involves
iniquity and its overthrow. And this plan for history, already in operation but not yet complete, affects the whole universe:

> For the created universe waits with eager expectation for God's sons to be
> revealed. It was made the victim of frustration, not by its own choice, but
> because of him who made it so; yet always there was hope, because the uni-

verse itself is to be freed from the shackles of mortality and enter upon the liberty and splendour of the children of God. Up to the present, we know, the whole created universe groans in all its parts as if in the pangs of child-birth (Rom. 8:19–22).

And finally the full growth of Christ himself must be achieved. It is not just that all men must pass before him. The growth must be completed in history as a plan:

> He who descended is no other than he who ascended far above all heavens, so that he might fill the universe . . . So shall we all at last attain to the unity inherent in our faith and our knowledge of the Son of God—to mature manhood, measured by nothing less than the full stature of Christ (Eph. 4:10–13).

> Then comes the end, when he delivers up the kingdom to God the Father, after abolishing every kind of domination, authority, and power. For he is destined to reign until God has put all enemies under his feet; and the last enemy to be abolished is death. Scripture says, "He has put all things in subjection under his feet." But in saying "all things," it clearly means to exclude God who subordinates them; and when all things are thus subject to him, then the Son himself will also be made subordinate to God who made all things subject to him, and thus God will be all in all (1 Cor. 15:24–28).

Thus this whole process of subjection is of a gradually progressing meas-ure, the measure of the full Christ which gradually takes shape between the Ascension and the second coming.

But it is primarily in his letters from prison, probably in Rome, that Paul unfolds the vision, both historical and eschatological, which is ours today in this world:

> With this in mind, then, I kneel in prayer to the Father, from whom every family in heaven and on earth takes its name, that out of the treasures of his glory he may grant you strength and power through his Spirit in your inner being, that through faith Christ may dwell in your hearts in love. With deep roots and firm foundations, may you be strong to grasp, with all God's people, what is the breadth and length and height and depth of the love of Christ, and to know it, though it is beyond knowledge. So may you attain to fullness of being, the fullness of God himself (Eph. 3:14–19).

This love of Christ, operating in this universe whose dimensions have already been described, is the whole mystery of God's plan of love:

> With this I make my prayer, I, Paul, who in the cause of you Gentiles am now the prisoner of Christ Jesus—for surely you have heard how God has assigned the gift of his grace to me for your benefit. It was by a revelation that his secret was made known to me. I have already written a brief account of this, and by reading it you may perceive that I understand the secret of Christ. In former generations this was not disclosed to the human race; but now it has been revealed by inspiration to his dedicated apostles and proph-ets. . . . To me, who am less than the least of all God's people, he has granted of his grace the privilege of proclaiming to the Gentiles the good

news of the unfathomable riches of Christ. . . . This is in accord with his age-long purpose, which he achieved in Christ Jesus our Lord (Eph. 3:1–11).

And this mystery, summed up in a few words, is this:

> For in Christ our release is secured and our sins are forgiven through the shedding of his blood. Therein lies the richness of God's free grace lavished upon us, imparting full wisdom and insight. He has made known to us his hidden purpose—such was his will and pleasure determined beforehand in Christ—to be put into effect when the time was ripe: namely, that the universe, all in heaven and on earth, might be brought into a unity in Christ (Eph. 1:7–10).

The Epistle to the Colossians, which reiterates many of the themes found in the Epistle to the Ephesians, also presents us with the historical-eschatological mystery of the plan willed by God:

> Through him God chose to reconcile the whole universe to himself, making peace through the shedding of his blood upon the cross—to reconcile all things, whether on earth or in heaven, through him alone (Col. 1:20).

One final passage may help us to appreciate the twofold character (i.e., both eschatological and historical) of the divine plan that is carried out in history between the Ascension and the second coming of Jesus. Let us take resurrection, or victory over death, as an example of this reconciliation. If we do, then here is the eschatological aspect:

> Were you not raised to life with Christ? Then aspire to the realm above, where Christ is, seated at the right hand of God (Col. 3:1).

And, by the same token, here is the historical aspect:

> All I care for is to know Christ, to experience the power of his resurrection, and to share his sufferings, in growing conformity with his death, if only I may finally arive at the resurrection from the dead (Phil. 3:10–11).

Struggle and conflict do not rule out the sureness of victory. It is a victory so complete that we cannot even imagine it:

> Now to him who is able to do immeasurably more than all we can ask or conceive, by the power which is at work among us, to him be glory in the church and in Christ Jesus from generation to generation evermore! Amen (Eph. 3:20–21).

C. THE CHURCH AND THE PROBLEM OF BEING A SIGN

1. One problem of the Church in Corinth was to integrate freedom, sin, and the task of being a sign.

The Christian communities were soon faced with the problem of pointing out what sin was. The problem came up in Corinth, and Paul spread his teaching to the Church of Rome, which he did not know personally. One of the concrete issues here concerned eating meat that had been sacrificed to idols. Paul worked up this general proposition in connection with this particular issue:

"We are free to do anything," you say. Yes, but is everything good for us? "We are free to do anything," but does everything help the building of the community? (1 Cor. 10:23).

But this proposition is of general application. It applies to what we have already seen regarding the Christian and the law. Paul reiterates it even when it concerns a clearcut matter, such as that of sexual immorality (1 Cor. 6:12–14).

What Paul is trying to say is this. To find our true moral perspectives, we must not look primarily to see whether a thing is permitted or not. Instead we must try to see whether it is advantageous with respect to the overall plan we are trying to understand:

Let us therefore cease judging one another, but rather make this simple judgement: that no obstacle or stumbling-block be placed in a brother's way. I am absolutely convinced, as a Christian, that nothing is impure in itself; only, if a man considers a particular thing impure, then to him it is impure (Rom. 14:13–14).

Thus in trying to form a sure conscience we must operate in terms of that which is the fulfillment of the law: i.e., love of neighbor:

He who loves his neighbour has satisfied every claim of the law. For the commandments, "Thou shalt not commit adultery, thou shalt not kill, thou shalt not steal, thou shalt not covet," and any other commandment there may be, are all summed up in one rule, "Love your neighbour as yourself." Love cannot wrong a neighbour; therefore the whole law is summed up in love (Rom. 13:8–10).

To form a proper conscience is to arrive gradually at this summation of our moral conduct, by examining the advantageousness of every action with respect to this plan. Hence this two-edged concrete response to the problem posed:

Certainly food will not bring us into God's presence: if we do not eat, we are none the worse, and if we eat, we are none the better. But be careful that this liberty of yours does not become a pitfall for the weak (1 Cor. 8:8–9).

The weak are those whose faith is poorly formed or not formed at all. Paul goes on to discuss this in greater and more concrete detail:

"We are free to do anything," you say. Yet, but is everything good for us? "We are free to do anything," but does everything help the building of the community? Each of you must regard, not his own interests, but the other man's. You may eat anything sold in the meat-market without raising questions of conscience; for the earth is the Lord's and everything in it. If an unbeliever invites you to a meal and you care to go, eat whatever is put before you, without raising questions of conscience. But if somebody says to you, "This food has been offered in sacrifice," then, out of consideration for him, and for conscience' sake, do not eat it—not your conscience, I mean, but the other man's. "What," you say, "is my freedom to be called in question by another man's conscience? If I partake with thankfulness, why am I blamed for eating food over which I have said grace?" . . . give no offense to Jews, or Greeks, or to the church of God (1 Cor. 10:23-32).

Thus the moral conscience of the Christian is intrinsically social and sign-bearing. And it is by progressing in one's moral conscience that the Church is enabled to carry out her mission as a sign.

2. But it can also happen that steps must be taken to recover the sign-bearing function. This happened in Corinth with respect to another issue posed to Paul. When asked about a case of incest, Paul offered a simple answer: expel the offender from the community:

For my part, though I am absent in body, I am present in spirit, and my judgement upon the man who did this thing is already given, as if I were indeed present: you all being assembled in the name of our Lord Jesus, and I with you in spirit, with the power of the Lord Jesus over us, this man is to be consigned to Satan for the destruction of the body, so that his spirit may be saved on the Day of the Lord (1 Cor. 5:3-5).

But we must keep in mind three things if we are to understand and appreciate this decision.

Firstly, it is not a question of human frailty but a matter of principle. Paul is talking about a stable situation which the Corinthians have not reacted against and which is intermingled with pride. When discussing the case of Thessalonians who were not working, Paul distinguished clearly between human frailty and basic principle:

If anyone disobeys our instructions given by letter, mark him well, and have no dealings with him until he is ashamed of himself. I do not mean treat him as an enemy, but give him friendly advice, as one of the family (2 Thess. 3:14-15).

Secondly, this position is necessary if the Church is to carry out its mission as a sign to those outside. And this mission involves a twofold obligation: nearness and clear visibility:

In my letter I wrote that you must have nothing to do with loose livers. I was not, of course, referring to pagans who lead loose lives or are grabbers and swindlers or idolaters. To avoid them you would have to get out of the world altogether. I now write that you must have nothing to do with any so-called Christian who leads a loose life, or is grasping, or idolatrous, a slanderer, a drunkard, or a swindler. You should not even eat with such a person (1 Cor. 5:9-11).

Thirdly, we must be sure that we are not sacrificing the sinner for the sake of the purity of the Church or for its mission as a sign. Note what Paul adds to the decree of excommunication, if we may call it that:

This man is to be consigned to Satan for the destruction of the body, so that his spirit may be saved on the Day of the Lord (1 Cor. 5:5).

The Church does not save people by holding them inside somehow. She does it by carrying out her universal mission as a sign.

3. In this way we can see how the complete reality of the Church is articulated and shaped. Like Paul, Apollos, Cephas, life and death, it is placed at our disposal even as is the whole universe of institutional religions:

> All of them belong to you—yet you belong to Christ, and Christ to God (1 Cor. 3:23).

But this whole Church is also Christ who, as the whole Christ, belongs to God:

> When all things are thus subject to him, then the Son himself will also be made subordinate to God who made all things subject to him, and thus God will be all in all (1 Cor. 15:28).

If, by contrast, we switch Paul's terms inside out and view man as being *for the sake of the Church,* then the latter will be deprived of its sign function and will not be able to carry out its function of subjecting all reality to Christ, to the whole Christ.

APPENDIX III

Springboard Questions

The theology of the Church presented in this volume was shaped and formed through real-life seminars (see the Introduction). In our experience with these seminars we found that it was absolutely necessary to prepare questions for the discussion periods.

Such questions were not meant to encourage passivity on the part of the participants. Their purpose was not to get the participants to "recall" or review what has been said in lectures or texts. They were meant to broaden the outlook of the participants by getting them to think out the logic of what they have heard in terms of real-life problems and situations. In short, they were meant to produce a confrontation between what they have experienced and what they supposedly believe and know.

We felt that our readers might like to see the type of question we proposed, and to understand the rationale behind it. So here we offer some of the questions we proposed in connection with each chapter topic, together with an explanation accounting for our choice of these questions.

Chapter One

QUESTIONS

Here is the statement of a contemporary author: "Christian love involves thinking about another person, caring greatly about his welfare, putting the concern of others first. Now it seems to me that this full love cannot be attained outside Christianity. Why, after all, should people get married for the sake of another person instead of their own happiness, outside of the whole framework of love that Christ communicated to us?"

Does the first part of this statement seem correct to you? Does the second half of it seem correct to you? If you were the author, how would you formulate a definition of Christian love and of the situation of the non-Christian with respect to it?

EXPLANATION

The purpose of the question is to inspire a radical change in the language that the Christian currently uses. It should become clear that the first part of the author's statement above is a definition of *authentic* love, not of *Christian* love. The new element added by the latter is not authenticity but knowledge of love's mysteriousness. The second half of the author's statement presupposes that "Christ's gift" and "Christianity" are one and the same thing. It overlooks the love which Christ communicated to all humanity even beyond the limits reached by the Christian message. In discussions we often find that people begin to ask whether it is valid to make a distinction between charity and philanthropy. And they suggest that the former may be constituted by the intention which makes it *supernatural*. On this, see CLARIFICATION II of Chapter I of this volume.

Chapter Two

QUESTION

Do you think it is correct to distinguish two ways of obtaining salvation: namely, an *objective* way through faith and the sacraments and a *subjective* way in which God takes account of the secret intentions of men?

EXPLANATION

Chapter II tries to offer a radical change in our picture of the Church. But many people still tend to cling to the notion that salvation comes to Christians because objectively they do what they are supposed to do, following the path traced out by God and utilizing the means provided by him; and that it comes to non-Christians *despite* what they do objectively because they are guided by a good intention into which God sees. So even though they do things that are wrong (e.g., remarrying or not going to Mass), they are saved by the good intention. But reflection on the content of Chapter II will suggest another outlook. It indicates that there is one *objective* salvation for all men that involves practicing love of neighbor. The building up of the world in love is the one common objective work that is capable of putting man in touch with salvation. But of course God does take account of men's intentions which he alone knows—both with regard to the non-Christian and the Christian. If one feels that the salvation of the non-Christian is effected in some unknown way, then a service-oriented Church becomes impossible. Even without wishing it, the Church will again turn into a conquering Church.

QUESTION

What do you do or say when a person asks why he should become a Christian because he is already sacrificing his life for others?

EXPLANATION

This question complements the first one. If the necessary and sufficient objective task insofar as salvation is concerned is the building up of the world in love, then can we "rest content" with engaging in that task? What can we say to such a person to show him that there is a further step to take? The aim of these questions is to see to what extent the individual has grasped the function of faith and the sacraments *in relationship to love,* and not directly in relationship to such notions as salvation, perfection, superiority, etc. The responses will show whether they associate them with a *responsibility,* i.e., with an unheard-of potential for love. This paves the way for the topic treated in the next chapter, and for the theme treated in CLARIFICATION III of Chapter II.

Chapter Three

QUESTIONS

Do you think that a balance should exist between human development and the development of the Church in a given country? Is it always desirable that we have the greatest possible development of the Church and its proper functions (dioceses, parishes, number and quality of priests, facilities for catechetics, etc.)? If you answer "no" to the first question, explain why. If you answer "yes," what concrete criterion would indicate when the desired balance is present?

EXPLANATION

The aim of the questions is to make more concrete the idea that the whole objective of the internal ecclesial community is to guarantee effective dialogue between the questions raised by love and the responses that full-fledged faith has for them. It is quite possible that all the responses will be affirmative. But it is not so readily true that people will see that the criterion is an ongoing dialogue between the Church and the rest of mankind, in which they deal with the same problems in the same language. One way of fleshing out this problem is to pose a hypothetical case. Suppose we were being sent to some scarcely civilized island inhabited by pagans, and that we had all the money we needed to carry out any type of project of aid. What would we do? Another subsidiary but related question is this: Do you see an intrinsic relationship between the mission of the Church and the historical epoch and place in which she was founded?

Chapter Four

QUESTIONS

What do you think about excluding someone from the community of the Church? In other words: Are such exclusions being used? Should they be used more? Or not used? Or used better?

EXPLANATION

The aim of the question is to get people to reflect on the interrelated aspects of this chapter. First of all, despite the fact that they may have grasped intellectually the import of the obligations facing the Church, their emotional feelings may still operate within an older outlook. They may feel that people should not be expelled from the Church because that would harm them. Such expulsion is not regarded with favor (see CLARIFICATION II of Chapter IV). Secondly, the question may help people to realize that purifying the Church's function as a sign may come to involve excommunication as Paul indicated, but that in day-to-day life it is exercised in the sacrament of penance. We cannot go to Communion until we have re-entered the community through contrition, firm resolve, and divine and ecclesial pardon. It is absolutely necessary for people to realize that this prerequisite is not based on a concern about "sacrileges" but on the obligations incumbent on a Sign-Church. The question will also help people to see that Christianity must be lived out in authentic communities that place deep-rooted obligations on their members. If it is not, then any obligations leading to expulsion will be legalistic and external, opening the way for much worse countersigns in the Church.

Chapter Five

QUESTIONS

Do you feel that the Church must involve herself more in national problems in order to truly dialogue with the world and be a sign in its midst? If yes, how should she do this? If no, why not?

EXPLANATION

One purpose of this question is of course to make the ideas of this chapter more concrete. But its purpose is also to get people to distinguish the two poles of the Church's sign function and her commitment in the world. Those two poles are the hierarchy and the laity. The reader should appreciate that the hierarchy is meant to stress the supratemporal aspect of the message while the laity are meant to stress its temporal aspect. There is an intimate connection between the two. While authority is more bound up with the first pole, the *raison d'être* of the Church is more centered in the second pole, as the Council tells us (see Appendix I, conciliar passages cited under Chapter V).